Pedagogy for Religion

Pedagogy for Religion

Missionary Education and the Fashioning of Hindus and Muslims in Bengal

Parna Sengupta

UNIVERSITY OF CALIFORNIA PRESS
Berkeley · Los Angeles · London

University of California Press, one of the most
distinguished university presses in the United States,
enriches lives around the world by advancing
scholarship in the humanities, social sciences, and
natural sciences. Its activities are supported by the UC
Press Foundation and by philanthropic contributions
from individuals and institutions. For more information, visit www.ucpress.edu.

University of California Press
Berkeley and Los Angeles, California

University of California Press, Ltd.
London, England

© 2011 by The Regents of the University of California

Library of Congress Cataloging-in-Publication Data

Sengupta, Parna, 1971–
   Pedagogy for religion : missionary education and the fashioning of Hindus and Muslims in Bengal / Parna Sengupta.
     p. cm.
   Includes bibliographical references (p.) and index.
   ISBN 978-0-520-26829-6 (hardcover : alk. paper) —
   ISBN 978-0-520-26831-9 (pbk. : alk. paper)
   1. Education—India—Bengal—History. 2. Hindus—Education—India—Bengal—History. 3. Muslims—Education—India—Bengal—History. 4. Church schools—India—Bengal—History. I. Title.
   LA1154.B4S38 2011
   371.071'25414—dc22   2011006067

20 19 18 17 16 15 14 13 12 11
10 9 8 7 6 5 4 3 2 1

To my parents, Banasree and Dipankar Sengupta

Contents

Acknowledgments ix

Introduction: Pedagogical Frames and Colonial Difference 1
1. The Molding of Native Character 23
2. A Curriculum for Religion 40
3. An Object Lesson in Colonial Pedagogy 61
4. The Schoolteacher as Modern Father 81
5. Teaching Gender in the Colony 102
6. Mission Schools and Qur'an Schools 123
   Conclusion: Pedagogy for Tolerance 150

Notes 161
Bibliography 189
Index 205

Acknowledgments

Acknowledgment is far too inadequate a word to express my gratitude to the teachers, mentors, colleagues, and friends who have made this book possible. My research and writing has been funded at various stages by a number of organizations, including the Social Science Research Council, the Mellon Foundation, the Spencer Foundation, the National Academy of Education, and Carleton College.

I am grateful to have had the chance to work with Richard Candida-Smith, Fernando Coronil, Kali Israel, Aamir Mufti, Sumathi Ramaswamy, and Ann Stoler at the University of Michigan. Nick Dirks introduced me to the larger field of South Asian studies and the relevance of anthropology for the writing of history. Sankaran Krishna gave me a very early opportunity to present my work at the University of Hawaii and Itty Abraham was critical to the early funding of this project. Barbara Metcalf and Tom Metcalf have been wonderful critics, readers, and mentors. Most of all, I want to thank Tom Trautmann, who has not only taught me a tremendous amount about the world of early India but has also served as an exemplary model of the type of scholarly rigor, creativity, and intellectual curiosity to which I can only aspire.

My work has benefited tremendously from the intellectual exchange, friendship, and camaraderie of many, including Laura Bear, Tom Foster, Tyrone Forman, Will Glover, Tom Guglielmo, Anne Hardgrove, Riyad Koya, Amanda Lewis, Karuna Mantena, Rama Mantena, John McKiernan-Gonzalez, Farina Mir, Gita Rajan, Shimul Rahim, Anupama Rao, and the late Anjan Ghosh. My research in Kolkata would not have been possible without the home-away-from-home provided by my Choto Pisi, and Pisa, Deepak and Pritha Ray, and my cousins, Partha and Kaushik. In Dhaka, I was welcomed into the home of the Rahmed family, and for this I owe a great debt to Nipa Rahim. I am grateful to Caitlin Adams, Subham Basu, and Bhaskar Mukhopadhyay for helping me make my way through the archives of the British Library and the restaurants of London.

I am deeply indebted to my colleagues and students at Carleton College, especially Scott Bierman, Andrew Fisher, Annette Igra, Adeeb Khalid, Jessica Leiman, Lori Pearson, Alexander Persaud, Sabrina Singh, Dominic Vendell, Choua Vu, Serena Zabin, and Eleanor Zelliot. At Stanford, the support and encouragement of Shahzad Bashir, Nancy Hill, Sangeeta Mediratta, and Ellen Woods has been tremendous. This book has been vastly improved by suggestions from various journal editors and anonymous reviewers and I would like to especially thank Antoinette Burton, Tom Metcalf, Cynthia Talbot, Tom Trautmann, the anonymous reviewers at UC Press, and my editor, Niels Hooper.

My family has been a constant source of support, love, and encouragement. My interest in education is in no small part because of the value my own parents placed on learning and this book is dedicated to them. My sister, Tesha Sengupta-Irving, is a model of what engaged teaching and research should look like and I continue to learn from her example. I am grateful to the rest of my family, the Irvings, Ghoshes, and Sinhas, for their love, support, and good advice. The arrival of Arjun has blessed our lives and has made this a truly spectacular year.

Acknowledgment seems an especially inadequate word to express my gratitude to Aishwary Kumar. Our conversations constantly push my own thinking—on history, on writing, on reading, and on politics—in unexpected and wonderful ways. I thank him for all the cooking, the ideas, the books, and the sheer joy and love that he brings into my life every day.

Introduction

Pedagogical Frames and Colonial Difference

This book challenges one of the most compelling historical fictions: that Western rule secularized the non-West. I confront this idea by demonstrating how the sustained involvement of missionaries in the expansion of modern education ultimately reinforced, rather than weakened, the place of religion and religious identity in the development of Indian modernity. My research questions the conclusions drawn by theorists of historical and contemporary imperialism who describe the missionary role as a "self-consciously modernizing project . . . the Victorian 'NGO.'"[1]

In describing missionary activity in this way, scholars are able to temper a general critique of Empire by emphasizing its humanitarian contribution to the welfare of the non-Western world. One of the commonly cited examples of this "self-consciously modernizing project" is the introduction of Western education, an imperial undertaking broadly credited to missionaries, who, as members of a "Victorian NGO," were able to globalize the norms of Western liberalism.

My research reveals the paradox that the pursuit and adaptation of modern educational techniques and institutions, mainly exported to the colonies by Protestant missionaries, opened up new ways for Hindu and Muslim leaders and the colonial state to reformulate ideas of community along religious lines.[2] That is, Western forms of schooling brought with them the foregrounding and standardizing of certain kinds of knowledge and forms of identity—particularly religious identity. Nineteenth-century pedagogic theories and models of teacher training can be read as efforts to teach ordinary Indians what it meant to be a modern religious subject in ways that combined explicit religious beliefs with a set of implicit cultural practices and hierarchies.

In spite of the status accorded English education in colonial society and among historians of colonial India, my book demonstrates the centrality of vernacular education as a space in which missionaries and native leaders could theorize and ultimately propagate the practices and norms required of a properly modern society. Through a careful archival study of the methods, books, and institutions created by Christian, Hindu, and eventually Muslim educators in Bengal, my research reveals the ways the materials and institutions of vernacular education became a means to argue for a vision of community and identity based on religious affiliation.

By foregrounding education, I shift away from the conventional reliance on conversion, sacred text, or ritual practice as the primary means to understand religion and religious change. Rather, this book suggests that the very ordinary activity of learning to read in the modern school, through language primers and schoolteachers, became an exercise in individual and community religious self-fashioning in the colonial period. The pedagogic subject and the religious subject were, in these moments, wholly coterminous; thus, instruction in science also became a means to instruct the Indian child, whether Christian, Hindu, or Muslim, about the primacy of reason and rationality over superstition. The emphasis on literacy and reason as the heart of modern religious epistemology was part of a more general nineteenth-century reformist impulse all over the world. Modern education did not secularize religious traditions in India as much as it reformulated definitions of religion and religious community as a part of a more global process.

An example of the twinning of the pedagogic and the religious subject can be seen in one of the most famous texts produced during the colonial period, W. W. Hunter's *The Indian Musalmans: Are They Bound in Conscience to Rebel against the Queen?* Hunter, a civil servant in Bengal, wrote the book in 1872 to answer a question initially posed by Lord Mayo, the viceroy of British India. Mayo wanted to assess the loyalty and status of the Muslims in British India—a task deemed especially important after the Indian Mutiny and Rebellion of 1857 and a series of trials on the putative Wahhabi conspiracy in the 1860s.[3] Hunter felt that the colonial state had sadly neglected its pedagogic responsibility to its Muslim subjects, creating a whole class of "backward" and potentially seditious Muslim peasantry. He argued, "A system of purely secular education is adapted to very few nations. In the opinion of many deeply thinking men, it has signally failed in Ireland, and it is certainly altogether unsuited to the illiterate and fanatical peasantry of Muhammadan Bengal."[4] Hunter's book reflects the more general comparative imperial perspective adopted by the British Empire as it considered the options for dealing with its "illiterate and fanatical" subjects, whether Bengali Muslim or Irish Catholic. Among his various other recommendations, Hunter emphasizes that the loyalty of Muslims can be best assured by providing them greater access to modern education and specifically religious education. The advancement of secular schooling, for Hunter, is a luxury that a Protestant government can no longer afford.

Hunter was explicit about the political stakes of institutionalizing religious-based education, in which religious belonging was linked to imperial order. More surprisingly, however, his perspective came to be mirrored in the growing sentiments among Indians themselves. Rather than connecting modern forms of religiosity to imperial subjectivity, the primary focus of Hindu and Muslim leaders was to relate it to national belonging. It was the growing concern with the definition of national identity in the twentieth century that came to be the most fraught aspect of developing a system of elementary vernacular education. Debates over education functioned as parallel, and at times surrogate, discussions about political representation and religious identity. The modern school was a powerful metaphor for both community and nation and thus became the grounds to explore unresolved questions about the place of religion within the world of modern politics. The displacement of complex political conversations into the arena of education can be seen most clearly in the mid-twentieth-century writings of Bengali Muslim leaders, the *ashraf*, the group with which Hunter (for wholly different reasons) had been so concerned. Specifically, Muslim Bengalis were drawn to the idea of the separate funding and development of schools as a means to preserve the distinctiveness of their religious and linguistic community, particularly against the dominance of upper-caste Hindu society. From the mid-nineteenth century on, upper-caste Hindus, or *bhadralok,* had opened many of their own schools and monopolized government institutions. For Muslim leaders, then, religious education became essential to creating and claiming a space as a religious and political community, in contrast to Hunter, who had seen it as an antidote to insurgency.

Yet what was paradoxical in the demand for Muslim education in Bengal was that Muslim reformers were equally insistent that the need for separate religious education did not necessarily translate into the need for wholly separate schools, or nations. That is, the possibilities offered by modern education for Bengali Muslims did not begin and end with a call for a divided education (or a divided nation). Rather, this book suggests that modern education offered Indian educators and leaders the opportunity to work through, in a highly sophisticated manner, a more pluralistic vision of community and nation. It was no longer a question for Indians that school should impart religious training at the primary level, but rather a question of determining how this might happen with children from many different backgrounds. The demands for more multireligious (rather than secular) schoolbooks and trained teachers from multiple religious backgrounds all became occasions to rehearse the arguments for and implementation of possible political futures.

My study begins in 1854 with the passage of Charles Wood's "Despatch," a document that marked a new interest by the colonial state in expanding vernacular education, and it ends with the early-twentieth-century debates between Hindu and Muslim leaders over culture and mass education.[5] In the first part of the book, I look at how new kinds of school materials and pedagogic methods introduced into India in the nineteenth century allowed Protestant missionaries and upper-caste Hindus, the *bhadralok*, to theorize new ideas about religious epistemology and effect social and cultural transformation. While missionaries intended that literacy would inevitably lay the groundwork for eventual Christian conversion, *bhadralok* reformers aimed to use schooling to inculcate new forms of upper-caste rationality and respectability. In fact, by the mid-nineteenth century, *bhadralok* educators working for the Department of Public Instruction (DPI) began challenging the missionary dominance of elementary schooling by publishing their own competing versions of Bengali-language schoolbooks and object lessons and helping establish *bhadralok*-run normal schools for teachers. I show that in the process of developing a parallel system of education, notions of what constituted appropriate cultural, gender, familial, and religious conduct were themselves transformed.

Uncovering the experimental nature of modern education in the colonies leads to one of the most unexpected findings of my book: that late-nineteenth-century pedagogic institutions and theories informed the development of broader religious and social norms in colonial India. Although the metaphor of education is liberally used in histories of nineteenth-century gender and religion, few scholars look seriously at how the materials of modern schooling actually shaped the language and models of reform deployed by native leaders. At the level of epistemology, the translation of textbooks and pedagogic methods by *bhadralok* educators rehearsed the broader efforts of Bengalis to change the underlying Christian orientation of Western conventions and reorient Bengali gender habits.

In spite of the best efforts of evangelicals, the colonial state and local society always regarded mission schools as foreign institutions working to propagate Christian norms and belief. In contrast, *bhadralok*-produced educational materials and institutions were regarded by the Department of Public Instruction as truly "native." In the last part of the book, I show how this easy equation of upper-caste Hindu norms with an authentically Bengali culture was challenged in the late nineteenth century by urban Muslim leaders, the *ashraf,* who pointed out the caste and religious biases of village-level and Anglo-vernacular schools in Bengal. I examine the various ways that Bengali Muslim leaders, from the 1890s on, contested the Hindu orientation of everything from language primers to the makeup of the school inspectorate in order to make a case for a separate system of religious education for Bengali Muslims. *Ashraf* leaders and the colonial state ultimately borrowed the highly evangelical-inflected language of "backward" and "nominal" religiosity amongst Muslims (especially rural Bengali peasants) to argue for separate Bengali Muslim schools.

The paradox of the influence of mission paradigms on Indian religious education was that even as sectarianism and sectarian schooling increased in the late nineteenth century, what constituted effective modern religious instruction simultaneously became more standardized. A number of Muslim groups in Bengal organized around the issue of education and literary production and began developing and demanding their own separate schools, echoing arguments made by other North Indian Muslim leaders. My interest in this process is how the recommendations made by the state and by Muslim leaders to transform Muslim elementary schools, like the Qur'an schools and the *maktab,* were less connected to traditional forms of Islamic education and more informed by the mission school in terms of their pedagogic methods and goals.

By the early twentieth century, the colonial state, missionaries, and Indian educators assumed that at the curricular and institutional levels, mass schooling should be connected to the proper reproduction of particular religious and caste identities.[6] This made education one of the primary ways in which Bengalis, whether Christian, Hindu, or Muslim, came to identify and ultimately divide themselves. In fact, the effort to develop, at pedagogic and institutional levels, distinct systems of education based on religious and cultural identity became an exercise in pondering the possibilities for an integrated and equitable educational network—an effort that was clearly not divorced from the possibilities of imaging the same for the Indian nation. While the mid-nineteenth-century interest in vernacular schooling had focused on religious and social reform, by the early twentieth century, educational policy came to be seen as a proxy for political policy. As a result, modern education became a crucial part of debates leading up to the partition of the subcontinent into India and Pakistan in 1947. But in drawing attention to twentieth-century debates over mass primary schools, I resist any teleological narrative that might take us from the mission school to partition. In fact, this book suggests that rethinking the nature of the vernacular school, particularly the question of how to offer a modern education to a religiously diverse group of students, reflected a both pragmatic and hopeful effort by educators and reformers to imagine the future of India as a pluralistic and integrated society.

REHISTORICIZING EVANGELICAL PEDAGOGY

Why is it important for a historian of Empire to understand pedagogy? The conventional answer would link colonial schooling, particularly missionary schooling, to imperial (Western) ideology and dominance—succinctly captured in the title of Sanjay Seth's wonderful work, *Subject Lessons*.[7] That is, education tells us something about the epistemological and ideological assumptions of the "West" in which modern and Western come to be seen as almost synonymous. This Western education is assumed to be widely disseminated throughout the colonies, and in the process, natives learn only too well the lessons of their masters—a common imperial dynamic that both leads to the emergence of nationalist movements and leaders and traps the non-West forever in Western paradigms of thought and knowledge. Colonial education, from Tanzania to Sri Lanka, has been understood as an exercise in precisely this dynamic of the dissemination of imperial ideology and the eventual emergence of a nationalist leadership—a story that captures the process of colonization and decolonization.[8] As metaphor, it works to reveal to the historian something fundamental about the power and weakness of nineteenth- and twentieth-century modern empires.

But this book argues something quite different about the relationship between education and Empire; namely, that one of the most underappreciated aspects of colonial pedagogy was its relationship to the transformation of religion and religious community. Vernacular schooling was not simply a handmaiden of the Raj or a vehicle for Christian proselytizing; it was a dense nexus of state, missionary, and local demands and desires.

Although centered on colonial Bengal and education, this book has theoretical and political implications for other parts of the subcontinent as well. Primary vernacular schooling in Bengal anticipated many of the political, cultural, and religious issues that emerged all over India and the world. This was the result, in part, of the fact that the goals of modern education were neither wholly universal (the creation of a single modern subject) nor completely particularistic (the creation of a distinctly Bengali, upper-caste subject). In the tension between the two, pedagogy offered a space that allowed for endless malleability and self-fashioning. Thus an institution that began with evangelicals interested in producing Christian subjects was eagerly taken up by many different kinds of caste, religious, and linguistic communities as the means to modernize and preserve their own particular traditions. My study suggests that this particularly volatile mix of identity and schooling ensured that modern education remained a critical political arena in twentieth-century mass politics—a space in which issues of national identity and culture were constantly renegotiated.

All over India, education became a site for intense internal debate and organization—from the formation of educational societies to the publishing of reformist tracks on the need for women's education. Thus, it provides an ideal field in which to explore what has become a recent interest among colonial historians: the complex relationship between vernacular culture and colonial intervention, from local history publications, to new forms of poetic and musical genres and even market cultures.[9] *Pedagogy for Religion* demonstrates the oblique ways that missionaries and Indian reformers helped redefine essential aspects of vernacular culture in an institution that is conventionally seen as connected to state control. Modern education may initially seem like an unlikely place to explore forms of local culture since it is primarily studied in highly bureaucratic ways or as a site of imperial (state) ideology, but vernacular schools became just such a space. By drawing attention to the historical role of elementary schooling, I highlight technologies, institutions, and dynamics in which the colonial state was only mildly involved and interested, yet proved crucial in the eventual creation of Bengali modernity. For instance, through the production of language primers—done largely through the private publishing efforts of missionaries and *bhadralok* educators—a modern prose Bengali was developed and propagated. The creation of a standard written prose language proved indispensable for later cultural and political mobilization. This process was more generally true, from the changes in Punjabi literary traditions to the teaching of Sanskritized Hindi.[10]

In spite of the reciprocal influences between missionary and local educators, a peculiar disconnect separates the scholarship on missionaries and the scholarship on nineteenth-century Bengali history—a field that tends to obscure the place of evangelicalism in colonial society. Early-nineteenth-century missionary activity is acknowledged, yet evangelicals disappear from later nineteenth-century social and cultural histories.[11] Instead, historians study the development of colonial modernity almost exclusively as the product of either state intervention or debates wholly internal to native culture. While histories of the *bhadralok* (upper-caste Hindus) routinely employ missionary sources (particularly James Long's extensive writings) and missionary histories refer to various efforts of *bhadra* society to oppose or impede evangelicalism, there is little about the interaction or movement of ideas between these two kinds of reformers.

On the other hand, the work on colonial education remains overly focused on imperial ideology and evangelical proselytizing, with little effort to integrate Indian institutions or ideas. This is in part because of the continued overreliance on governmental and missionary English-language sources. To counter this historiographic tendency, I employ multiple kinds of sources in English and Bengali that demonstrate a far more interactive field of historical action. My research draws from missionary, state, and native publications to offer a rich and detailed picture of how ideas were negotiated, contested, and transformed in different institutions and among different communities. In the course of my research, I recreated some of the imperial circuits on which missionaries and their ideas traveled in the nineteenth century, from Calcutta to Birmingham and from Dhaka to Edinburgh. The reports, correspondence, and diaries of the Baptist Missionary Society (BMS), Church Missionary Society (CMS), London Missionary Society (LMS; Congregationalists), and Scottish Free Church missionaries offer a glimpse of the daily practices of the mission classroom. I then put missionary educational activities within the larger context of colonial schooling by systematically reading them alongside the reports of the director of the DPI, *bhadralok*-produced educational material, and the writings of Bengali Muslim reformers.

The subject of missionaries provokes considerable scholarly and political disagreement. Unlike other aspects of colonialism, missionary work continues unabated in the postcolonial present. Evangelical organizations maintain schools, churches, and hospitals in the third world, where they are simultaneously lauded and resented by governments and native populations. In India, this is especially true as evidenced by heated debates over the legality of proselytizing, the anxiety over conversion, and the recent violent attacks on missionaries and churches by right-wing Hindu groups.

On the scholarly side, this is paralleled by the general emphasis on conversion as the main feature of the evangelical encounter. This focus has produced two very divergent sets of studies: Church historians who write teleological accounts of the founding of a particular mission or church, and anthropologists who examine the conceptual and theoretical meanings of "conversion."[12] Not surprisingly, much of this work tends to be geographically focused on South India, which saw the growth of the largest number of churches and converts.[13] While I have been tremendously influenced by this work, my interest in this book has been to highlight some of the less obvious, but nonetheless foundational, institutional and epistemological ways that Indian society was shaped by the "evangelical" encounter.

Historians of missions, meanwhile, are slightly less concerned with the conceptual meanings of conversion than with the assessment of evangelicalism's place within imperial expansion.[14] The differences between various studies are largely about approach, captured in the titles of Andrew Porter's book *Religion versus Empire?* and Catherine Hall's *Civilising Subjects*.[15] Even as there seems to be a general historical agreement that there is no single way to assess the *general* question of missionaries and Empire, scholars still tend to come down on one side or another of the debate. Porter, for instance, after tracing the general historical arc of British missionary activity, ends by noting, "Whatever the ambiguities of the relationship between missions and empire and notwithstanding missionaries' own lack of a steadfast imperial commitment, the *possibility* remains that missionaries might still be effective imperialists."[16] Porter's comment is striking less because he denies missionary involvement, however ambiguous, with Empire, than because of his subsequent need to question whether they should be understood as "imperialists."

This discomfort with imperialism is in contrast to the work of John and Jean Comaroff or Catherine Hall, who similarly acknowledge the tensions inherent in evangelical ideology, its universal aspirations, and its highly imperial and racist formulations without needing to defend missionaries from their roles in the larger imperial project at home and abroad.[17] My research suggests that missionaries in India, even as they consistently critiqued the ways the British Raj continued to perpetuate certain kinds of hierarchy (notably caste), nonetheless saw their ultimate success as linked to imperial expansion in the subcontinent. Moreover, missionaries were crucial in shaping the popular ways that the metropolitan British public perceived not just India but also, crucially, Indian religions as "barbaric" and "backward."

To return to the question with which I began this section, one of the reasons that historians of Empire need to be attentive to pedagogy is that the influence of Christian evangelicalism on colonial society can be seen far more clearly in the development of modern forms of education than in the percentage of the population who chose to convert. While evangelicals had expected that their schools would serve as proselytizing vehicles, in fact the schools (particularly the English-medium schools in urban areas) were largely used by non-Christians who clearly had no intention of converting. In fact, missionaries became better known and more influential for educational change than for any other endeavor, religious or social. Mission schools included a wide range of institutions that educated (and continue to educate) communities as diverse as Santhal *adivasis* (tribals) and upper-caste, urban Hindus. The colonial state consistently held up missionary institutions as models to which other kinds of local and indigenous schools had to compare themselves. Thus, not only were mission schools attended by large numbers of Indians but also the schools themselves became connected to the funding (and thus the legitimacy) of other institutions.

Missionary educational expansion in Bengal and the rest of India differed from the history of missions both in other European empires and within parts of the British Empire itself. When compared to either the French (who had an explicit policy of *laïcité*, the absence of religion from governmental institutions) or the Portuguese (where the Catholic Church monopolized education), there were many more mission schools, representing a broad range of Protestant and Catholic sects, in the British Empire. But even within the British Empire, India stood out in contrast to the educational pattern in colonial Africa and Australia, where education was dominated by the government or missionaries and produced highly segregated and substandard "vocational" schooling. In India, in contrast, the limited expansion of modern schooling led to the funding of numerous kinds of nonmission schools, initially established by upper-caste Hindus but increasingly by Muslims and other communities. This precluded the kinds of racial segregation and dominance that characterized institutions like the boarding schools for aboriginal children in Australia.

These larger contextual patterns are significant because they explain the reasons for the more dynamic and competitive educational atmosphere in India, an atmosphere that led to greater challenges and exchanges between state officials, missionaries, and native educators. The Oxford History of the British Empire series, titled *Missions and Empire*, acknowledges this situation by noting that "the appearance of missionaries produced a backlash of religious revitalization among Hindus, Buddhists and Muslims."[18] While religious revitalization was certainly a core aspect of the expansion of modern education, the use of the term "backlash" assumes a historical dynamic in which European missionaries are seen as the primary actors while native communities simply react, in an almost unthinking manner, to the challenge posed by Christianity. Such a formulation does not capture the fact that the expansion (and funding) of modern vernacular education in India meant that ideas about religion, pedagogy, community, and nation had a life of their own amongst various communities. Such a linear narrative, the "backlash" that produces "revitalization," also does little to describe the radical ways that ideas and practices were transformed, were displaced, and become almost unrecognizable within the colonial context. In fact, I would characterize this period as one where Christian, Hindu, and Muslim schools were all reformulating what it meant to be a modern religious subject. In the colonial context, Christianity itself was religiously revitalized by the sudden expansion of missions and the need to incorporate Christians from all over the non-Western world, many of whom challenged, as much as non-Christians, a number of core beliefs and practices of Western Christianity.

But the exchange and transformation of pedagogic and curricular ideas were not confined to the colonies; rather, the growth of popular education in metropolitan Britain was also connected, in direct and indirect ways, to the ideas and policies enacted in India. Nineteenth-century educators and missionaries shared a belief that their ideas were universally transportable and applicable. The ubiquitous parish Sunday school could be opened in Calcutta, rural Ireland, or southern Africa and be expected to educate Indian, Irish, and African Christians in much the same way that British children were educated. But mission schooling was never a wholesale importation of a British system into the colonies. Instead, the colonies were often used as a laboratory in which to test out new philosophical, political, and pedagogic ideas.

This process is illustrated in Gauri Viswanathan's *Masks of Conquest*. Viswanathan convincingly shows that an English literary curriculum in India enabled "the humanistic ideals of enlightenment to coexist with and indeed even support education for social and political control."[19] She points out that a number of early-nineteenth-century Protestant missionaries and sympathetic parliamentarians, like Charles Grant, critiqued the East India Company's policy because of the non-Christian orientation of the English literary canon; this is a debate, Viswanathan argues, the missionaries ultimately lost. While the missionaries may have lost the debates over elite English schooling, my book looks at Bengali education to demonstrate the success of the mission school model in popularizing modern religious education aimed at the "masses." This was, of course, a rather bittersweet success since it was not the content of Christianity but the form of the Christian school that ultimately became normative.[20]

MISSIONARIES AND THE CONSTRUCTION OF EMPIRE

For ordinary nineteenth-century Britons, missionary activity was one of their main connections to Empire. Nineteenth-century Dissenting Protestantism was the religion of the emerging middle classes, a group who defined themselves through respectability rather than wealth or pedigree. This group effectively redefined what it meant to be a good Protestant because of their interest in voluntary philanthropy and religious humanitarianism. Both Established and Nonconformist congregations organized agencies to deal with pressing humanitarian issues that were seen as a clear commitment to Christ and Christianity.

One of the earliest and most profound articulations of this new orientation was William Carey's famous pamphlet, *An Enquiry into the Obligations of Christians to Use Means for the Conversion of the Heathen*, in 1792. Carey argued that if English traders managed to surmount "all those things which have generally been counted insurmountable," for the sake of overseas profit, the possibility of Christian conversion should offer an even greater incentive for ordinary Britons to venture abroad.

Carey explicitly connected "trade and preaching," since both involved "insinuat[ing]" oneself into the favor of native peoples.[21] For Carey, the expanding British trading empire did not merely provide greater opportunities for instruction in the gospel, but also it made it the *obligation* of every nineteenth-century Christian to support the conversion of the "heathen," those very populations who were being enslaved and colonized by the British Empire.

Carey's writing galvanized the British public, coming as it did on the heels of the late-eighteenth-century evangelical revival, the movement to abolish the slave trade, and the expansion of the second British Empire. Indeed, the language of abolition was usefully deployed by Protestant missionaries to raise money for those "enslaved" by caste in India. This led British Protestants to sponsor over 20 foreign missionary societies. Among these, the most important in Bengal were the BMS, LMS, CMS, and Scottish Missionary Societies (both Free Church and Established Church). These various organizations worked on the domestic and imperial fronts, but it was clear that the possibility of converting and educating the "heathen" abroad offered a special challenge and adventure to British evangelicals and their middle-class supporters.

The province of Bengal was the center of the East India Company and later the British Raj and had a special status within evangelical circles and the broader British Empire. Protestant missionaries like William Carey, who understood their success as closely tied to the expansion of the East India Company into the subcontinent, inaugurated the modern mission movement by sailing to Serampore, Bengal, in 1793.[22] This in part accounts for why missionaries continue to see Bengal as important in their work even though the actual number of converts and the Christian community were relatively small.

Thus, from an early period, both the colonial state and missionaries were invested, financially and politically, in establishing formal schooling in the province. Bengal is distinctive in another way in terms of its educational development: it had the dubious honor of having more privately funded schools than the other presidencies. That is, both missionary and upper-caste Hindu leaders actively expanded education through small grants-in-aid from the government. This resulted in a relatively dynamic system of Bengali-language schooling. This also makes Bengal a particularly good place to see how ideas and institutions were adapted by Indian leaders and developed within a relatively autonomous situation.

THE PLACE OF BENGALI EDUCATION IN COLONIAL SOCIETY

One of the most important debates over cultural policy in the Indian empire was in 1835 between the Anglicists and Orientalists. The occasion for the debates on language policy was the earmarking of Rs. 100,000 by the British Parliament for the education of its colonial subjects. It was an inconsequential sum but symbolically important because of the debate over whether Britain's subjects should be educated in English or the classical languages of Sanskrit and Persian. The differing views of the Orientalists and Anglicists related to different administrative goals and forms of governance of the British East India Company. Orientalists, under Warren Hastings, merged their classicism with an administrative pragmatism that depended on training Muslim *maulavis* and Hindu *pundits* to interpret native legal traditions for the company. Thomas Babington Macaulay decisively threw his weight behind the Anglicist position and wrote one of the most important and historically quoted documents: the "Minute on Indian Education." In his "Minute," Macaulay argues that a proper English literary education would help create "a class of interpreters between us and the millions whom we govern—a class of persons Indian in blood and colour, but English tastes, in opinions, in morals and in intellect."[23] It is not surprising that Macaulay's provocative words have prompted multiple studies by historians and postcolonial literary theorists. But by focusing too narrowly on the debates between the Orientalists and Anglicists, scholars reproduce the colonial government's own diffidence toward the development of vernacular education, a field that involved a great many more Indian actors.

While the East India Company primarily funded English-language schooling, Protestant missionaries began publishing Bengali Bibles, Christian tracts, schoolbooks, and dictionaries. The lack of state competition in Bengali schooling meant evangelicals were able to dominate the field of formal vernacular education in the first half of the nineteenth century through generous funding from their Home Committees. The growing missionary project in the colonies was parallel to the inroads the evangelical movement was making in mid-nineteenth-century British society and politics.

But in 1854, the Department of Public Instruction decided to nominally increase the funding of Bengali-language schooling. In fact, the DPI specifically wanted to offset the impression that they were unduly favoring Christians, and so they encouraged native leaders to establish their own Bengali and Anglo-vernacular schools. Missionaries continued to receive funding from Home Committees and the DPI for their pedagogic endeavors, but they now had to compete with the alternative publishing and schooling developed by native educators. In 1914, colonial officials, in response to fears of growing nationalist agitation in Indian schools, noted that in Bengal, conditions varied "more widely from those obtaining elsewhere in India ... while elsewhere they [Anglo-vernacular schools] owe their existence mainly to Government or to local funds and occasionally to individual munificence, here they have been and are being principally established *by private effort.*" Repeatedly, educational officials noted the extensive privatized system in Bengal, a system dominated by "the Bengali *bhadralok,* or clerical classes and small landholders."[24]

The consequences of the aversion of the colonial state (and, until the late nineteenth century, also the metropolitan state) to any system of centrally funded schooling resulted in an Empire run on the cheap—in spite of the pedagogic pretensions of imperial discourse. A later education report benignly called this neglect the adoption of "an attitude of practical non-interference in regard to private enterprise."[25] This statement belies the systematic underfunding of basic schooling by the colonial state and, more insidiously, the slow dismantling of various precolonial systems of village-level education.

An equally profound, albeit less historically acknowledged, effect of the private grant-in-aid system was the degree to which vernacular education came to constitute a crucial part in the development of the colonial public sphere and civil society. British Protestant churchgoers, regularly visited by missionaries with stories of successful school building and grateful letters from native orphans, could never have imagined the ways Protestant-based ideas and methods were being "translated" into native schools. For missionaries and the evangelical congregations who supported them, literacy laid the groundwork for the transformation of belief and behavior among native populations. Funding missionary schools in the colonies meant spreading Christianity and Christian-based cultural and gender norms to the larger native population. However, this lesson was learned only too well by mid-nineteenth-century native reformers who modified Christian-based pedagogic tools to disseminate new forms of religious and gender sensibilities in keeping with new definitions of modern Hinduism and Islam.

The decision by the Department of Public Instruction in 1854 to set aside funds to encourage native leaders to open (or expand) their own schools coincided with a burst of interest and activity in Bengali language publishing and printing.[26] Within the dominating and coercive regime of the British imperial state, vernacular education became a space in which missionaries and the emerging class of urban, educated *bhadralok* were given some autonomy to imagine and plot a different kind of society. *Bhadralok* leadership had little access to political power and thus focused their energies on reforming cultural and social practices within their own households and their own communities.[27] Education *as a subject* became one of the crucial sites for natives to articulate a vision of a modern society and culture. That is, elementary education was important to local leaders not just because it produced a literate native public but also because the indifference of the colonial state made it a relatively autonomous arena in which new religious practices and gender norms could be debated and introduced. As one missionary noted about the production of Bengali schoolbooks, "[T]hey [colonial officials] are not likely to interfere in a matter in which Bengalis are chiefly interested."[28]

In fact, two of the most important mid-nineteenth-century *bhadralok* reformers, Iswar Chandra Vidyasagar and Bhudev Mukhopadhyay, began their careers within the department of public instruction helping to develop a modern, non-Christian vernacular educational system. The investment in Bengali education for individuals like Vidyasagar and Mukhopadhyay, no less than for Protestant missionaries, reflected their conviction in the possibilities of elementary education to transform Bengali society.

Missionaries and *bhadralok* reformers sometimes explicitly contested the meaning and content of education through correspondence and speech. But more often, this was a dialogue that took place implicitly through the creation of competing curriculums and institutions. Rather than a wholly equal exchange of ideas, this process was closer to what Dipesh Chakrabarty has described as the translation of concepts between the West and the non-West. That is "neither an absence of relationship between dominant and dominating forms of knowledge nor equivalents that successfully mediate between differences, but precisely the partly opaque relationship we call difference."[29] Missionaries and native reformers saw the project of translating modern education into colonial India as parallel to and constitutive of the creation of a specifically Bengali modernity. The use of the vernacular school by *bhadralok* reformers as a means to theorize and introduce new social norms paralleled missionary pedagogic labors that similarly aimed to train native converts into new forms of worship and models of familial behavior.

HIERARCHY, SCHOOLING, AND THE ARTICULATION OF COMMUNITY IDENTITY

Although upper-caste reformers liberally borrowed from evangelical methods and materials, they were unwilling to adopt the model of social mobility embedded within Baptist and Methodist pedagogy. Instead, *bhadralok* reformers took great pains to differentiate themselves (and their cultural practices) from those whom they perceived as *abhadra* or *choto* (unrespectable, uncultured, or uncivilized). These included lower-caste Hindus, tribal communities, and Bengali Muslims. Not surprisingly, for many *bhadralok* leaders, limiting access to modern education became a critical component of maintaining the class and social distinction they claimed for themselves.[30]

But the "modern" of modern education was precisely its radical promise of increased mobility and social transformation for those traditionally marginalized from formal education. To some extent, this is what Christian schools in the colonies offered. Missionary vernacular schools, in contrast to *bhadralok*-run schools, were attended by native Christians, the majority of whom were from lower-caste and tribal communities, precisely the *abhadralok* or "uncultured" groups against whom the *bhadralok* defined themselves. This was especially true of mission schools in smaller towns and tribal areas, where limited numbers of lower-caste men and women were not only given access to formal education but also trained to be teachers, administrators, and preachers.

By the 1880s and 1890s, other minority communities also began to see the cultural importance of elementary education. Lower-caste Namashudras and Bengali Muslims began demanding their own schools and greater recognition (and funding) from the colonial government.[31] Although the *bhadralok* classes represented only a small part of the Bengali population, they dominated government-funded education and their schools reflected their particular religious and cultural perspective. The discrepancy between population and access to resources became more visible after the 1872 census, which revealed that over half the population of Bengal was Muslim, not Hindu.

This prompted leaders of other caste and religious communities to develop their own systems of education—ones that provided greater access for their community but also represented their distinctive cultural norms. This was especially true for the Bengali Muslims, who were coming into their own as a political community during the later nineteenth century. Education became one of the ways in which urban Muslim leaders articulated a responsibility toward and the right to be spokesmen for their co-religionists in the countryside. I see the argument for Muslim schools, as a means to transform the religious practices of "backward" rural Muslims, as parallel to the late-nineteenth-century evangelical anxiety over the need to expand basic Christian schooling to raise the status of "nominal" native Christians.

Popular religious education, I will argue, was an especially ideal site for Bengali Muslim leaders to articulate a relationship between the "ethnic" (Bengali) and religious (Muslim) self-perception. Modern Qur'an schools were meant to be conducted in Bengali (rather than Urdu or Arabic) and were meant to teach village children what it meant to be a modern Muslim—the proper rituals, texts, and morals. In this way, my study demonstrates what Suffia Uddin, in her book *Constructing Bangladesh*, describes as some of the key moments through which "language and popular ritual life" helped form a "hyphenated, mutually influencing ethnic and religious communal self-perceptions" among Bengali Muslims.[32]

For many religious communities in India, education became an essential part of constructing a "vision of community." For example, one of the more common events of the late nineteenth century was the organization of large public meetings by religious leaders to debate educational advancement. One British visitor observed that every major holiday of Sikhs, Hindus, and Muslims was "sure to be marked by an educational conference in one of the larger towns, and hundreds pour in . . . to sing, recite scripture and pass resolutions on the importance of education for women."[33] In this way, reform, and particularly educational reform, actually became a part of the practice and ritual of modern religion. Any public celebration and assertion of a religious identity were simultaneously a display and enactment of a commitment to change and modernization.

Inevitably, the debates over access to and control over education became a part of growing political demands for representation and economic justice by minority religious and lower-caste communities. For Bengali Muslims, in particular, the question of the dominance of upper-caste Hindus in government schools was seen as metonymic of their power in colonial society more generally. The close connection between education and political representation is perhaps best exemplified in the history of the All-India Mohammedan Educational Conference, an organization initially set up to increase support for Muslim educational needs. In 1906, the organization changed its name to the Muslim League and became far more active in direct representational politics. This transformation coincided with the first partition of Bengal into an Eastern territory and a Western territory. As David Ludden has pointed out, support for the 1906 partition of Bengal "deployed a *demographic* vision of the Indian nation that complicated and contested the Congress *territorial* vision."[34] That is, Bengali Muslim organizations (like the Mohammedan Educational Conference) argued for both a separate system of education and a separate territory because they felt the needs of their demographic, the Muslim community, were being consistently ignored by the arguments for a territorially undivided (but Hindu-dominated) Bengal.

By the 1940s, the Muslim League (which had started out as the All-India Mohammedan Educational Conference), under the able leadership of M. A. Jinnah, became one of the key players in Indian nationalism and the eventual partition of the subcontinent. The league's history, from an educational organization to a political organization, suggests the ways that the subject of education (and educational access) provided one of the key initial spaces for Muslims to articulate a separate identity.

SOURCES AND CHAPTERS

What sets apart my research is its focus on how the mundane aspects of schooling, rather than debates between religious leaders, transformed the everyday definitions of what it meant to be a Christian, Hindu, or Muslim in the nineteenth century. In spite of the limited expansion of vernacular education during the nineteenth century, it became one of the unanticipated ways that missionaries and native reformers participated in the project of making a modern society. My reading and assessment of vernacular schoolbooks, teacher-training manuals, newspapers, stories, and memoirs help me better understand the multiple ways Bengali educators and reformers engaged with evangelical ideas as they set out to shape Bengali education. I delineate the exchange and subsequent transformation of ideas and practices between missionaries and their native interlocutors. My study explores not only the ideas but also the men, women, and children who peopled the nineteenth-century Bengali classroom.

The first part of the book examines how ideas about modern religion, particularly religious epistemology, were theorized by missionaries and *bhadralok* reformers through different pedagogic models. I argue that by successfully decoupling modern education from Christianity as a religion, *bhadralok* reformers demonstrated the possibility of creating an upper-caste Bengali modernity. In spite of the fact that missionary schools underlined the potential for Protestant conversion inherent in literacy and object lessons, *bhadralok* educators created competing materials and methods (many of them for government schools) that reflected their own modern upper-caste sensibilities. *Bhadralok* educators translated European schoolbooks and methods (many originating in evangelical schools) to secularize explicitly Protestant language and insert examples of upper-caste cultural practices in place of (or in addition to) European ones. Bengali educators effectively created an alternative set of "modern" educational tools that emphasized reason as the mark of scientific, rather than Protestant, thinking. In some instances, the materials produced by *bhadralok* educators were seen by missionaries themselves as superior to the vernacular Christian materials they were using and led to the unlikely outcome of the use of *bhadralok*-produced schoolbooks in Bengali Christian schools.

The second section of *Pedagogy for Religion* details how the gender norms of the missionary classroom, structured by notions of religious respectability, influenced the cultural ideas of the indigenous elite. I open up the literature on gender history in nineteenth-century India by using teacher training to study the construction of "modern" colonial masculinity and the overlooked histories of non-elite native women. The evangelical belief in the fundamental difference between boys and girls led them to insist that schooling at the primary level should be sex segregated (a practice that was otherwise not commonly practiced in Bengali village schools). This was accompanied by a new need to train men and women who could teach in the (now) sex-segregated schools and serve as models for appropriate gendered comportment. Teacher training manuals and institutions thus offered missionaries and *bhadralok* reformers an opportunity to articulate what "appropriate" gendered comportment should look like and how it could be introduced into native families. I show how good teaching came to define the qualities of good parenting in colonial Bengal.

After examining the complex and contradictory ways that missionary ideas were adopted by native society, I turn in my final section to the longer term effects of this historical dynamic for twentieth-century politics. I examine how debates among Hindu and Muslim leaders over primary schooling became a deliberation over the religious and national identity of India itself. Muslim educators criticized the dominance of upper-caste Hindus in government schools and the construction of the government curriculum. This led Muslim leaders, along with the colonial government, to argue for the necessity of a system of religiously separate schooling for the "backward" members of their community along the lines of the mission school model. The failure of Hindu educators to adequately respond to or even acknowledge the religious and cultural biases of their schools prompted Muslim leaders to argue for separate education and eventually for a separate nation.

My conclusion considers how the close connections between mass schooling and the reproduction of modern religious identity had long-term effects for both education and religion. On the one hand, by connecting religious identity so closely to modern schooling, the definitions of what constituted Christianity, Hinduism, or Islam became more narrowly defined through the standardizing of particular texts and rituals. In a colonial context, this meant that a (Protestant) imperial state effectively made itself the arbiter of what constituted an authentically modern Muslim education and, I would argue by extension, an authentically modern Muslim.

In the broadest possible sense, the purpose of modern schooling was as much about the production of new religious sensibilities as it was about the production of colonial subjects. This historical dynamic resulted in the increased politicizing of religion within schools—a characteristic that has sadly become one of the many shared aspects of global modernity. A historical perspective allows us to contextualize contemporary debates about the "excessive" religiosity of non-Western communities against the putative secularism of Western societies. We continue to see particular educational systems as standing in for the "qualities" we impute to particular religions. Muslim education is an obvious example of this historical blindness. Like W. W. Hunter, with whom I started this introduction, we are told that Muslim communities are predisposed to "fanatical" and "anti-American" tendencies—tendencies that are inculcated through Muslim *madrassahs* and *maktabs*.

But the simple binary of West and non-West on which such assertions rest is historically untenable. Religion, my study suggests, is written into modern education and not evidence of a sudden erupting of primordial identities by "backward "communities. The sustained involvement of missionaries in the development of mass schooling in both the West and its colonies meant that religious identity was always already a part of modern education. It is hardly surprising, then, that education globally remains one of the critical spaces for public debates over religion and culture as evidenced by the controversies over the wearing of headscarves in French schools or the teaching of Hindu histories in India. Thus the Sunday school and the Qur'an school must be seen in the same analytic frame, a part of the historical legacy of the imperial and missionary encounter.

CHAPTER 1

The Molding of Native Character

The title for this chapter comes from a study done in 1832 by the Unitarian missionary William Adam. Lord Bentinck, the governor-general of Bengal, had asked Adam to conduct a survey on the educational status of Bengal's villages both to determine the level of literacy in the Bengal countryside and to find out how rural schools were funded.[1] Adam's report was relatively comprehensive, detailing the different types of institutions for vernacular education, the levels of literacy, and information on school attendance. Adam had initially come to India as a Baptist missionary in 1818 but, under the influence of the early nineteenth-century Bengali intellectual Ram Mohan Roy, had become a Unitarian and active abolitionist. His growing social radicalism led him to support the educational "uplift" of ordinary villagers through basic education in the vernacular: Bengali or Hindi. He advocated a theory of general rural education based upon the indigenous village school, the *pathshala*, and in his work he attempted to demonstrate the vitality of the system in Bengal and Bihar. Though he was critical of what he perceived as the lack of moral instruction in indigenous schools, Adam felt that financially backing the existing system of *pathshalas* offered the East India Company the most effective (though expensive) means to modernize education in colonial Bengal.

Adam's report challenged the Calcutta-centered nature of the educational debate; while Anglicists and Orientalists might differ as to the language in which Bengalis should be educated, there was never any question that its center should be the city. Adam, in contrast, wanted the company to consider their responsibility to all of their colonial subjects. His highly detailed and careful study tried to make a case that any funding set aside for education should be expended for the vernacular schooling of the cultivating classes in villages. For Adam, a *pathshala*-centered strategy would ensure that children in every part of Bengal, cities, towns, and even small villages, would be able to benefit from enlightened British rule. Adam's report, so important to later historians, was largely ignored, and in 1838 he left India to join the abolitionist movement in the United States and Britain.

The interest and investment in primary schooling should not be confused with any real commitment to mass education. Bengali-language schooling, always in tension with English education, never received enough private or public funding to make it truly expansive. The colonial state remained, until 1854, wholly committed to a policy of elite English schooling. But Adam's report reflected an important facet of nineteenth-century Christian thought and activism. For reform-minded evangelicals like Adam, basic literacy (in the vernacular) was an essential part of the religious and social uplift of society, whether one was speaking of poor parishioners in the East End, Bengali villagers, or slaves in the West Indies.

In this chapter, I trace the paradox at the heart of the evangelical advocacy for primary education. On the one hand, Protestant missionaries like Adam, consistently framed basic education in terms of the eradication of larger social hierarchies—class or caste or slavery. At the same time, the historical experience of Nonconformist Protestants in Britain made them wary of any state involvement in education and prompted them to push for a more decentralized, private school system. Thus, the history of primary education in Bengal demonstrates the tension between these two mid-Victorian values of humanitarianism and voluntarism. The paradox lies in the fact that the privatization of education ensured that it would never be fully funded or supported. At the same time, a largely privatized system meant the active involvement of multiple constituencies in the development of a crucial modern institution—the school.

In Bengal, the conflict between voluntarism in school funding and the potentially socially radical impulses of mass education was most stark. Initially, the East India Company assumed that the small class of Indians they were willing to educate could be convinced to take up the cause of basic education for their peasant brothers. But this remained a chimera;

the English-educated Bengali *bhadralok* were, in Ashok Sen's words, "bound in the nexuses of subordinate activities and wealth of the colonial economy." Thus, they offered little support for the real expansion of vernacular education to the masses, particularly when "it would be encouraged at the cost of their own facilities for English learning, the only means of living and respectability available to them."[2] For missionaries, this resistance was not only economic but also a reflection of the deeply entrenched caste hierarchy at the heart of Hindu culture. The potential for social (and caste) mobility through education was not realized through the *bhadralok*, but instead got taken up by missionaries and lower-caste Hindu and Muslim communities themselves, who embraced the potential of social transformation through the broadening of educational options.

EVANGELICALISM AND THE GROWTH OF MODERN ELEMENTARY SCHOOLING

The religious revival in Britain began in the mid-eighteenth century in the form of Wesleyan and Calvinist Methodism. It was a popular movement originating from genuine religious impulse and striving toward the creation of a new kind of society. As one historian of missionaries describes it, the idea of being born again in Christ was "the working of inner spiritual experience with a sudden illumination . . . coming after the consciousness and repentance of sin."[3]

Initially, Christian revivalism was influenced most by the activities of Nonconformist Protestants, the name commonly given to Protestant Christians who refused to "conform" to the rituals and rules of the Church of England. But anxiety and fears engendered by the French Revolution led the Church of England to become more open to the appeal of evangelicalism in the Anglican Church as well. Victor Kiernan has suggested that the tension within early-nineteenth-century British religious culture was "of religion as the formulary of an established society, its statement of faith in itself; the other as a catastrophic conversion of the individual, a miraculous shaking off of secret burdens."[4] The nineteenth century can be seen as a constant effort to contain the enthusiasm and potential rebellion of the "catastrophic conversion of the individual" in order to ensure the stability of "established society."

Both Established and Nonconformist congregations organized agencies to deal with the pressing humanitarian issues of the period: poverty, education, and slavery. In fact, the very definition of what it meant to be a good Christian became inextricably tied to the notion of doing good works: "in the public mind the word 'philanthropist' became all but synonymous with 'evangelical' and 'philanthropy' was applied to the good works that appealed most to evangelical tastes."[5] Evangelical Christians were involved in a variety of activities that could be variously described as philanthropic or political—the line consciously blurred.[6] But the evangelical project that is most critical in this study is the development and expansion of mass schooling that began with the Nonconformist Sunday schools in Britain and extended to the establishment of a wide network of mission schools in Africa, the Middle East, and Asia.

British Sunday schools became important institutions not only for expanding the access of the poor and working classes to literacy (and thus to the word of God) but also as a place for popularizing missionary activity and Empire more generally. For example, one of the most popular subjects for the missionary biographies taught in Sunday schools was William Carey, the first Baptist missionary in Bengal. William Carey's life trajectory bears out Hobsbawm's colorful description of Nonconformists as coming from "among those who were about to rise into the new middle class, those about to decline into a new proletariat, and the indiscriminate mass of small independent men in between."[7] Born in Northamptonshire in 1761, Carey's father (a handloom weaver) sent him off to be a shoemaker's apprentice, and it was there that he became an evangelical Baptist.[8] Biographies of Carey make his humble background the center of his greatness; his success and stature as a missionary were not marked by his high status, but by his personal conversion, his love of science (especially botany and geography), and his desire to read other great imperial works, like James Cook's *Voyages*.

In India, Christian schooling and pedagogic practice were meant to "awaken" the Hindu masses and eventually result in the transformation of native society through conversion but also through an open attack on caste and gender segregation. Evangelical missionaries understood Hinduism, as they did other non-Christian religions, through a literal reading of Genesis. Since Adam's fall, his descendants had moved away from the true teachings, but its traces could still be detected in Hinduism. It was the responsibility of missionaries to bring non-Christians back into the fold.[9] But the equally important role of Christians was to end various religious practices that they argued defined Hinduism: sati (the immolation of widows), female infanticide, and caste.

Caste, in particular, was seen by Protestant missionaries as the main obstacle to Christian conversion since it tied individuals to not only their families but also whole communities and livelihoods. From the early nineteenth century, as Protestant evangelicals began looking toward India to proselytize, they circulated the notion of caste as a form of slavery. The social and ritual hierarchy of caste made Hindus subservient to the machinations of the Hindu priest and the cruelty of the Brahmin. In 1808, for instance, the *Christian Observer* noted, "A Brahmin may seize without hesitation, if he be in distress for a subsistence, the goods of his Sudra slave, for as that slave can have no property, his master may take his goods."[10] The arbitrary power of the Brahmin seemed analogous to the arbitrary tyranny of the slaveholder.

Protestant missionaries challenged the caste system in a number of different ways: publishing anticaste pamphlets, agitating against Untouchability, and starting schools open to all castes. Even the Church Missionary Society, which was highly invested in promoting class stability in Britain, was openly critical of the stratification of the caste system. For native Christians, a number of whom were from lower-caste and Untouchable communities, the Christian school provided them with their first opportunity to be formally educated. The missionary decision to educate lower-caste communities was a direct challenge to one of the core principles of upper-caste discriminatory practice—retaining the exclusive right of upper-caste men to literacy. Evangelical interest in establishing modern education served two purposes: a genuine effort to proselytize through schools as well as an effort to dismantle caste hierarchy through literacy and mobility. It was this latter project that provided one of the most important distinctions between Christian schools and those run by the colonial state and *bhadralok* educators. The caste bias of Bengali schools proved quite intractable, and both government and *bhadralok*-run institutions were dominated by the traditionally higher, literate castes: Brahmins, Kayasths, and Baidyas.

ELEMENTARY SCHOOLING IN BENGAL

In his report, Adam noted the various kinds of indigenous learning systems in Bengal. There were Persian schools catering to Hindu and Muslim students training them for Mughal administrative positions. There were also Hindu religious schools (*tol*) meant to impart Sanskrit liturgical knowledge. But the most widespread rural education was provided by *pathshalas*, which taught rudimentary "reading, writing, arithmetic . . . zamindari and mahajan accounts."[11] The *pathshalas* were organized around agricultural work schedules, meeting in the morning and evening so the students could return to the fields during the day. The *tols* (Hindu liturgical schools) and *madrassahs* (Muslim religious schools) offered a higher education in grammar, rhetoric, law, literature, philosophy, medicine, and astrology. The *tols* and *madrassahs* were more dependent on wealthy benefactors and religious elite than were *pathshalas,* which were strictly local institutions. Although *pathshalas* were widespread, they were not truly vehicles for "mass" education. They tended to educate male, Hindu, upper-caste (but non-Brahmin) boys and were not as "democratic" as later nationalist writers would argue.[12]

Missionaries were critical of the native *pathshala* for both the quality of the education it offered and its exclusive focus on upper-caste and male children. The *pathshala* lacked many of the outward trappings of modern education (a permanent schoolroom, punctual attendance, etc.) and offered a perfunctory education that did little to mold good character or behavior in students. In contrast, missionaries argued that their educational efforts captured the true spirit of modern pedagogy: the inculcation of moral nature and thus the social transformation of society.

The establishment of vernacular rural education was attempted early on, mainly by Nonconformist Protestants. Well before Adam's report, William Carey, the Baptist missionary, had already begun experimenting with Sunday schools in Serampore. Carey's own conversion history, from a poor cobbler to a highly respected missionary in India, convinced him of the importance of literacy and basic education—in this case, aimed at rural Bengalis. From the early nineteenth century, he and his compatriots, William Ward and Joshua Marshman, focused on establishing printing presses to publish Bengali-language Bibles and schoolbooks, and opened primary schools for native children in Serampore, Chinsura, Burdwan, and Calcutta.[13] As the Serampore missionaries translated the Bible into Bengali, Baptists in Wales were similarly translating and educating the population in Welsh.

Mission educators, unlike company officials, were concerned with the long-term solutions to the problem of vernacular schools in India. They devised a number of alternative plans to extend their model of modern schooling to compete with *pathshalas.* For instance, Thomas Thomason, the Anglican chaplain for the East India Company, in 1814 devised "the first detailed and comprehensive plan for education in the Bengal Presidency."[14] He suggested opening government high schools to teach English and modern science, a normal school to train teachers, and primary vernacular schools in villages. Although some of Thomason's ideas would be later taken up by the colonial state, there was little money or interest among company officials in extending primary schools.

The relative indifference of the East India Company to questions of elementary schooling, and the fact that the Established Church did not have the same monopoly in India as in Britain, meant Nonconformist missionaries had greater autonomy to experiment with more radical pedagogic techniques. In contrast, in Britain, the Church of England and Parliament were wary of the possibilities that pedagogic radicalism would lead to political radicalism. Particularly in the early nineteenth century, conservative thinkers like Hannah More believed that teaching working-class children to read was acceptable as long as they mainly read Church-sanctioned catechism and were not taught to write. Thus, anxiety over class conflict influenced the degree to which English schools were willing to employ new forms of pedagogy.

Missionaries in India, on the other hand, were able to create a much broader and more liberal curriculum in early-nineteenth-century Bengal because they wanted to "awaken" the masses to Christianity. The Serampore missionaries found that they had complete autonomy in devising their Sunday schools and thus felt no compunction about breaking with English educational systems and turning their attention to Scotland, which had a more innovative pedagogic and institutional system for elementary education. Scottish parish schools, endowed and financed by local landowners in each parish, provided more stable financing and a more standardized educational system than the more haphazard English one.[15]

Not all evangelicals were convinced that investment in vernacular schooling was the best way to proselytize and convert India. In fact, Carey's work in vernacular education was directly challenged by Alexander Duff, a Scottish Presbyterian missionary.[16] For Duff, it was foolhardy for missionaries to ignore the education of the higher classes, leaving them at the mercy of the various "secular" experiments with English college education funded by the company and Parliament.[17] Missionaries needed to make inroads into this class of natives who would one day wield power and influence in the economy and society. Duff argued that while "the soul of the humblest and most illiterate peasant may be as precious, in the sight of God, as the soul of the most powerful," in terms of "the great interests of a realm (say Scotland) one Knox is worth ten thousand illiterate peasants."[18] Duff questioned the purpose of educating large numbers of illiterate peasants, as Carey was doing in the Serampore countryside, since any native Knox (the theologian responsible for the Calvinist reformation in the sixteenth century) would invariably have to come from educated and more elite Bengali society.[19]

Within missionary circles, the language debate was never clearly won by either Duff or Carey. The differences between the Anglicist and vernacularist evangelical positions led to very different kinds of mission schools: the urban, English-medium secondary institutions and the rural, Bengali primary schools. Naturally these two types of schools also served different communities. The rural schools increasingly became the place where native Christians and lower-caste children were educated, while Christians training to be catechists and schoolteachers and the Hindu *bhadralok* attended institutions like Duff's Free Church School and College in Calcutta. The divide between Duff's institution and the various semirural vernacular day schools started by both the Baptists and Methodists demonstrated the inherent tension within Christianity itself—between its imperial aspirations and its message of equality and brotherhood.

"WOOD'S DESPATCH" AND MODERN VERNACULAR EDUCATION

Before 1854, the colonial government not only ignored but also actually helped dismantle vernacular education, particularly the village *pathshala* system. Colonial land reforms had disrupted the *pathshala* system since declining agricultural revenue and loss of local control decreased villagers' abilities to support their local school. Thus, while missionaries continued to expand and extend their network of rural primary schools with little regulation from the government, the *pathshala* system suffered from lack of funds and support from either the government or local landowners.

Meanwhile, the company continued to fund upper-level English-language institutions mainly attended by the children of upper-caste families, particularly those families who worked for the East India Company. The English-language schools, in keeping with the government's commitment to religious neutrality, were run as secular institutions, but the company made no such provisions at the primary, vernacular level.

In response to the secular schools run by the company in India, missionaries petitioned Parliament to fulfill their Christian and moral duty by withdrawing from their godless secular experiments and giving direct aid to missionaries to help create a comprehensive system of primary and secondary Christian schools. The missionaries hoped to recreate in India the dominance they enjoyed in Britain, where Nonconformists established a parallel private system of schooling that eclipsed state efforts. In India, however, missionaries found themselves in direct competition with the putatively Christian imperial state. The relationship between missionaries and the colonial state deteriorated further after the Mutiny of 1857, when it became even more important for the government to reiterate its commitment to religious neutrality.[20]

When the government finally adopted a system of grants-in-aid for vernacular education, it was not for the purpose of supporting mission education, but to encourage native Hindus and Muslims to open their own schools. In 1853, when the company's charter was being renewed, the House of Commons held an extensive inquiry into educational developments in India. Their findings, published in 1854 as "Wood's Education Despatch," criticized the official government policy of downward filtration inherent in Macaulay's Anglicist position. In "Wood's Despatch," the colonial government publicly acknowledged that it had, at least rhetorically, a responsibility to educate its colonial subjects.[21]

The grant-in-aid rules were set up to ensure that the state retains its religious neutrality and that private organizations, missionary and native, benefit from government funds. The establishment of grants-in-aid mirrored educational policy in Britain, where from the 1840s various schemes were created to combine secular instruction and religious education. As one essayist suggested in the *Calcutta Review,* "The cardinal principal of the Government in England in education has been grants-in-aid, helping men to help themselves."[22]

"Wood's Despatch" laid out a series of educational objectives funded through both private and public means. This included the establishment of a Department of Public Instruction (DPI) in each of the five provinces. The department was headed by the director of public instruction, who would be assisted by a series of inspectors and assistants. The despatch also legislated that a certain amount be spent on opening universities in the main urban areas and schools for training teachers. In terms of primary education, the despatch had two main features: establishing a network of graded schools (from *pathshala* to the university) and creating a system of grants-in-aid to fund these institutions.

"Wood's Despatch" reflected not only a particular educational vision but also the sentiments and ideology of mid-Victorian Britain more generally. That is, the despatch was concerned that every individual should receive the education suited to his or her station in life: English for the elite, vernacular for the masses. The mid-Victorian ideal was best reflected in the voluntarism that underlay the despatch. The colonial government did not want to increase the small sum it set aside for colonial education, so it expected that native leaders would open and extend schooling through grants-in-aid from the state. The government provided one-third to one-half of the cost of opening a school. Governmental aid was to be given to any and all schools that imparted a good secular education (any religious instruction offered did not figure into grant decisions), was well managed, submitted to inspection by the government, and levied a fee from the students.

In their annual reports, entitled the *General Reports on Public Instruction*, the inspectors in the DPI maintained a yearly record of the grants-in-aid they awarded. For example, in 1868 in Bengal, we learn that 318 missionary institutions, 52 "Other Christian bodies," and 1,245 "native" schools received grants from the government.[23] While the 1868 report suggests that there was rough equity per student (with the notable exception of "Other Christian bodies," which received almost three times per student), a comment from a school inspector in an 1864 report suggests otherwise: "The grants to the Christian school are by far the largest in proportion to the number of students under instruction and missionary schools receive nearly 50% more for each of their students than the schools under native managers."[24] The reason for this bias was actually structured into the system itself. The grants-in-aid were awarded based on the degree to which individual schools were seen to meet the definition of a "modern" education. The ostensibly "objective" set of criteria was shaped by the elementary school models in Britain—schools that had been developed by Protestant Nonconformists. In real terms, this meant that indigenous pedagogic practices were dismissed out of hand as "backward" and inappropriate for a modern education.

Although missionaries disproportionately benefited from the grant-in-aid policy, they were nonetheless hesitant about accepting state aid. State intervention meant that schools run by natives and schools run by missionaries would be judged by the same guidelines, and that the government could continue its own "Godless" experiments by opening secular government primary schools. Unsure of how to respond to the despatch, missionaries hoped that the experience of Britain would be their guide. In Britain, the peculiar mix of private and public funding for education was at least partially related to the resistance of Nonconformists to any purely state-run system. Historians of education in Britain argue that Nonconformists (Baptists, Methodists, etc.), who were seminal in inaugurating primary education, effectively sabotaged any success of a national education system. The fear of the Nonconformists was that any national schools would de facto come under the influence of the Church of England.

Unlike in Britain, the ecumenical sentiments of Indian missionaries (in a "heathen" country, they were all Christians) made them more open to government support. But the colonial government was determined to retain its religious neutrality and expected missionaries to apply, alongside natives, for government grants-in-aid. In spite of the indignity of being treated in the same manner as non-Christians, missionaries in India seemed to lean toward accepting the grants-in-aid from the colonial state. This was in spite of their Home Committee's skepticism of the dangers of state intervention. The Church Missionary Society (CMS), as a branch of the Church of England, did not hesitate at all. However, the home societies of the Congregationalist London Missionary Society (LMS) and the Baptist Missionary Society (BMS) were more circumspect and hesitant about state support. Edward Storrow, an LMS missionary in India, wrote to the directors in London encouraging them to accept "Wood's Despatch." "You will perceive that the education we now give is in no sense interfered with, we are simply encouraged by pecuniary aid to increase the number and efficiency of our schools."[25] Storrow argued that the Scottish Free Church (under Duff) had accepted the funding, and he felt that the LMS mission would fall behind if they declined government aid. The correspondence between Storrow and the directors indicate that the Indian missionaries were more eager to accept the aid than the directors of the home societies in London.

The Baptist Home Society in Britain displayed a similar hesitancy, but acknowledged that the colonial situation was different than the relationship of Nonconformists to the state in Britain. Specifically, the missionary Home Committee in Britain was committed to "the principle of not accepting government money," but they recognized that "India was deemed an exceptional case . . . [they shall] leave the Christian liberty of the missionary untouched."[26] The committee simultaneously expressed its displeasure and recognition of the special case of India (and probably other colonies), where there was a greater financial and political need for government money and support.

"WOOD'S DESPATCH" AND THE FAILURE OF VERNACULAR EDUCATION

After 1854, the DPI recognized that the *bhadralok* community would (or should) be a primary player in the extension of vernacular education. It was not only that the colonial state gave grants-in-aid to various *bhadralok* educators but also that some of the major nineteenth-century upper-caste reformers, particularly Iswar Chandra Vidyasagar and Bhudev Mukhopadhyay, were actually employed by the DPI.

It was routinely observed within the DPI that Bengal had most successfully met the goals of "Wood's Despatch" because of its extensive privately funded schooling system. But rather than leading to the successful expansion of primary-level education, the difference between government expenditure on lower-class schools in Bengal and that in other provinces was marked: Bengal spent 103,000 rupees, Bombay spent 393,000 rupees, North West Provinces spent 337,000 rupees, and Punjab spent 167,000 rupees.[27] The large disparities in educational funding created a curious historical situation. Bengal, which had long been known for its renaissance and the importance of its intellectual elite, actually had a system of schooling that was very shallow. It had a small, highly educated elite and larger numbers of illiterate peasants than almost any other part of India. It seemed that wherever English was taught, it eclipsed and drew away support from any other forms of education, especially vernacular, primary schools (and even lower-grade *pathshalas*). While the *bhadralok* had enthusiastically taken up the private expansion of education, their efforts were not exactly what the DPI had hoped for. Instead of a large number of primary schools in rural areas, in Bengal there were many more Anglo-vernacular institutions that almost exclusively educated the children of the *bhadra* classes.

The Department of Public Instruction noted four types of schools in Bengal that were funded through "Wood's Despatch." They were, in order of how much direct assistance they received from the colonial state, *Zillah*, or district, schools (completely funded by the state); aided Anglo-vernacular schools; aided vernacular schools; and indigenous schools (completely unfunded and unregulated—various kinds of informal village institutions). The degree of state funding directly influenced how elite a school was considered by the native population and the kinds of children who were allowed access to them. For instance, *zillah* schools were dominated by the children of those who worked for the government: tax collectors, magistrates, educational inspectors, and so on.

Anglo-vernacular schools tended to be filled with children of *talukdars* (small landholders), clerks, *banias* (merchants), and so on. Poorer, lower-caste, and more rural communities sent their children to the aided vernacular (which, by receiving some funding from the state, were still popular) and indigenous schools.

Though "Wood's Despatch" was initially hailed as a challenge to the notion of downward filtration, in fact it instantiated the hierarchy of languages and class in colonial India. This is evident in the section on the relationship between English and the vernaculars. The despatch concludes that "while the English language continues to be made use of as by far the most perfect *medium* for the education of those persons who have acquired a sufficient knowledge of it to receive general instruction *through* it, the vernacular languages should be employed to teach the far larger class who are ignorant of, or imperfectly acquainted with, English."[28] In "Wood's Despatch," English remained the perfect medium for a general modern education. The status of English, against the vernaculars, was not lost on the *bhadralok*, who were more interested in funding separate Anglo-vernacular schools that would offer them the possibility of teaching their children English without succumbing to a purely "Western" education. As the 1863 *Report on Public Instruction* brutally remarked, "[T]he teaching of English brings resources and money along with it which a good vernacular school simply doesn't."[29]

In spite of the relatively low status of Bengali, compared to English, the Anglo-vernacular school still remained the most popular form of modern education among the *bhadra* (cultured) classes. While it was important for individual upper-caste children to learn English, it was critical for Bengalis, as a community, to modernize their own language. The education of students in Bengali, in addition to English, would ensure that education would not merely be a form of "Westernization" but rather a form of "modernization." The cultural anxiety over retaining one's culture, however reconfigured, in the face of colonial culture was one that marked all colonial societies, and the Anglo-vernacular school provided the *bhadra* classes with one solution.

SLAVERY AND EDUCATION: THE DEBATE OVER EDUCATION FUNDING AND TAXES

The colonial government, interested most in stabilizing its land policy, was nonetheless concerned about instilling at least a modicum of duty in the landowning classes, particularly since education for the masses was largely privatized. The educational report of 1856 lamented the *zemindars*, who had no "proper sense of their duties and responsibilities," and thus refused to promote "the establishment of improved vernacular schools among the poorer class."[30] The education report put the problem squarely on the shoulders of the colonial government, which had failed to reward (or punish) *zemindars* for fulfilling (or failing to fulfill) their educational duties and responsibilities to their peasants. Yet the very permanence of the land taxes made it virtually impossible to financially coerce the *zemindari* classes to defray the cost of vernacular mass education.

In the 1870s, the whole question of the Permanent Settlement and funding for mass education was revisited in the reorganization of colonial administration and fiscal management. Between 1854 and 1870, the colonial state had created a very centralized system of financial administration, where the budget allotted to any one province had no relation to the actual revenue generated there. But in 1870, certain departments, including education, were decentralized and kept a part of their tax receipts and a lump sum from the government to finance various programs. Although there were changes in the levels of centralization and decentralization, educational funding did not increase. The only opportunity to get more funds for education came at the time of the revision of the land settlements, once every five years. Thus, in 1870, there was a debate in Bengal over the possibility of increasing the funding for vernacular schools through a land cess (tax) and shifting some of the resources devoted to English schooling to vernacular education.

The debate over increasing tax funding for mass education in the vernacular pitted missionaries against *zemindars* (landowners) and reflected two quite distinct orientations on the question of the purpose and logic behind modern schooling. The Permanent Settlement (ostensibly the reason that taxes on the land could not be increased) represented for the *zemindars* the great triumph of property ownership and civilization. But for the missionaries, the Permanent Settlement had created a situation of abject poverty and slave-like working conditions in the rural areas.

Zemindars argued that the Permanent Settlement represented a promise between the colonial government and the Bengali landowners to respect a fixed tax that could not be arbitrarily raised, which is what was being proposed in the educational cess. The key to successfully creating trustworthy landed elite was to ensure that the fiscal demands of the state would not unduly burden the *zemindars*. Baboo Rajendra Lall Mitra succinctly captured the promise inherent in the settlement, in which the "benign and liberal English rule, has taught the people the value of property and the constitutional means of defending their rights."[31] The Permanent Settlement, English-based education, and the voluntarism of "Wood's Despatch" were part and parcel of a system in which a benign and liberal colonial state would *teach* natives the fundamental values of mid-Victorian Britain: property, Western learning, and a noninterventionist state.[32]

In a *zemindari* propaganda pamphlet published during the cess debate, Thakurdas Chakraborty bemoaned the folly of supporting any form of mass primary education. He pointed out that only the upper strata, which he defined through caste (Brahmins, Khetrees, Boidas, and Kavists), could benefit from schooling. The lowest castes (Harees, Bagdees, Doms, Chandals, Moochio, Kowras, etc.) "are forever doomed to a life of wretchedness and misery. They do not appreciate education."[33] Rather than seeing education as a means by which the lowest and most untouchable castes in Bengal could be "uplifted" from their wretchedness and misery, Chakrabarty echoes centuries of Hindu caste prejudice in asserting that it is their low status that makes them fundamentally unworthy of schooling itself. But what makes Chakrabarty's pamphlet, entitled "Popular Education for Bengal," modern is the perceived need to actually justify reasons to deny mass education in the vernacular to the lower castes, a fact that was rarely raised in earlier periods.

In contrast to Chakrabarty, Reverend James Long, an Anglican missionary with the CMS, had a very different view of the effects of both English education and the Permanent Settlement.[34] Long claimed that the colonial state had to consider the claims of all its colonial subjects, especially the humble *ryot* or peasant. The Permanent Settlement, like English education, resulted in strengthening the position of the *zemindars* and unintentionally allowed the development of a tyrannical, autocratic class of landowners. In the process, the Bengali peasant had become increasingly impoverished and uneducated—a victim to the machinations of *zemindars* who were opposed to his education or the amelioration of his existence. Long noted that after a "quarter century's residence in Bengal," he had rarely known any *zemindars* or educated natives who would "do anything *to raise the Bengal ryot to the status of a 'man and brother'*. The Supreme Government, therefore, as the gurit-purwa (the protector of the poor and helpless) ought not to forego it[s] functions in this case."[35]

The evocation of the antislavery movement's most famous battle cry, "Am I not a man and a brother?" was not accidental.[36] It recalled the powerful metaphor of caste hierarchy (in this case, the peasant castes against the urban upper castes) as a form of enslavement. The Permanent Settlement had created, in the view of Long and many of his missionary counterparts, a system of semi-unfree labor that only exacerbated the caste hierarchies in native society. This situation, comparable some argued to that of the West Indian slave, was made worse by the lack of a vernacular education, which made it virtually impossible for the *ryot* to learn his rights and protect himself against the tyranny of the *zemindari* class. Both the *zemindars* and missionaries, in making their arguments to the colonial government, relied upon notions of humanitarianism and voluntarism. The *zemindars* resisted a compulsory cess by insisting that they had already contributed to, and would continue to privately contribute to, the education of the benighted masses. The missionaries, while supporting an educational cess, based their argument on the notion of a state as the protector of the weak and helpless.

CONCLUSION

I want to conclude by considering a slightly different argument about mass education proposed by Reverend Lal Behari De, one of the most important native Christian leaders (belonging to the Scottish Presbyterian Church) and social reformers in Bengal. Lal Behari De felt colonial education was ultimately funded through the labor of the peasant classes themselves. Thus, the colonial state's various plans for mass education should not be viewed (as Long suggested) as a part of charitable largesse and imperial humanitarianism. Reverend De indignantly asserted that defining the funding of mass education as a form of charity was "a strange sort of charity . . . to receive in return an infinitesimal fraction of millions of pounds sterling which we pay every year in hard cash!"[37] Reverend De pointed out the obvious reality: the rural masses *subsidized* the British imperial state, and in return the paltry sum set aside for education went to English education of the elite. Thus, it was not charity that should move the colonial state to improve vernacular schooling but duty and a modicum of responsibility.

In reading the debates between missionaries and *zemindars* over the question of mass schooling, it is easy to see the colonial state as a neutral arbitrator and administrator. But the colonial state, through the Permanent Settlement and "Wood's Despatch," had made it virtually impossible for elementary mass education to ever be realizable. It was an inherent contradiction between the "humanitarian" and "colonial" imperatives of the government. There was, in fact, no material reason for the middle classes to support mass education since they themselves were unsure of their employment prospects. In spite of their rhetoric, it was also not in the colonial government's interests to spend their "profits" or "taxes" on the education of the masses. Ultimately, as one writer in the *Calcutta Review* noted, in the United States the success of popular education was that it was not based on philanthropy but on citizenship.[38]

In spite of the failure of mass education to be ever truly realizable during the colonial period, schooling in the vernacular remained a compelling and important issue for missionaries and their *bhadralok* interlocutors. The lack of any real state effort to expand and extend education created the conditions in which private organizations, largely based on caste or religious affiliation, felt responsible for establishing schools for their "own" children. The next four chapters will look at how the semi-privatized school system led to a highly creative proliferation of educational materials and technologies. This meant, in part, that ordinary language primers and teacher-training manuals were able to capture the cultural aspirations and prejudices of various communities in a rapidly changing colonial society.

CHAPTER 2

A Curriculum for Religion

In the traditional village school, the *pathshala,* the purpose of numeric and alphabetic literacy was to teach children a set of skills to meet "the practical demands of life."[1] *Pathshalas* taught account keeping and reading so students knew how to write letters and keep land and financial records. *Pathshalas* rarely employed books; instead, they taught through dictation, memorization, and writing on palm and plantain leaves. The few manuscripts used in the *pathshala* were books on Hindu devotion or grammar—texts that students learned and then recited back to their teacher or *guru.* Thus, the introduction of schoolbooks into mid-nineteenth-century Bengali vernacular and Anglo-vernacular schools represented a wholly new way to teach literacy. But schoolbooks did not merely represent the introduction of a new technology into the *pathshala.* The modern language primer and reader denoted a new sensibility about the ultimate purpose of reading itself—the shaping of religious character.

The earliest Bengali schoolbooks were published by missionaries in the first half of the nineteenth century. Evangelical educators, unlike the *pathshala guru,* believed that reading was inextricably connected to the cultivation of the moral Christian self. Literacy's role transcended the purely functional in evangelical Protestantism; just as important as knowledge of Scripture was the actual act of reading. The practice of reading was a means for constructing and improving the new Christian subject.

In 1817, the Calcutta School Book Society was established to supervise and standardize schoolbook publications. The organization was made up of European and Indian scholars and educators (in a 2:1 ratio), including Muslim *maulavis,* Hindu *pandits,* and Protestant missionaries.[2] Again, this reflected the imperial common sense that education should remain under the purview of religious scholars, even though this did not reflect the complexity of the educational picture in precolonial Bengal. While the Calcutta School Book Society continued to fund the publication of Bengali language material into the 1860s, their work was soon eclipsed by the private publishing efforts of missionaries and upper-caste Hindu educators, the *bhadralok,* by the mid-1850s.

Initially the Baptist missionaries in Serampore began writing and printing readers to help reach potential converts and introduce new ways to teach basic Bengali literacy. However, unlike in Britain, where various Christian groups continued to retain some dominance in schoolbook publishing, by the mid-nineteenth century, *bhadralok* educators successfully took up the new educational method. Although missionaries had introduced the modern language primer and reader into colonial Bengal, *bhadralok* writers and publishers made the practice truly profitable. Bengali language schoolbooks, mainly written by upper-caste Hindus with connections to the colonial government, shared with the earlier evangelical texts the need to connect literacy with the molding of moral and religious character. Basic language primers and readers offered *bhadralok* schoolbook writers the opportunity to teach both a new form of prose Bengali as well as lessons meant to produce a modern Bengali, upper-caste subject.

Among the great number and variety of language primers and readers available in the later nineteenth century, by far the most widely used in schools were those of Iswar Chandra Vidyasagar, the preeminent social reformer and educator. Vidyasagar's midcentury schoolbooks, particularly his primer *Barnaparichoy (An Introduction to Letters),* became the template for almost all other language primers. The crucial role of Vidyasagar in the creation of primary language instruction is attested to by the decision of a number of missionary schools to adopt his texts for their own Bengali schools, replacing Christian Bengali readers and primers that they had previously employed.

There have been some wonderful studies of Vidyasagar's life and work, but these have largely focused on how he "vernacularized," through a Brahminical filter, the moral lessons of colonial modernity.[3] But my goal in this chapter is somewhat different. I am less interested in how Vidyasagar's work informed a particular moment in the formation of *bhadralok* culture and more interested in the meaning and resonance of Vidyasagar's readers and primers for non-*bhadralok* educators—specifically missionaries. I see the evangelical debates over the use of Vidyasagar's books in Christian schools as having significance beyond Protestant mission circles. In the process of attacking or defending the use of Vidyasagar's primers and readers, missionary educators articulated and anticipated many of the arguments that would structure colonial debates about how best to educate a religiously plural society.

On the face of it, it is unclear why Bengali literacy should be such a contested subject. There seemed to be widespread agreement among many communities in the mid-nineteenth century that a modern Bengali society, seen to be made up of Hindus, Christians, and Muslims, needed to be literate in the vernacular language.[4] Yet, as I will show in this chapter, the actual history of language primers and readers, everything from the form of modern Bengali to the sentences employed to teach the language, were seen to be inextricably connected to questions of religion and religious identity. The debates over literacy and religious subjectivity that began in the midcentury between *bhadralok* and missionary educators were continued into the twentieth century among Hindu and Muslim reformers.

This chapter focuses primarily on the conflict over language and religious identity among Protestant missionaries in the mid-nineteenth century: a conflict that reflected two distinct orientations to the question of how to teach literacy within a multireligious cultural context. On one side of the debate was John Murdoch, a prominent Indian missionary and founder of the Christian Vernacular Education Society (CVES), who accused missionaries in Bengal of abandoning the central goals and purposes of Christian education by adopting Vidyasagar's book. Since Protestant epistemology emphasized the production of religious character through reading, Murdoch argued that the use of non-Christian books would produce a nominally Hindu subject.[5] At first, he directed his concerns to Vidyasagar (and the larger *bhadralok* educational establishment) himself, critiquing what he perceived as the overly difficult, highly Sanskritzed prose Bengali that Vidyasagar was employing in his language primers. Murdoch was frustrated that Vidyasagar's version of modern Bengali, with its roots clearly in the world of the Brahmin literati, should be so eagerly embraced by local educators, the government, and even missionaries. Ultimately, Murdoch's critiques were ignored by other *bhadralok* educators, and so he turned his attention to local missionaries in Bengal, who seemed to be using Vidyasagar's texts in larger numbers. Murdoch instigated an investigation into the use of *bhadralok*-based texts in mission schools and attempted to get Protestant home societies to pressure the committees in Bengal to use more explicitly Christian material.

On the other side of the debate, and as a response to Murdoch's attacks, Bengali mission schools defended their use of Vidyasagar's texts by questioning the relationship between reading and the formation of a specific kind of religious subject. Missionary teachers argued that Vidyasagar's texts were far superior to any Christian-produced texts because the language was more "authentic" and the examples and stories more pedagogically effective in producing morally upright subjects. In spite of the opposition of Murdoch and the home societies, missionaries in Bengal continued to use *bhadralok*-produced texts and effectively defied the evangelical orthodoxy that a Christian education meant a curriculum completely oriented around Christian books and methods. Instead, Protestant missionaries tried to address Murdoch's concerns by reconfiguring their curriculum to teach Christianity as a separate subject using biblical exegesis and catechistical texts. Missionaries in Bengal were criticized by home societies for this decision since it seemed to capitulate to the forces of secularism rather than merely being a pragmatic movement toward ecumenicalism in a religiously plural colonial environment.

While the debates over the use of Vidyasagar's texts had largely dissipated among missionaries by the later nineteenth century, they were revived again in the early twentieth century. Specifically, Murdoch's early critique of the caste and religious bias of *bhadralok*-produced texts was picked up and made even more forcefully by Muslim reformers. Bengali Muslim educators, like evangelical educators before them, rejected the existing Bengali schoolbooks because they taught a *pandit* Bengali through Hindu idioms. Like Murdoch, members of the urban Muslim elite, or *ashraf,* wanted schoolbooks that were written in *dobhashi* or *Mussalmani* Bengali and contained stories and references to greater pan-Islamic culture. The *ashraf* repeatedly raised the concern that Muslim schoolchildren who attended the local Bengali *pathshala* and learned Bengali from *bhadralok*-produced texts would emerge as "Hinduized" Muslim subjects.

The first part of the chapter traces the development of language primers and readers from metropolitan Britain to colonial Bengal—in particular the exponential growth of Bengali publishing among upper-caste Hindus, in response to the growth of vernacular schooling in the mid-nineteenth century. I then examine the consequences of the debate engendered by John Murdoch's challenge to the use of Vidyasagar's texts in Christian schools. The chapter concludes by considering how missionary debates about the relationship between language and religious identity helped constitute two crucial aspects of later Bengali political discourse. On the one hand, the evangelical accusation of upper-caste bias in popular Bengali primers was echoed by later Muslim Bengalis who similarly opposed the Sanskritized language being taught in village schools. On the other hand, the ecumenical sentiments expressed by local Bengali missionaries, that there was an inherent educational and literary worth in using books that were not written by Christians, opened up the possibility for a broader imagining of the relationship between religious identity, education, and language that would become important in both British and Indian forms of pluralism.

THE EVOLUTION OF THE EVANGELICAL SCHOOLBOOK

Initially among Christian educators, the Bible represented the most complete text in terms of its theology and pedagogy. But the nineteenth-century expansion of Sunday schools (in metropolitan Britain) and mission schools (in colonial India) prompted the demand for and production of separate Christian schoolbooks. Nineteenth-century Protestant missionaries were especially interested in the relationship between knowledge and the inculcation of morality and belief. The main purpose of the early Sunday schools was to teach rudimentary literacy so the children of the working classes could read Scripture. Reading, which allowed the individual direct access to the word of God, was more than an exercise of the intellect, and Luther's. The practice of reading became a way in which the moral (evangelical) self could be monitored and improved, and was thus constitutive of the new Christian subject. The "conversion of the individual" was made possible through literacy.

The religious importance given to the teaching of reading led many Christian groups to expand into the field of educational publishing; they eschewed the use of catechisms and Scripture stories since these were no longer considered "reading books" by modern educators but rather books for religious instruction.[6] Instead, they began writing and publishing separate language primers (meant to introduce students to the alphabet) and readers (meant to teach reading). Evangelicals worked to ensure that the acquisition of written language through these new kinds of schoolbooks remained connected to the production of an explicitly Christian identity.

In the early nineteenth century, the education materials published by the National Society and the British and Foreign School Book Society (associated with the Anglican and Dissenting movements, respectively) were primarily concerned with conveying to students "the 'correct' moral and religious tenets."[7] Educational organizations scrutinized readers to ensure that their students were not exposed to any "wrong" readings of biblical passages or catechisms.[8] Furthermore the monitorial method, based upon a system of rote question-and-answer and memorization, did not require separate reading books for each child. This limited the kinds of schoolbooks available to non-elite British schoolchildren in the early part of the nineteenth century.

But by the 1840s, the National Society and the British and Foreign School Society began producing a wider range of educational materials for their primary schools. The British and Foreign School Society (and eventually the National Society) were in part inspired by readers published in another imperial location, Ireland. The religious context in Ireland in the mid-nineteenth century created a need for nonsectarian Christian schoolbooks. In addition to Christian religious passages, Irish readers contained rudimentary lessons on political economy, geography, and science. The addition of various "secular" subjects inevitably led to a decrease in the proportion of biblical passages and explicitly religious subjects, a change that was welcomed in Ireland but was met with some anxiety by evangelical educators in Britain. This did not mean, however, that religious education disappeared. Instead, the books continued to emphasize such moral values such as industry, cleanliness, honesty, obedience, and so on in a distinctly Christian idiom. By the 1860s, the acrimonious debates among educators over the "sectarian" nature of schoolbooks gave way to a consensus on a basic set of Christian norms that would be imparted through primary educational materials.[9]

The emergence of modern readers in England was not wholly divergent from their emergence in Bengal. As in Britain, some of the earliest examples of printed Bengali schoolbooks were published by Nonconformist evangelicals like William Carey and his fellow Baptist missionaries in Serampore. As Michael Laird notes, the Welsh periodical "Drysorfa Ysbrydol had its Bengali counterpart in JC Marshman's *Samachar Darpan*; and the modern development and use of Bengali owes almost as much as Welsh to evangelical concern for the salvation of souls."[10] But the creation of a modern prose Bengali was also the result of the collaboration between Protestant missionaries and local Bengali *pandits*. William Carey, for instance, had to rely on the *pandit* Mrityunjay Vidyalankar to help write the early Bengali-language texts published by the Serampore press, including *Kathopakathan* (*Dialogue*) and *Itihasmala* (*Collection of Stories*). In turn, Mrityunjay, born in Midnapore, Bengal, in 1796, got into the business of writing Bengali schoolbooks only because of his association with Carey. Both Brahmin literati and missionaries came out of school-going and textual traditions, and their collaboration was oddly complementary: the evangelical desire to expand literacy by publishing Christian works in the vernacular depended upon the Sanskrit-based training of Hindu *pandits,* like Mrityunjay, who were the linguistic experts.

Drawing upon what was most familiar to him, Mrityunjay became best known for his Bengali versions of *Batris Sinhasan* and *Hitopadesha,* stories that were regularly taught in *pathshalas* (village schools). The two texts were regional versions based on Sanskrit manuscripts: *Batris Sinhasan* related stories about the great virtues of the mythic king Vikramaditya, and *Hitopadesha* consisted of fables of animals and people that imparted moral lessons to children. Although these were stories that were widely known, Mrityunjay's printed schoolbook represented a significant departure from the ways in which *pathshalas* employed such stories. In the *pathshala,* mythological and religious stories were typically orally imparted by the *guru* or teacher; they were not meant to be used to teach the Bengali language itself.

While the early-nineteenth-century British schoolbook was pulled between the ideological imperatives of evangelicalism and utilitarianism, the Bengali schoolbook was further filtered through the ideology of Brahminical Hinduism. Soon after Carey's first forays into writing language readers, a number of other evangelical schoolbook publishers became involved with printing vernacular educational materials that attempted to adapt Brahminical stories and moral codes into schoolbook form.[11] But all of these texts, suggests Brian Hatcher, "tended to be highly Sanskritic . . . or to be overly burdened with figures and lessons drawn from European history."[12]

When the colonial government affirmed a commitment to vernacular education in 1854 (through "Wood's Despatch"), neither the "European" nor the "Brahminical" texts that had been published were considered appropriate for a modern vernacular school-going population. The need for proper vernacular schoolbooks not only was felt by officials in the Department of Public Instruction (DPI), but also became a concern for missionary societies. Unlike the traditional stories used in *pathshalas,* these were books that were meant to teach morality through the acquisition of basic literacy. It was the connection of these two goals that created the need for modern Bengali primers and readers.

THE CREATION OF MODERN BENGALI

As early as 1857, the largest number of books being published in Bengali were described as "educational," suggesting a whole range of primers, readers, and study guides.[13] Thus, alongside the expansion in cheaply printed material was the expansion of vernacular education itself. Recent studies have demonstrated the importance of the burgeoning print market to the development of a growing Bengali-language public sphere. That is, the wide range of reading practices and the various efforts to standardize and shape literary production were crucial parts of a Bengali civil society.

By the 1870s, the writing and publication of Bengali-language educational materials outstripped those of any other language, including English. This market was dominated in Bengal by the group of inexpensively printed pamphlets and books that emanated from the Battala publishers. As Anindita Ghosh, in *Power in Print,* has recently demonstrated, the size and range of the Battala publications (which included almanacs, popular Puranic and Persian stories, and religious manuals) indicate a much larger literate public than educational or employment statistics would suggest.

The Bengali used in the Battala publications was pejoratively described as "simple" because it was closer to the regional spoken vernaculars. The popular-publishing world of Battala comfortably accommodated the linguistic, religious, and regional differences within Bengal without needing to resort to a standardized language or a prescribed set of genres. Popular publishing demonstrated continuity between the oral, aural, and manuscript traditions that had prevailed in precolonial Bengal.

In contrast to the diversity and variety of Bengalis published by the Battala presses, the books published for educational purposes were more standardized and scrutinized because they were meant to be used in government-aided schools. Nonetheless, they constituted a fairly significant section of the publishing market. In fact, the DPI noted that "Bengali books are published by author on their own responsibility, and without any inducement held out by Government, except in the case of a few medical works." This was especially true for schoolbooks, which were published in large editions. In fact, the report marveled that "one Bengali primer had in a single edition of 100,000 copies; more than a dozen had 10,000 copies or upwards in one edition while [those with] 5,000 in an edition were very numerous."[14] The exponential growth in publishing, "without any inducement held out by Government," reflected the growing market for printed schoolbooks.

The various educational texts and schoolbooks did not demonstrate the same continuities between oral and written culture. Instead, schoolbooks, particularly language primers and readers, were invested in creating a standard Bengali and producing texts that were appropriately modern. The striking thing about the wide range of readers published from the 1860s on was their consistent conviction that learning to read was also a process through which one learned to be a moral person. This notion was as true for Christian readers for mission schools (with generic titles like *Barnamala* or *Nutan Barnamala*) as it was for language readers used in governmental and native vernacular schools (where the majority of the students were upper-caste boys).[15] The creation of a moral student was thus divided by religion and gender. The assumption underpinning these broad divisions was that literacy should be taught through lessons on how to be a girl, a Christian, or (although rarely marked) an upper-caste Hindu boy. For example, the preface to the language reader entitled *Bala Bodh* (1874) notes that it is meant as a text for "the education of small girls to read non-compound words through moral poetry and prose."[16] In the process of becoming familiar with noncompound letters and words, the *Bala Bodh* also taught girls to be charitable, disciplined, and obedient and to wear modest clothing.

In various ways, the Bengali readers assumed an upper-caste and Hindu audience, as much as the Christian readers addressed themselves to Christian schoolboys and -girls. However, unlike the Christian readers, the books produced by *bhadralok* writers were never explicit about the religious or caste basis of their texts. Nonetheless, the forms of Bengali and the cultural idioms and norms used suggested the upper-caste and Hindu underpinnings of even the most general moral aphorism. Eventually, missionaries and the DPI came to be seen as "standard" Bengali and part of a "modern" curriculum, but, as I show in the next section, this assumption was not wholly uncontested.

LANGUAGE PRIMERS AND RELIGIOUS IDENTITY

In mid-nineteenth-century Bengal, language primers were not merely vehicles for the transmission of an already formed language but were instead the actual means through which a new prose Bengali was being created. The crucial place of the primer in both the creation and propagation of a particular form of the Bengali language helps explain why John Murdoch, a Presbyterian missionary and educator, decided to directly intervene in their production. In this section, I will examine the public letter written by Murdoch to Iswar Chandra Vidyasagar, the author of the popular *Barnaparichoy*. *Barnaparichoy* served as a template for most other published primers and also helped create an early version of a "standard" prose Bengali. I read Murdoch's letter as an example of an alternative evangelical theory of creating an (equally) artificial written prose that would facilitate mass literacy rather than cultural renaissance.

Iswar Chandra Vidyasagar and John Murdoch were roughly contemporaries: Murdoch was born in 1819, and Vidyasagar in 1820. Although coming out of very different cultural and intellectual traditions—evangelical Presbyterianism and Brahminical Hinduism—they both became interested in transforming vernacular education in Bengal. Murdoch's interest in improving missionary education through publishing in the vernacular grew out of a desire that schools in South Asia function as proselytizing agencies. Iswar Chandra Vidyasagar's goals were no less grand. As a Sanskrit scholar, social reformer, and inspector of schools, Vidyasagar saw the writing and publishing of Bengali primers and readers as an opportunity to develop a modern prose Bengali and by extension a modern vernacular culture.

John Murdoch was one of the more prolific and influential men in nineteenth-century missionary education in India. Murdoch attended the University of Glasgow and while there entered the Normal Seminary started by David Stow in 1836.[17] Murdoch, considered one of the most accomplished of Stow's pupils, was assigned the post of headmaster of a government school in Ceylon. Unlike in India, the colonial state in Ceylon allowed the explicit teaching of Christianity. But rather than exploiting this fact to further evangelize, Murdoch resigned from his position as headmaster because he felt the state should have no part in the religious education of native Ceylonese. He rhetorically asked, "Is the religious training of the people a part of the duty of governments? Is it just in a government to compel the people to pay for the teaching of what the great majority of them consider deadly error?"[18]

In his quest to evangelize, Murdoch toured the churches and schools on the subcontinent and found that the vernacular Christian schoolbooks available to mission schools were pedagogically inadequate. He returned to Scotland to establish a schoolbook society that would specifically address the needs of Christian schools in India. Murdoch's conviction was supported by the United Presbyterian Church in Scotland, and in 1857 he formed the Christian Vernacular Education Society (CVES). The CVES, a nondenominational organization, was funded through contributions by evangelicals specifically interested in Christian educational efforts. In an 1881 report, Murdoch reported that the organization had published almost 730,000 books and pamphlets during the year, the majority of which were schoolbooks. The CVES schoolbooks principally addressed "the great doctrines of the Gospel, others illustrate Christian duties; some of them teach cleanliness; the advantages of vaccination; and other things calculated to promote the physical well-being of the people."[19] As is evident from this list, the "Christian" topics were wide-ranging: some were pointedly religious (great doctrines of the Gospel) while others reflected public health concerns (vaccinations, and cleanliness).

Iswar Chandra Vidyasagar did not have the same kind of institutional backing as John Murdoch. He established his printing press by using his wages from his work teaching in the Sanskrit College and working in the DPI. The most successful books published by Vidyasagar were his primers and readers, texts that found an immediate market in Anglo-vernacular and vernacular schools.[20] The press allowed Vidyasagar "to write, publish and sell books that embodied his curricular vision." He expanded the typical vernacular curriculum through schoolbooks that introduced various scientific subjects and imparted "morality" tales that were shaped by bourgeois and Brahminical norms.

Vidyasagar was also instrumental in some of the earliest nineteenth-century attempts to mold Bengali into a language that was appropriate for modern uses. His educational endeavors proved important in this respect since he could use his published primers and readers to more widely disseminate this new language. *Barnaparichay*, his first primer published in 1855, reflected Vidyasagar's background and training as a Sanskrit scholar. In it, he employed a highly erudite and Sanskritized version of the Bengali vernacular: *sadhu-bhasa*.[21] In a general situation of low levels of literacy, a very small proportion of the population could either read or write Bengali, and Vidyasagar's Bengali was further removed from any of the spoken vernaculars, the *chalit-bhasha,* that were more widely employed. *Sadhu-bhasa* instead represented a "new" language reinvented for a new society.

In effect, Vidyasagar's schoolbooks represented not only a new form of teaching literacy but also a new form of the vernacular itself. This becomes clear when we look at his introduction to the first part of *Barnaparichay*. In it, Vidyasagar explains that the Bengali alphabet traditionally has 16 vowels and 34 consonants. However, he has decided to change this to 12 vowels and 35 consonants, and his introduction carefully details the reasons for adding and subtracting each letter, mainly having to do with the frequency with which certain letters are used. In the second part of *Barnaparichoy*, which introduces compound letters, Vidyasagar chooses to focus on the method of teaching by describing how a teacher might actually use the primer in a classroom. He suggests that the teacher, the *shikhak mahashoy*, encourage pupils to learn and identify the consonants, memorize the spelling, and ignore the meanings of various words. Attempting to learn both meaning and spelling simultaneously would only frustrate teacher and pupil, so teachers should focus on meaning in the short reading sections rather than the spelling sections.[22]

Vidyasagar's primers became immediately popular (his connections to the DPI being very useful at this point) in government schools, *pathshalas*, and missionary schools. The ubiquity of Vidyasagar's texts, especially in mission schools, prompted John Murdoch to write to Vidyasagar in 1864 to express his dissatisfaction with the usefulness of his primers for basic written literacy. Although written to Vidyasagar, Murdoch addressed himself to the larger community of social reformers, "educators like Babu Bhoodeb Mookherjea, to the intelligent Principals of the government vernacular Normal Schools, to the Bengali Press and to the entire educated community." Murdoch continued that "whatever my own countrymen may think of the proposal, they are not likely to interfere in a matter in which Bengalis are chiefly interested." Murdoch was acutely aware that the colonial government granted great autonomy to the "educated community" to reform and shape the Bengali language and Bengali culture. However, as an evangelical educator, Murdoch felt equally invested in the efforts to "modernize" Bengali. He further recognized that Vidyasagar, who wielded great influence on vernacular schoolbook product, had to be his main interlocutor. Thus, by appealing to Vidyasagar, Murdoch hoped to convince him to further simplify prose Bengali and help create a linguistic vehicle that would be appropriate for mass education.[23]

Murdoch's letter expressed his concern that the Sanskrit-based Bengali primer was too difficult because of its orthographic complexity. Murdoch admitted that he knew almost nothing of the Bengali language itself, but it was precisely for this reason that he had insights into the difficulty of acquiring the language. "A child poring over the spelling book knows his sorrows much better than a learned professor."[24] Murdoch had very specific suggestions to make Bengali orthography simpler and easier to learn and that it was incumbent on him to push Vidyasagar even further in this direction.

Murdoch's perspective on language drew upon a nineteenth-century evangelical orientation toward literacy. He wondered if Vidyasagar could "in the slightest degree render it easier for the toil worn ryot to trim his lamp in the evening, or for the mother to snatch a few minutes while her babe is asleep, to acquire knowledge through books, especially that which is 'able to make wise unto sanction.' "[25] Deploying the conventional set of images familiar to any Victorian audience—the hardworking peasant, the poor mother, and the hungry child—Murdoch dramatized the plight of the student of *Barnaparichoy*. For evangelical Christians like Murdoch, the purpose of reading primers was to facilitate mass literacy so that anyone, from infant to old peasant, would be able to one day read the Bible. Most poor Bengalis, Murdoch pointed out, spent a very brief period in school, and thus it was critical that they learned to read as quickly and simply as possible.

In the best possible scenario, Murdoch wanted Bengali (written in a script derived from Devanagri) to be Romanized into what he perceived as a far simpler and more accessible form in order to encourage vernacular literacy. While Murdoch's suggestion was certainly radical, and reflected his own ethnocentrism, it would be wrong to see it as qualitatively different from Vidyasagar's reconfiguration of the language. Murdoch's suggestions did, however, represent a significant departure from not only the desires of upper-caste reformers but also missionary practice itself. After all, William Carey, Mrityunjay Vidylankar, and the Serampore missionaries remained assiduously committed to printing books in the Bengali script, *not* a Latinized script.

Murdoch himself must have recognized the difficulty of succeeding in Latinizing the Bengali alphabet, and so he came up with alternative ways Vidyasagar could simplify his primers in ways that would lead to greater mass literacy. The main orthographic complexity and primary difficulties of Bengali were the compound letters. Compound letters are mixtures of two or even three letters that often take a distinctly different form from either of the original letters. In modern Bengali, for instance, there are upward of 400 compound letters in addition to the regular consonants. Faced with this particular problem, Murdoch argued for dispensing altogether with compound letters and simply putting the two (or three) letters side by side. He justified this radical departure by drawing attention to the different contexts in which Bengalis might learn to read, "though the compound letters may seem easy enough to pundits, the case is very different with children and with the poor whose period of education is brief . . . considering the millions of India yet untaught, and the short period many can remain at school, it is most desirable to remove obstruction to progress in learning to read."[26] Again, Murdoch emphasized the notion of literacy as a means to produce the largest number of readers, a process that demanded that the norm not be the "pundit" but the "poor."

Murdoch seemed to make little headway with other *bhadralok* educators, but he found another outlet in which he could experiment with the Bengali language: the primers he published for the Christian Vernacular Education Society. The CVES primers employed a very instrumental vision of language instruction as a means to further basic literacy so Christians and non-Christians could read the Bible. Paradoxically, despite Murdoch's critique of *Barnaparichay*, the CVES primer, *Barnamala*, stayed fairly close to Vidyasagar's model, introducing all of the consonants and vowels before making short sentences with them. The major difference was that the second part of *Barnamala* did not bother with compound letters. Instead, CVES publications used the *biram* to indicate compound letters.[27]

In spite of Murdoch's constant exhortations, the majority of missionaries working in Bengal continued to use Vidyasagar's books in their schools. The most striking example of this is the comment by James Long, an important evangelical voice in nineteenth-century Bengal, who lauded Vidyasagar's Sanskritized Bengali as an example of the democratizing of elite culture itself: "He has taken the noble Sanskrit away from being the weapon of superstition and Brahminical enthrallment, to be the lever for giving dignity to the language of the masses."[28] Unlike Murdoch, who saw the heavily Sanskritzed language as an impediment to mass literacy, Long assumed that Vidyasagar's Bengali would eventually come to represent a "language of the masses" that was nonetheless truly "dignified."

The irony of Long's observations was that Vidyasagar's Bengali was conceived of and developed as a formal, written language, not a replacement for the *chalit-bhasa*, or spoken vernacular of the "masses." Nonetheless, his comments reflect the perspective shared by many missionaries who similarly believed that Vidyasagar's version of the Bengali *sadhu-bhasha* was closer to "real" Bengali than the language found in most other texts. This helps account for the multiple reports from various mission societies, including the Wesleyan Methodist Society, that they were using *Bodhodoy,* Vidyasagar's translation of *Rudiments of Knowledge,* to examine European missionaries on "colloquial Bengali and pronunciation."[29] Although Vidyasagar's Bengali would later be superseded by far less Sanskritized versions of the language, the popularity of his schoolbooks ensured that his vision of a "literary" vernacular would dominate the ways in which nineteenth-century schoolgoers (and missionaries) were taught their "mother" tongue.[30]

PRODUCING THE CHRISTIAN SUBJECT

In the face of what he perceived as the decreasing space allotted to religious instruction within metropolitan British schools, John Murdoch expected colonial mission schools to be more explicit in their Christian education. But, as I will show in this section, Murdoch's expectations were confounded by the success of Vidyasagar's vision of language and literacy within evangelical circles. When he first began his tours of India, Murdoch encouraged missionaries in Bengal to avail themselves of every opportunity to evangelize in their schools. He insisted that "a far more weighty reason [to print Christian schoolbooks], was that in missionary schools, Christian truth may be more fully stated than it is in most school books published at home."[31] The tense relationship between the Established Church and Dissenting Societies in Britain circumscribed the degree to which explicit Christian instruction could be offered because of the ever-present possibility of conflicts between competing sectarian interpretations of religious ideas and biblical knowledge. Murdoch felt that in India, the absence of the same level of sectarian conflict and the presence of multiple non-Christian traditions meant that missionaries should employ schoolbooks that were openly religious—explicitly evoking Jesus and introducing children to Christian theology.

While the sectarian differences between Protestants in India were far more muted, government involvement in Indian schools led to a similar kind of scrutinizing of texts. This was in part because in the centralized school-leaving exams taken by students from government and private schools, "no marks are given for religious knowledge, [which] causes the students to regard this subject as utterly valueless."[32] At the lower levels, it was not the standardized exam but the commitment of the state and organizations like the Calcutta School Book Society to religious neutrality that prompted a similarly secularizing impulse. This extended to missionary organizations, which felt compelled to adopt some government books, especially in English schools, because they competed with government schools for grants-in-aid. For example, schoolbook committees might replace "'From that young Christian's life' . . . [to] 'From that young soldier's life.' "[33]

The removal of explicitly Christian material from schoolbooks was in part a reflection of the cautious mood after the 1857 Rebellion and Mutiny. The widespread perception among colonial officials was that the rebellion that spread across North India was prompted by fears that the British East India Company was trying to proselytize to its native subjects and force them to convert to Christianity. Not surprisingly, in its aftermath, the British Raj felt the need to repeatedly articulate its commitment to religious neutrality and dampen the power and enthusiasm of missionary activity, including educational activity.

In light of governmental reluctance to introduce Christianity into India, John Murdoch decided that he should redouble his efforts to expand Christian education through the Christian Vernacular Education Society (CVES), an organization established to publish Christian schoolbooks in all the major vernacular languages in India. Murdoch hoped that the CVES books would be adopted all over India and thus help standardize the elementary vernacular education being given in mission schools. Murdoch was interested in producing reading books for two reasons: first, because in the majority of schools "the reading book is the only one a child has since all other subjects are taught orally"; and, second, because "heathen" parents were uncomfortable with the use of printed catechisms and Scripture, and so the reading book offered the greatest chance for proselytizing to non-Christians in elementary schools.

In spite of Murdoch's enthusiasm and the funding he received from the Scottish Presbyterian Church, the CVES books were routinely ignored by local missionaries, who preferred the non-Christian schoolbooks of Iswar Chandra Vidyasagar. The continued popularity of *Barnaparichoy* in mission schools, over the primers produced by the CVES, reflected the more general contempt that local missionaries felt toward Murdoch and the CVES. From early in its establishment, the CVES had become the target of criticism from some of the most influential Protestants working in Bengal. In an 1859 letter to the London Missionary Society, Archdeacon Pratt, Bishop Wilson, Alexander Duff, James Long, and Macleod Wylie expressed their reservations about Murdoch's appointment and his plans to standardize mission education all over India. They suggested instead that the CVES function like the DPI by giving grants-in-aid to already existing organizations: "I may as well just hint that the CVES is not as yet popular among Christian friends in India. Although its object is excellent it is apprehended, that from its institutions it will not work well."[34]

Protestant missionaries chafed at Murdoch's efforts to dictate local school policy from afar; he neither spoke Bengali nor resided in Bengal, and yet was convinced that he knew what was best for Bengali mission schools. Local missionaries felt that the CVES and Murdoch were trying to supplant their individual educational initiatives in Bengal and, as mentioned above, felt that his society should supplement, rather than supplant, missionary endeavors by providing grants-in-aid.

The tensions among missionaries working in Bengal and the CVES eventually erupted over school readers. John Murdoch accused Bengali mission schools of rejecting Christian schoolbooks (particularly those published by the CVES) for "heathen" readers (by Hindu educators), in the process abandoning their duties as evangelicals for Christ. This set off a series of letters and ultimately resulted in a group of missionaries sending out a questionnaire to determine which reading books were used in Christian schools. The questionnaire, written by Duff, Mullens, Fyfe, and Storrow, listed the books currently used by schools throughout Bengal.

One of the initial goals of the CVES had been to publish primers and readers that were specifically written for India rather than being translations of metropolitan schoolbooks. The CVES published both short Christian stories with titles like *Tinti Bipad* (Three Obstacles) and language primers like *Barnamala*. For different reasons, neither of these kinds of publications enjoyed great popularity in mission schools. Instead, the statistical table compiled by the Bengal missionaries showed the widespread use of translations of older Christian texts rather than the newer stories published by the CVES.[35] A few older texts like *The Old, Old Story; Bart's Bible Stories; Peep of Day;* and *Line upon Line* dominated the evangelical curriculum. "These are Christian reading books in the strictest sense of the term. It is maintained by competent judges that these are superior to those which have been prepared by Dr. Murdoch and in the case of 'The Old, Old Story,' supply what he has not supplied, a poetical reading book."[36]

In the standard reading primer published by the CVES (*Barnamala*), there were a series of short passages to assist students with their reading. The first few sentences were general "moral" aphorisms such as "Never be envious" or "Guilt cannot be hidden." By the end, such general character-building sentences gave way to more explicitly Christian proclamations: "We all sin . . . God let his only son die for us."[37]

Murdoch was frustrated that CVES books were not even used as general education books. It seemed that local missionaries found the Bengali CVES texts overly didactic and inappropriate in the social and cultural climate of late-nineteenth-century Bengal. They argued that the more conservative spirit (after 1857) made such stridency a dangerous proposition and increased the chances of angering the colonial government, to whom missionaries looked for funding. Missionaries had to be more circumspect and cautious in what they could and could not publish in India. For example, the Bengali primer written by Reverend Bomwetch, the principal of the Krishnagar Normal School for teacher training, steered clear of explicit Christian messages. Instead, Bomwetch's reader, *Nutan Barnamala (New Alphabet)*, imparted more general Christian values such as charity. For example, one of the simpler reading sections begins with a question about a boy named Kedar. Soon after learning his name, we are told (by the speaker), "He does not have a mother or father. My mother takes care of him."[38]

The missionary rejection of CVES primers was not only the result of fears about governmental or native reprisals. In, fact the CVES texts were abandoned not only for older Christian texts but also for non-Christian primers written by prominent Bengalis, like Vidyasagar. The table compiled by the missionaries makes clear that the most popular books were the non-Christian readers—Vidyasagar's *Bodhodoy* (a translation of *The Rudiments of Knowledge*), O. C. Dutt's *Chaurapat* (lessons on natural history and astronomy interspersed with biographies), and *Kathamala* (a translation of *Aesop's Fables*). The missionaries defended their use of non-Christian primers by arguing that the CVES books were lacking in clarity and relevance. "Let us have books equal in style and usefulness to the Chaurapath and we will use them."[39] One missionary reported that his attempts to replace the non-Christian books with Murdoch's readers were unsuccessful, and he had reverted back to *Barnaparichoy, Kathamala*, and *Bodhodoy*.[40]

CURRICULUM FOR RELIGIOUS PLURALITY

The controversy between the Bengal missionaries and the CVES was not merely intramissionary squabbling.[41] It represented an important moment in the creation of a pluralist Indian curriculum. Christian missionaries, in making an argument for treating religion as a separate school subject, opened up the possibility for imagining an educational system that was not necessarily divided into separate Hindu, Christian, and Muslim schools. Rather, Hindu, Muslim, and Christian schoolchildren could attend the same modern primary school if it offered distinct religious classes for each community during some part of the day.

The missionaries, usually so critical of the attempts of the government to regulate and standardize their schoolbooks, questioned the necessity of an explicitly "Christian" book to teach reading and writing. In a letter in *Church Missionary Intelligencer* for August 1872, Murdoch blasted Christian schools for secular teaching. The missionaries in Bengal promptly replied that "we do not dread what is commonly called secular teaching, when restricted to reading, writing and arithmetic ... so long as concurrently with this missionaries can daily teach scripture and inculcate religious dogmas in their schools." This separation (of the secular subjects from the holy) ensures that "Bible teaching should ... be hallowed teaching, intermingled in afterlife with pleasant recollections."[42] What the Indian missionaries suggested was a significant shift in the purpose of a Christian education away from a notion that the whole school curriculum should be consciously imbued with the Christian spirit. Primary education in Britain, for example, continued to stress a "sound religious education" rather than a secular one.[43]

The missionaries further pointed to their own recollections of learning how to read. "We think it would have been difficult to have discovered the religious views of Dr. Mavor or Mr. Carpenter from the spelling and reading books, which most of us have used when children."[44] It was a startling admission, and one testifying not only to the vernacularizing of British texts into Bengali, but also to the process by which the British missionaries uncoupled the religious content of a schoolbook from the religious affiliation of the author. Thus, missionaries in Bengal were untroubled by the Brahminical context of Vidyasagar's books because they were perceived as pedagogically superior to anything being produced by the CVES.

While early-nineteenth-century missionaries in Bengal had feared that an English literary education that was not explicitly Christian would lead to irreverence and radical skepticism, by the late nineteenth century, evangelicals embraced non-Christian and non-British schoolbooks. Missionaries were drawn to Vidyasagar's primers as representing a more authentic, and ultimately more prestigious, form of the Bengali language. In metropolitan Britain and colonial India, missionaries accepted that modern pedagogy demanded that they no longer "consider catechisms and scripture stories *reading* books. They are classed as books for *religious instruction*."[45] It seems that the need for pedagogically appropriate schoolbooks had successfully trumped the necessity for texts that actively proselytized.

DOBHASHI BANGLA AND PANDIT BANGLA

This chapter has traced a debate over language readers that, although internal to the Protestant missionary community, managed to raise larger cultural issues that became increasingly central in late-nineteenth- and early-twentieth-century nationalist politics. At some level, Vidyasagar and his *bhadralok* counterparts "won" the language debate: *Barnaparichoy* remained the most widely used language primer in government, missionary, and aided primary schools. However, the consensus over the text was short lived, and by the late nineteenth century the question of the relationship between religion, culture, and language acquisition exploded in a very different and more politically pointed way.

Specifically, as Bengali Muslim leaders in the 1870s contemplated the expansion of basic primary education for their fellow co-religionists, they consistently pointed to the religious and cultural biases of the language readers used in government and village schools. Muslim educators and reformers challenged the claim that *pandit* (Brahminical) Bangla, the highly Sanskritized language taught in midcentury primers, represented the whole of the Bengali linguistic or cultural world. In fact, the kinds of critiques that John Murdoch had earlier leveled against Vidyasagar were echoed in the concerns raised by various Muslim urban leaders. Like Murdoch before them, Muslim reformers were frustrated with the Hindu orientation of the stories, ideas, and norms that were a part of the *pathshala* curriculum.

Instead, Muslim leaders wanted to introduce schoolbooks that employed *Mussalmani* or *dobhashi* Bengali—distinguished by the high use of Persian, Arabic, and Urdu words.[46] The degree to which this represented a wholly different language is debatable—there does not seem to be a single Muslim Bengali any more than there was a single Hindu Bengali. The different linguistic practices in Bengal were regional and based in social class rather than a reflection of distinct sectarian religious identity. But Muslim educators and leaders became committed to "Islamicizing" Bengali, in much the same way that Vidyasagar had Sanskritized the language, so that it could serve as an appropriate vehicle for imparting religious and cultural knowledge. As I discuss later in the book, the question of religion and language would become a highly divisive political issue in the twentieth century.

The particular social, religious, and political landscape of colonial Bengal ensured that schooling remained a site in which larger social and cultural debates were played out. Thus, the use of new tools for teaching vernacular literacy, language primers and readers, was fundamentally mediated by questions of religion and religious identity. As I will show in the following chapters, this was equally true of other modern pedagogic and instructional theories and methods introduced into Bengali schools.

CHAPTER 3

An Object Lesson in Colonial Pedagogy

The following lesson on rice appeared in the 1860 text, *Object Teaching and Oral Lessons,* by David Stow, the Scottish educator and evangelist. In the lesson, Stow describes the high starch-to-gluten ratio of rice, and its concomitant characteristic of being "less stimulating and nutritious." Stow then gets to the heart of the lesson and encourages teachers to ask their students, "What nations live on rice—what is, in general, their disposition? Can you trace any connection between their soft, dull, phlegmatic temperament, and the food on which they live?"[1] Stow's object lesson on rice assumes a fundamental connection between the empirical observation of an object, rice, and the hidden qualities of those who consume that object. There is no escaping the highly gendered adjectives that Stow chooses to describe rice and rice-eating cultures. They are "soft" (womanly), placid cultures in contrast to the hearty, energetic (masculine) cultures of those who devour (presumably) bread. In Stow's object lesson, the essential qualities of rice come to be shared by those who consume rice, effectively making food metonymic of culture and cultural difference.

David Stow's lesson book represented his interpretation of a pedagogic technique first developed by Johann Pestalozzi (the famous Swiss educator) in 1798 at his school in Stanz, Austria. Object theory, as articulated by Pestalozzi, postulated that the best means to instill higher thinking in children was through the observation, description, naming, and classification of objects. By presenting children with a series of objects and asking increasingly complex questions, teachers could cultivate the natural path of a child's mental development from lower to higher levels of perception. Ultimately, children would learn to think and reason abstractly, moving from objects to ideas (or ideas contained in objects).

In order to accomplish this, the teacher first encouraged children to observe the objects presented to them and carefully describe their observations. The initial set of adjectives used to describe rice, for instance, are ones that children were meant to come to by themselves. However, Stow's book then encourages teachers to carefully guide students through a series of almost catechistical questions and answers in order to direct them to (rather than having them discover) the larger cultural observations about phlegmatic rice eaters.

I begin with Stow's lesson on rice to demonstrate the peculiar mix of empiricism and cultural prejudice that structured this popular nineteenth-century pedagogic technique. While Pestalozzi, in his school at Stanz, had used objects found in the natural environment (like shells and leaves), British object lesson books routinely replaced these with objects found in the colonies, like rice. But earnest and moralistic nineteenth-century object lesson books were not solely aimed at the metropolitan imperial imagination of British schoolchildren. The object lesson was exported to the British colonies at the same time that it became popular in Britain. It was quickly adopted in evangelical classrooms and by the 1850s made its way into Bengali teaching manuals and schoolbooks written by *bhadralok* educators. Just as nineteenth-century educational theory linked literacy to the molding of religious character, similarly the object lesson, an otherwise fairly ordinary pedagogic method, came to be seen by evangelical and *bhadralok* educators as fundamental to the transformation of religious epistemology.

In the most general sense, evangelical and *bhadralok* educators saw the object lesson as teaching one of the fundamental tenets of modern (Western) thinking: the subordination of the object to the subject.[2] Yet this was meant to be done almost counterintuitively, using concrete objects (or pictures of objects) to help children think abstractly. The cognitive paradigm at the center of the object lesson, positing a natural path of learning that started with objects and then moved to abstract ideas and categories, was assumed to be the "natural" path through which religions and cultures modernized. Thus, for Protestant evangelicals, the falsity of other religions and faiths could be in part attributed to their relationship to concrete objects and concrete ways of thinking. The religious practices and thinking of fetishistic Africans, idolatrous Hindus, or even crucifix-wearing Catholics could be placed on an evolutionary continuum comprising a movement from objects (fetishes, idols, and the crucifix) to words (the Bible).

Meanwhile, the popularity of object lesson books among *bhadralok* educators was related to the fact that they were seen as the preeminent means to teach rationality and science, and, through this, a rational approach to culture and religion itself. *Bhadralok* educators successfully ignored the evangelical aspects of the object lesson by choosing to use more scientifically oriented metropolitan schoolbooks. But just like Stow's rice lesson, science lessons in Bengali object lesson books were interspersed with cultural and anthropological lessons on appropriate social, familial, and religious modes of thought. Ultimately, in the process of translating object lessons on the natural world into Bengali, *bhadralok* educators could not escape incorporating Hindu paradigms of culture and religion in place of or in addition to the British ones.

The abstractions that children were meant to learn from objects in British and Indian classrooms ranged from systems of Linnaean classification to the "truth" of Protestant Christianity and the cultural models of a reformed upper-caste Hinduism. In the first part of the chapter, I trace the ways mission teachers tried to use object lessons to wean Hindu children from what they perceived as fetishistic and idolatrous practices; the object lesson rehearsed the shift away from heathenism (the worship of objects) to the truth (and abstraction) of Protestant Christianity. Missionaries in Bengal assumed that Hindus, like children, attributed purpose and intention to objects rather than to the laws of God and nature. Missionaries felt that the "heathen" propensity to anthropomorphize was most clearly reflected in the central place of idols and fetishes in their worship.

The second part of the chapter explores how teacher trainees and schoolchildren in mid-nineteenth-century Bengal were introduced to object theory through translations of British object lesson books and the incorporation of object lessons into training manuals. This reflected the broader religious reform efforts of midcentury *bhadralok* who were invested in emphasizing a more "enlightened" Hinduism, one that rejected backward religious rituals and unthinking idolatry.

What was shared in the development of various object lessons by evangelical and *bhadralok* educators was the consistent placement of instruction in higher levels of thinking, often scientific thinking, within a religious or cultural evolutionary framework. Evangelicals had assumed that through object lessons, they could raise non-Christians to higher levels of thinking, and simultaneously assumed that abstract thinking was inherent to Christians. In a parallel fashion, *bhadralok* educators assumed that through object lessons and formal education, anyone could be "civilized." Yet their books consistently reinforced the notion of the inherent cultural backwardness of various lower-caste and tribal (*adivasi*) communities. As Kaushik Ghosh, and more recently Prathama Banerjee, have observed, lower-caste or *adivasi* communities consistently served as the cultural (and temporal) other against whom the *bhadralok* asserted their own rationality and religious modernity.[3] It was not Hindus, but *adivasi,* who were fetishistic and irrational—a seeming displacement of *bhadralok* anxieties about their own unstable position within the social and political hierarchy of colonial Bengal.

Intellectual historians rarely examine such pedestrian techniques as object lessons.[4] Compared to the high educational ideas of Locke and Rousseau, object lessons, in spite of their ubiquity, appear unimpressive. But in the nineteenth century, object lessons were used in classrooms, museums, and churches to shape the ways ordinary Britons and their colonial subjects understood and interacted with the world.[5] But this chapter suggests that embedded in this popular pedagogic technique were powerful cultural and epistemological paradigms that drew upon an unlikely combination of nineteenth-century Protestant evangelicalism and rational empiricism. Regardless of whether the object lesson was meant to lead to Christianity or science or rational Hinduism, the method allowed both Protestant missionaries and *bhadralok* educators to project arguments about stages of civilization that reproduced their own particular religious and cultural prejudices and hierarchies.

THE ORIGINS OF THE OBJECT LESSON

The putative originator of the object lesson, Johann Pestalozzi (1746–1827), was born in Zurich and spent his life researching and experimenting with children's education. Pestalozzi's theoretical approach was shaped by his exposure to the empiricist theories of Locke and Hume, and the rationalist (and psychological) views of Leibniz and Kant. His writings were meant to be practical applications of empiricist and psychological insights he gleaned (and cobbled together) from both British and Continental philosophers. For Pestalozzi, direct perception of the world was effective only to the degree that it is explicitly connected to "natural" laws thought to govern a child's mental development.

Pestalozzi felt he improved upon the catechistical method by drawing out children's natural inclination and teaching them in a manner that took into account their internal development. His most important and new principle was the notion of spontaneity or self-activity. Children should not be given ready-made answers but should arrive at questions and solutions themselves and thus cultivate their own perceptions, thinking, and intuition.[6]

Thus, the purpose of schooling was to develop a child's *anschauung* (sense impression or sense perception) through the critical categories of number, form, and language. This method worked by presenting children with concrete objects, like a ball, having them notice the sensual qualities of that object (the number, the shape, the texture, etc.), and then naming that object—a round ball. Pestalozzi's ideas were similarly based upon the notion that the development of *anschauung* had to precede the learning of abstract rules, laws, or concepts. Directly observing and experiencing the world through objects (rather than books) would prepare children for the next stage of learning—abstraction. For Pestalozzi, it was critical that early education start from objects before moving on to book learning. The lower form of thinking was the passive perception of forms and objects. Pestalozzi's method was meant to nurture a more active and higher apperception that allowed children to understand objects through "intuition" and "imagination."

Pestalozzi had developed his object theory as an argument about the innate curiosity and educational potential of all children, rich and poor alike. As the method traveled to Britain and its colonies, educators were clearly influenced by Pestalozzi's view of object theory as a central part of early education for the masses. However, the context of nineteenth-century modern education in Britain and colonial India led to two significant modifications in Pestalozzi's theory: the substitution of pictures of objects for actual objects in their lessons and the introduction of much more explicitly moral lessons. The use of pictures rather than objects minimized the encouragement of self-discovery (children handling objects for themselves) and allowed more didactic instruction to ensure that students learned the right lesson.

The opposition to the use of objects can be traced to the anxiety of many British educators, who were fearful that a wholly sensual education dependent on a child's "self-activity" (as envisioned by Pestalozzi) would threaten traditional structures of authority.[7] The danger with an open-ended system of learning was that educators, parents, Church authorities, and ultimately the state ran the risk of their students (and subjects) coming to a wholly different conclusion than the one that they expected or wanted. This fear was explicitly discussed in the primary schools run by Christian organizations. Although desiring progressive methods of education, evangelical Christians were wary of subverting authority (particularly God's authority). This partially explains why Pestalozzi's ideas, influenced by Enlightenment rationality, were domesticated into a highly empiricist, mechanized, and Christian-influenced method in the British object lesson. The British version of Pestalozzi's theory of *anschauung* discarded some of the fundamental concepts developed at Stanz; Burgdorf, Germany; and Yverdon, Switzerland. Rather than open-ended inquiry, observation, and intuition, object lessons in Britain seemed to emphasize everything stressed by a Protestant biblical education: asking catechistical questions and the use of images (rather than objects) inevitably framed by a book. That is, whereas Pestalozzi had been concerned to bring children into nature, to feel, smell, and (perhaps) taste objects, now the object lesson was based primarily upon differences and qualities one could see. Pestalozzi's primary goal had been for children to explore the natural environment and develop their skills of observation, and moral education was a very small part of his methods and books. But within evangelical object lesson books, there were far more explicit connections made between object lessons and the teaching of Christian "truth."

The object lesson was part of a more general shift in the curricular offerings at the non-elite (secular and Christian) schools attended by the working and lower classes. Although beginning in the 1830s and 1840s, this process continued into the early twentieth century. Jacqueline Rose, analyzing early-twentieth-century language theories, argues that this distinction between the subjects appropriate for elementary education (which was the end of schooling for most working- and lower-class children) and those appropriate for the higher classes was most clearly seen in the distinct ways in which language was taught.

Here, Pestalozzi's insistence on direct perception as the base of a child's learning was transformed into theories of class-based language education. Rose argues that working-class children in elementary schools in early-twentieth-century Britain were taught that language arose from a direct relationship with concrete objects. Thus, elementary schoolchildren, when presented with images of objects, were encouraged to focus on descriptions of the object itself, a form of "natural expression." Language instruction based on a utilitarian relationship to the concrete world was contrasted with the language instruction in secondary schools for the middle and upper classes, which tended to emphasize a classical education and an approach to language as style. Rose argues, "We can compare this [elementary language instruction] with the use of literature in the secondary school, where the child's consciousness is directed at the language of the author . . . the aim being to produce an attention to language itself rather than to bypass it in the name of the event which it records. . . . In the elementary school the stress [is] on the visible and manipulable aspects of physical experience, on concrete impression and on language as the direct extension of the visual sign."[8]

The distinction between concrete language and stylistic language also shaped the kinds of subjects studied by elementary and secondary school students. Ironically, missionary and state-run schools for poorer children were where the new subjects of Empire were being introduced. In contrast, elite public schools continued to emphasize a classical education in Latin and Greek. Rose suggests that this led to a paradox in which "the public school [i.e., where the elite were taught] remained the repository of the ideology of imperialism, but the subjects relevant to the Empire (geography, religion, and comparative ethnography) with their corresponding emphasis on empirical access to the real world, were only introduced into the state schools."[9] Although Rose identifies this trend during the period of late-nineteenth-century high imperialism, Mayo's and Stow's object lesson books demonstrate that an education based on an empirical and concrete apprehension of the world was already developing by the 1830s.

As the century progressed, object lesson books became more systematic, standardized, and "scientific." There continued to be lessons on some of the same objects discussed by Stow and Mayo (animals, vegetables, minerals, and other miscellaneous manufactured goods), but empire figured in object lessons in different ways. This can be seen in an object lesson on the "cocoa nut" as described by Mayo in the early part of the nineteenth century, and a similar lesson in *The Handy Book of Object Lessons from a Teacher's Note Book*, by J. Walker (the tenth edition published and edited in 1876).

Like the lesson on rice, Mayo's description of the coconut describes its consumption in the colonies: "The coca nut tree affords the Indians food, clothing and means of shelter. Before the kernel comes to maturity, it is soft and pulpy, may be scraped out with a spoon and offers the natives an agreeable and nutritious food . . . by soaking the fibrous trunk in water it becomes soft and can be manufactured into sailcloth . . . they are also used for umbrellas, mats, and various other useful articles."[10] Mayo's lesson emphasizes both the functionality of the coconut and the resourcefulness of those who grow and use the fruit. In contrast to this is the description of the coconut in Walker's 1876 book: "Suppose we were to go to Ceylon, which is an island S.E. of India. We should there find portions of land appropriated to the cultivation of coca-nut trees. Each of these plantations, as they are called, is enclosed by a high fence. At one corner of the plantation is a watch tower, in which a man is constantly stationed to keep guard over the plantation. The watchman is a Malay, and he is armed on account of the thievish nature of the Cingalese."[11]

The object lesson on the coconut, focusing as it does on the *plantation* where it is grown (owned by white plantation owners), seems to parallel the deepening colonial relationship between Britain and South Asia. Mayo's early nineteenth-century lesson discussed coconut cultivation only in terms of native use and consumption. The hidden qualities of the coconut were the other ways in which it was used by natives. One could argue that the changes in object lesson books were themselves a lesson in changing colonial relationships. In Walker's discussion of the coconut, in the late nineteenth century, British children were being taught how to manage the colonial products that were brought in as objects to metropolitan Britain. In order to have the coconut in the British classroom, the white plantation owner had to ensure that the "thievish" Singhalese population was vigilantly policed. The coconut thus became an object lesson in increasing production in a colonial economy. In the 1840s, the elite public schools, threatened by the democratizing possibilities of both Christian and state education, became a space for classical learning and literature. But a classical system was already being dismantled as British education officials realized that the running of an Empire, as evidenced in the coconut object lesson, demanded knowledge of the new subjects.[12] Good colonial governance depended on direct empirical observation, and experiential methods and object lessons prepared the ground for secondary schooling in the modern subjects of geography, religion, and comparative ethnography: subjects relating observable differences with cultural differences.

OBJECTS, IDOLS, AND FETISHES IN THE MISSION SCHOOL

The popularity of the object lesson was not limited to metropolitan Britain alone. As evidenced by the very name of Mayo's publisher—the

Home and Colonial School Society—and the objects used in the lessons, educational reform and pedagogic change in Britain occurred within an explicitly colonial framework. Thus, as early as 1833 (just four years after Elizabeth Mayo's book appeared in England), a reference to object lessons appeared in the report of an Anglican mission school in Calcutta. Mr. and Mrs. Perkins opened a vernacular infant school for native and Anglo-Indian children. The six native teachers who taught at the school used the "lessons prepared by Mr. Perkins [where] the names of objects or figures represented in the lesson cards is printed in Bengali."[13] The transformation of three-dimensional objects into two-dimensional drawings ensured that object lessons everywhere, from India to Britain, were the same—a set of uniform images printed on cards that effectively privileged the visual over any other sense.

The use of pictures of objects (and didactic teaching) allowed mission teachers to more explicitly introduce explicit moral lessons into the object lessons. For instance, in a late-nineteenth-century report from a North Indian missionary school (tellingly called "Dusky Darlings"), Frances Brockway described a typical object lesson in her class: "'Shut your eyes, children,' is the order and then I take out one of the pretty animals and stand it on a stool where all can see. . . . One day, I asked, 'What is the use of the cow's tail?' 'To pull,' was the ready answer—the only right one from anyone acquainted with the Indian bullock-*gari* driver and his habits. So I had to tell them that it hurts to have her tail pulled quite as much as it hurts a little girl to have her ear pulled."[14]

In a country filled with cows, Brockway chooses to use the picture of a cow sent from Britain in order to teach her students a lesson that she assumes must be similarly imported: the importance of Christian kindness toward all of God's creatures. Brockway's object in the lesson was to resignify (and thus rehabituate) in the minds of her "dusky darlings" the meaning of the cow's tail away from native cruelty toward Christian empathy. The use of the cardboard cow ensured that Brockway could polemically impart this lesson without fearing the "self-activity" that might lead a child to actually pull the tail of a cow should she be exposed to a real animal.

These examples of the explicit moral education afforded by object lessons obscure the more subtle but nonetheless crucial ways in which the lessons were connected to Christianity and Protestantism in particular. This was the evangelical belief that Western education, emphasizing as it did reason, rationality, and abstraction, would prepare the ground for the eventual conversion of "heathen" populations. The moral lessons learned by Brockway's students would, ideally, lead them closer to Christianity itself. The specific relationship of the object lesson to this endeavor is best understood through the concepts of idolatry and fetishism.

Nineteenth-century Protestants had a complex and troubled relationship with objects and worship. Medieval Catholics had distinguished between the proper and improper use of religious objects (by witches or non-Christians, for example) by making the Church the central and ultimate authority on what was a "sacred" versus an idolatrous object.[15] In part, Protestants defined themselves against Catholics by rejecting objects (idols) in their worship and deployed this same framework in understanding Hinduism. Hindus, Protestant evangelicals insisted, had a peculiar and literal relationship to religious objects—the Hindu idol. If we think of the object lesson as a metaphor, Hindus seemed to be stunted in their intellectual growth by fixating on objects (like idols) rather than learning to abstract and reason (as epitomized by Protestant Christianity).

For European intellectuals, idolatry was placed on the continuum between monotheism and fetishism. As William Pietz suggests about the truth of fetishism, it "resides in its status as a material embodiment: its truth is not that of the idol, for the idol[']s truth lies in its relation of iconic resemblance to some immaterial model or entity."[16] The idol, then, was understood to be iconic, to symbolize something outside of its immediate materiality. But for many Christians, including evangelical missionaries, these differences were often collapsed. Thus, Hindu ritual practice (which most nineteenth-century theorists of religion regarded as symbolically evoking some higher being) was understood by many missionary educators as a literal worship of material objects or animals.[17] Ideally, the object lesson would instruct Hindus to understand that their sacred objects were mere material artifacts with no power of their own. Paradoxically, the evangelical use of object lessons made objects both the problem and the solution to the problem of idolatry.[18]

For missionaries, idols could be metonymically used to illustrate Hinduism, itself.[19] In a missionary manual entitled *Object Lessons for Junior Work,* the author outlined the ways in which teachers and pastors could use the object lesson both to inspire their students for mission work and to critique false heathen gods. The author observes, "At one of the most interesting Junior Missionary meetings I ever attended, a little heathen idol was brought from the pastor's study and made the object lesson. We need only plan our meetings ahead, and with the determination on our part, God will supply the need."[20]

Though not explicitly stated, the purpose of the idol in the missionary meeting was to give young metropolitan Christians the opportunity to observe and handle as an *object* what others, like Hindus, regarded as a god. Rather than encountering the idol in a temple (where most Hindus would have seen it), the junior missionaries were given the idol in an object lesson, making the idol analogous to the spices manufactured in the colonies. By making the idol an object, like rice, the pastor could demystify and demonstrate the banality of non-Christian objects of worship and devotion. Furthermore, the idol, like rice, also symbolized, for a metropolitan audience, something essential about "heathens." Denying "heathens" an understanding of the symbolic or representational, Protestant evangelicals viewed the idol as a manifestation of the childlike literalness of non-Christian worship. Like children, "heathens" were grounded in concrete ways of thinking in which they literally believed that the idol had power.

The nuances of Hindu practice and religion were largely ignored in most nineteenth-century Western understandings of Hinduism. Instead, missionary writings abounded with references to the idolatrous proclivities of all native children, including their tendency to misunderstand the fundamental subordination of objects to the (thinking) subject. A rather humorous example of this was an anecdote reported in a late-nineteenth-century missionary journal. At the end of the year, missionary (and other "modern") schools routinely gave prizes for various academic and non-academic achievements, ceremoniously handed out by some local colonial official. But it seemed that even this common practice could be subverted by the fetishism of "heathen" children: "A vague and unauthenticated statement from a correspondent . . . [caused] much annoyance and trouble . . . the writer affirmed that 'mission dolls given as prizes to Indian children have been utilized by the heathen for their idolatrous worship. The matter was taken up by every society.' "[21] Although the report ultimately proved false, it engendered great anxiety about the instability of objects in the hands of Indian children.

Teachers had to be ever vigilant against such misappropriation of secular objects. But with the proper training, it was hoped that native children could learn to be skeptical of the power ascribed to their idols. One Methodist teacher related an object lesson she used in her school in rural Bengal that directly involved the local village gods. The teacher questioned the students' assertions that idols were really gods themselves and not concrete representations of gods. "At first some of the children were inclined to dispute the statement that idols have ears but hear not.

The students maintained that idols could hear and are alive, but one day the children in one village on their way home from school, ran into a little temple and went close up to one of the idols and then came out saying, 'No it doesn't breathe, we have been in to see.'"[22]

For the Methodist teacher, empirical observation of the idol, seeing that the idol did not literally breathe, would be enough to dispel the sacredness of the "fetish" object. This missionary, like many others, denied the symbolic role of idols and idol worship in Hindu practice. Instead, she believed that by proving to her students that the idol could not literally breathe, hear, or see, she could destroy their religious foundation and thus prepare them to hear the truth of Christ.[23]

Unfortunately for this Methodist missionary and for evangelicals in India in general, this was a fairly rare occurrence. Indians rarely converted to Christianity through attending mission (or other Western) schools. Instead, the Protestant-inflected orientation of the object lesson was effectively secularized by state and native educators. Object lessons and object lesson books became metonyms for modern Western education and the teaching of reason, not Christianity. The failure of the object lesson in terms of facilitating religious conversions should not obscure its success in privileging a particular epistemological orientation to the world.

OBJECTS AND OURSELVES

Bhadralok educators, like their evangelical counterparts, recognized the importance of Pestalozzi to the development of modern education, routinely equated with the "cultivation of the senses." But the translation of the object lesson in schools run by Bengalis eschewed the connection of abstract thinking with Christianity. In government and native non-Christian schools, it was empiricism and rationality, not Christianity, that was the ultimate goal of object lesson training. Moreover, just as British and missionary object lesson books implicitly reflected their cultural provenance, Bengali object lessons primarily found in *bhadralok*-produced texts similarly reflected their upper-caste and Hindu origins.

Government training schools for native teachers were some of the first places where object lesson training was disseminated. For instance, in the 1850s, Bhudev Mukhopadhyay, the headmaster of the Hoohgly Normal School, referred to Pestalozzi as the most important educational figure in his popular teacher-training book, *Sikshavidhayak Pastava: An Introduction to the Art of Teaching*. In Mukhopadhyay's training manual, he gave a sample object lesson that the *shikhah-mahashoy* (teacher) was meant to conduct in the *pathshala* or village school.

The lesson centered on rice, one of the most ubiquitous "objects" found in any Bengali village. Mukhopadhyay's lesson was far closer to Pestalozzi's original intentions for the object lesson than the evangelical texts. In fact, it is worth considering the differences between Mukhopadhyay's object lesson on rice with David Stow's lesson, with which I began the chapter. For Stow, the purpose of a lesson on rice was to connect its natural properties to the "dull and phlegmatic" nature of those who consumed the grain. In contrast, Mukhopadhyay's lesson focuses on rice as a part of the natural world, and he devotes far more time to the empirical qualities of the grain as it travels from the field to the kitchen. Mukhopadhyay begins by encouraging teachers to use rice to impart a rudimentary science lesson by demonstrating to their students the ways that heating the rice paddy allows farmers to more easily remove the brown hull. In Mukhopadhyay's object lesson, teachers are told that it is as important to teach students the various ritual uses of rice as it is to teach them any empirical observations on the natural properties of paddy and rice.

Ultimately, Mukhopadhyay's careful natural science lesson cannot help but reintroduce the social world—in this case, through descriptions of the ritual and cultural places of rice within Bengali Hindu households, a social world assumed to be shared between teacher and student. "Teacher: Is there any other kind of rice other than *shiddhya-chaul* (rice milled from parboiled paddy)? Student: Yes, there is. In our house, we place on God's altar a different kind of rice that is never mixed with the *shiddhya-chaul* we eat. Teacher: What is this rice? Student: (after numerous attempts) It is *atap chaul*. It is called *atap chaul* because it is milled from sun-dried paddy rather than parboiled paddy." Later, in the same lesson, the teacher uses the object lesson on rice to teach about agricultural seasons and also to insert another important ritual aspect of the rice harvest. "Teacher: Because rice is harvested during this season, it is the period when everyone has a *Lokhi* (Lakshmi) *puja* in their household. *Lokhi* is the goddess of rice."[24]

To what degree does Mukhopadhyay's object lesson on rice challenge Stow's imperial vision? On the one hand, Mukhopadhyay (unlike Stow) chose an object that represented the lived world of the students in the *pathshala*, ultimately staying much closer to Pestalozzi's original vision. Furthermore, echoing Pestalozzi's desire that students explore the natural world, Mukhopadhyay knows that the children who attend the *pathshala* will be far more familiar with the production of the food they consume than Stow's students living in the urban environments of Glasgow or London. While all Bengali children, regardless of religion or caste, would be familiar with the differences between parboiled and sun-dried rice, the lesson on rice assumes a shared set of religious rituals around rice and the goddess of rice. While Mukhopadhyay's rice lesson offers a far richer scientific and social meaning to the understanding of rice, it nonetheless yokes a lesson on the harvesting and consumption of a common object to a particular religious practice. The specificity of the religious rituals evoked in the rice lesson has the effect of including some (those who use *atap* rice in *puja* and pray to the goddess Lakshmi) and excluding others (all the Bengalis for whom the meanings of *atap* rice might be quite different).

Although Mukhopadhyay evoked Pestalozzi, like evangelical educators he suggested that the village teacher employ books on objects rather than objects themselves in their classrooms. This suggestion was echoed in the teacher-training manuals published by the Calcutta and Dhaka Normal School headmasters, Gopal Chunder Bandhopadhyay and Somnath Mukhopadhyay.[25] All three training manuals encouraged gurus to use other Bengali object lesson books, such as *Bodhodoy* (or *Nitibodh*) to conduct their lessons. Mukhopadhyay's suggestions ensured the widespread popularity of these particular texts in both Bengali and government schools. The object lesson schoolbooks referred to by Mukhopadhyay were extensively published from the 1850s through the 1870s. The books reiterated the relationship of objects, intelligence, and stages of civilizational attainment found in their British and missionary counterparts, illustrating the impossibility of non–culturally marked ways of teaching about objects or science.

One of the most popular object lesson books translated into Bengali was *Rudiments of Knowledge,* written and published by the Chamber brothers. *Rudiments* presented children with a series of descriptions (object lessons) on the natural world that would mimic the emerging scientific theories and methods. The Chambers were known for their support for and efforts to popularize to the general reading public the most contemporary and radical scientific ideas, from geological findings that challenged the age of the earth to Darwin's ideas of evolution. Joel Schwarz argues that the Chambers' articles gave a British reading audience "access to ideas that previously were available only to scientists who regularly attended professional meetings or read published transactions of such forums."[26] The scientific orientation of the Chambers' adult publications was central to their children's books. Here, books on objects, like *Rudiments of Knowledge,* were meant to introduce young children to Linnaean classification and abstract thinking that would culminate in scientific and religious rationality. It was hardly surprising that upper-caste educators were drawn to the scientific and rational orientation of the Chamber brothers' books. The writers of the two most important object lesson and sciences books, Iswar Chandra Vidyasagar and Akshay Kumar Dutta, were leaders in the liberal religious and cultural reform. Vidyasagar and Dutta's adoption of object lessons seems an extension of their efforts to transform social practices (e.g., by encouraging the remarriage of upper-caste Hindu widows) and to emphasize the traditions of rationality and reason within Hinduism.

But even the nonsectarian and "scientific" model of the Chambers brothers' work was based in a strongly Christian cultural paradigm. This prompted Vidyasagar, in his own translation of *Rudiments of Knowledge* entitled *Bodhodoy,* to change the original text in accordance with paradigms of upper-caste Hinduism. For example, an early object lesson, entitled "On Mankind," in *Rudiments* reads in the following way: "Mankind does not like to live alone. They are fond of living in families or with other persons and also to have neighbors in houses near them. Some people live in the country in cottages, but most people live in houses near each other in villages and towns and cities."[27] The Chambers' object lesson on humans describes various "natural" tendencies shared by all humans, like living in families. They note some differences between those choosing to live in the country and those in urban areas, a distinction no doubt reflecting the real shift of population from the country to the city during the nineteenth century.

The Chambers' text is translated by Vidyasagar in *Bodhodoy* in the following manner: "Humans don't like to live alone. They live with their mothers, fathers, brothers, wives, sons and daughters. . . . You also see this type, an individual who leaves human society and lives in the forest; but such people are rare."[28] Vidyasagar's rendition of the "natural" habits of humans departs from the Chambers' text in ways that suggests his awareness of the cultural specificity of *Rudiments of Knowledge.* For Vidyasagar, the "family" is not the immediate nuclear family, but the patrilineal extended family of "mothers, fathers, brothers, wives, sons and daughters"—sisters being absent since they have married into other families. An equally important change is the second part of the lesson. While the Chambers had focused on the rural and urban differences in habitation, Vidyasagar introduces the figure of the one who leaves human society to live in the forest. Within the Hindu system of *ashramas,* or stages of life, *dvijya* men (upper-caste or twice-born men) are expected to follow a specific life cycle. Vidyasagar's evocation of the forest refers to the third *ashrama, vanaprastha,* or forest dweller. The *vanaprastha* stage follows the stage of being a student and a householder, and precedes the ultimate stage of becoming a *sanyasin.*

Just as the *Rudiments of Knowledge* was a series of object lessons and knowledge based on particular cultural and social models (the middle-class Victorian family), Vidyasagar's *Bodhodoy* was informed by the objects and ideals of upper-caste Hinduism. Nonetheless, the two descriptions share an awareness of changing norms of society and culture. In the Chambers text, it is the shift to urban life in Britain, while for Vidyasagar it is the declining practice of *vanaprastha* and other Hindu *ashramas* in modern Bengali society that suggests a past that is being consciously left behind.

Later, in the section on "Mankind," Vidyasagar adopts a more explicitly comparative framework in translating *Rudiments.* The Chambers describe death and dying in the following way: "When life is gone, the body is an inanimate object, and is so unpleasing to look upon, that it is buried in a grave, where it rots into dust and is no more seen on earth. But although the bodies of mankind thus die and are buried, they have souls, which live forever, and which return to God who gave them."[29] The Chambers' description reflects the underlying Christian nature of their "universal" proclamations about human practice. Not only do they assert that it is universally (and scientifically) true that *all* bodies are inanimate and rot into dust, but they also assume that the only way to deal with death is burial.

Vidyasagar translates this section in a significantly different manner: "The dead body becomes unpleasant and discolored; if you see it you feel great sadness so people cremate the body without delay. Some kinds of people (*jatiya*) do not cremate, they bury the body in the ground."[30] Unlike the earlier description of humankind and human living habits, Vidyasagar not only suggests that cremation (rather than burial) is the normative manner of dealing with dead bodies, but also acknowledges that there are alternative ways to deal with death.

OBJECTS AND OTHERS

The implicit cultural model of the object lesson in mission schools was to link the development of sense perception to the evolution of cultural and religious forms of thinking. John Murdoch, a student of David Stow and a pioneer of Christian vernacular education in India, made this connection explicit in *Hints on Education in India,* a teacher-training manual translated into Bengali and used in mission training schools. In the section on the object lesson, Murdoch quotes Morell's *Elements of Psychology* and reminds the native Christian schoolteacher that "in a very early state of society, humanity itself is living the life of an infant; it is guided almost entirely by sense and instinct." He uses this to explain the development of native Indians. He suggests that tribal populations, "the rude Hill tribes," were in an "infantile stage," but the majority of Hindus should be "compared to children in whom the imaginative powers are largely developed.... A small proportion of the Hindus have advanced to the third stage, when there is a fondness for metaphysical speculation."[31] Thus, the object lesson proved ideal for the larger evangelical goal of converting imaginative (and idolatrous), and sometimes metaphysical, Hindu ways of thinking into an abstract faith in the one true God.

Murdoch's cognitive continuum from the tribal *adivasi* to the "small proportion of Hindus" reflected his evangelical and imperial orientation. But these same kinds of ideas seem to structure the ways that *bhadralok* educators developed their own object theory books. The figure of the *adivasi* dominates object lesson books as a metaphor for those "others" at lower levels of cultural or religious development in much the same way as in the Murdoch text, and similar to the way the "heathen" functions within missionary and evangelical texts. In part, this reflects British object lesson books and their fascination with "uncivilized" tribal populations, but *adivasis* figure far more prominently within *bhadralok* texts. I see this peculiar obsession as a response, in part, to evangelical and colonial assumptions about the religious and cultural backwardness of Hindus. That is, the fears that Hinduism might be collapsed into the "infantile stage" of cognitive development focused on the worship of objects seemed to prompt an obsessive need on the part of upper-caste Hindu educators to constantly distance themselves from tribal communities.

An example of the place of *adivasi* populations in *bhadralok* educational literature is the book *Charupath: Entertaining Lessons in Science and Literature* by Akshay Kumar Dutta. Dutta's book went into multiple editions and was one of the most popular texts used in higher primary Bengali and Anglo-vernacular schools. The book, a series of object lessons on the natural and human world, begins with a section on knowledge and education or *bidha-shikha*. The lesson on knowledge begins by enumerating the advantages of pursuing education for rich and poor and young and old alike. But the expansive possibilities of this sentiment are undercut by the next sentence, which suggests, "The primary reason for the negative conditions of mountain-dwellers, uncivilized people (referring to tribal populations) and inferior people everywhere is their lack of *bidha-shikha.*"[32] The introductory section suggests the single-minded focus of *bhadralok* educators on book learning and formal schooling as both the means and the mark of progress. But there is also a duality in the lesson on book learning since it seems initially to offer the possibility that *anyone* can be (and should be) educated even as it insists on distinguishing those Bengalis willing to get an education from those "others." In Dutta's text, the *adivasi* community's putative low civilizational standard is itself an object lesson for those Bengalis unwilling to educate themselves or their children.

In other object lesson books, the *adivasi* other is even more centrally the "object" of the lesson, and *bhadralok* educators use various objects to metonymically represent the truth of *adivasi* culture. *Ratnashar* (1870), by Kamakhacharan Ghosh, was an object lesson book divided into a series of lessons on rivers, the natural world (including solid, liquid, and gaseous objects), as well as animate beings.[33] In a section on "Mankind's Condition," Ghosh employed the same empiricism used to distinguish between gaseous and liquid objects to distinguish between the culture of those teaching and learning from *Ratnashar* (largely upper caste, Hindu, and male) and the other inhabitants of Bengal. "Those people who live in the forest, catching and consuming animals, wearing bark, animal skin or nothing at all, are uncivilized." In addition to tribal groups like the "Santhal, Kol, Kuki and Gond," whom Ghosh feels obviously fit this description, he also includes the lowest castes, mentioning the Dhangar "who clean the sewers in Calcutta."[34] Ghosh enumerates all those in Bengal who fall into the "class" of the uncivilized and the civilized. Ghosh's text mimics the book with which I began this chapter, David Stow's *Object Lesson,* which used the example of rice cultivation to draw a set of observations on the relationship between eating rice and the production of a phlegmatic and dull culture.[35]

For the Indian *bhadralok,* it was necessary to distinguish their culture as superior to those of other natives who did not have the same cultures of school-going. While the upper-caste Bengali may not have been as "civilized" as the English, his diet, housing, and clothing clearly pointed to his superiority over *adivasi* and lower-caste Hindu communities. The "uncivilized" are distinguishable, *Ratnashar* teaches, by the objects they wear and consume. But the ultimate reason for their backwardness is their lack of intelligence and reason. Like Dutta, Ghosh reminds his school-going audience that it is through intelligence and reason that civilized people are able to raise themselves up. But the constant evocation of the *adivasi* as representing a lower rung of cultural development suggests the ultimate impossibility of those "other" groups ever counting themselves among the civilized cultures.

CONCLUSION

The concern over objects and religion represents a consistent theme in evangelical and Hindu reform efforts throughout the early nineteenth century. Ram Mohan Roy, the early-nineteenth-century Bengali philosopher and activist, directed his energies at purging Hinduism of its ritual and idol-centered worship in order to reorient it in more "rational" and scriptural ways. Just as Pestalozzi's object theory incorporated the complex philosophical ideas of Hume and Kant, I see *bhadralok* writers of object lesson books, Bhudev Mukhopadhyay, Iswar Chandra Vidyasagar, and Akshay Kumar Dutta, incorporating into object lessons the philosophical and religious rationalism that marked their own ideas about cultural and religious reform. Many of the prominent writers of the popular object lesson books were active in various Hindu religious reform movements, and object lessons became one of the means to more widely disseminate notions of these ideas and introduce them into the classroom.

The general empirical and rational epistemology at the heart of object lessons easily created the conditions for them to become science lessons. By the turn of the twentieth century, colonial educators directly linked the empiricism of object lessons to science learning, and object lesson books became science primers for elementary schools. The Department of Public Instruction (DPI) reiterated the centrality of object learning to a modern curriculum in their 1905 report: "Children of this age are incapable of learning science, for generalizing from facts belongs to a later stage of mental discipline.... The cultivation of this power, which is the chief aim of the revised syllabus, is impossible, unless children are taught to observe, compare and contrast the objects which are around them."[36]

The use of object lessons as science lessons suggests the successful secularization of the evangelical orientation of the missionary books. But, as I have tried to show, the transformations in Bengali object lesson books by *bhadralok* educators did not result in a purely culturally neutral text.

Instead, upper-caste Hindu norms were normalized within the various "lessons," and instead of "heathen" it was now "tribals" that were seen as belonging to the earlier "stages of mental discipline."

It was not accidental that from the early nineteenth century, object lesson books were filled with the objects and the people of the British Empire. There were deep imperial and ideological assumptions embedded in educational theory, even in theories developed for progressive goals. The object lesson captures this dichotomy. Pestalozzi's school at Yverdon, Switzerland, was opened for orphans, for destitute children, and for training teachers in progressive pedagogy.[37] Yet in the colonies, the lesson was used by missionary and *bhadralok* educators to instruct new approaches to religion and culture as well as to employ the model of higher and lower levels of mental discipline to map out the religious and cultural hierarchies of colonial Bengal.

CHAPTER 4

The Schoolteacher as Modern Father

> The behavior between the guru and his students should be the same as between fathers and sons. But in this country, there is very little effort to encourage mutual affection and understanding between fathers and sons.[1]

The preceding observation by Bhudhev Mukhopadhyay occurs toward the beginning of his 1856 manual, *Shikha Vidyak Prasatava*, written for the Hooghly Normal School, a government-financed teacher-training institution headed up by Mukhopadhyay himself. In his manual, Mukhopadhyay bemoans the fact that while he would like to train the modern *guru* (teacher) to relate to his students as fathers relate to sons, the actual relationships in Hindu families make this impossible. For Mukhopadhyay, "mutual affection and understanding" should mark both the pedagogic and paternal relationship. But he sadly concludes that rather than awaiting a change in the behavior of native families, he and other upper-caste educators need to train native teachers to model within the classroom the kind of paternal affective behavior he desires within the home.

Mukhopadhyay's training system, as outlined in *Shikha Vidyak Prasatava*, was based on a method developed by David Stow in his Glasgow academy, an institution initially created to educate Christian instructors for missionary schools in the British Empire. Stow's method, variously described as "gallery lessons" or "the sympathy of numbers," was explicitly positioned against the mechanistic and repetitive monitorial method popular in the early nineteenth century.

In the previous two chapters, I have examined how some of the most innovative technologies of literacy and pedagogy became connected to the molding of new forms of religiosity. In this chapter, I will trace how *bhadralok* educators, like Bhudhev Mukhopadhyay, and missionary educators managed to catapult Stow's training system out of its narrow pedagogic niche and orient it toward the development of new forms of upper-caste Hindu and native Christian masculinity. In Bengal, *bhadralok* and missionary headmasters of normal schools (teacher-training academies) believed that their institutions were the ideal sites to propagate new forms of manliness based on the care and education of dependents, whether students or children.

Ironically, the dominance of Stow's theories among all educators meant that Mukhopadhyay, who was also headmaster of the Hooghly Normal School, came to use a Scottish Presbyterian theory of training teachers to help him articulate a model of enlightened upper-caste authority—one that was meant to transcend the classroom and transform the Bengali family and Indian society at large. Stow's model of teacher training was centrally focused on the single teacher in the schoolroom, a (male) teacher who governed his class based on sympathy and affection, rather than coercion. The engaged, sympathetic male pedagogue who listened, played with, and most importantly guided his students was explicitly compared by Mukhopadhyay to "traditional" fathers, who were seen as largely diffident and distant from their sons.

One of the consequences of Stow's theory of teacher training on the development of Indian masculinity was to underline a gentler patriarchal authority. The other, less obvious implication was that this model was ultimately based on a series of hierarchies: teacher-student; father-child; man-woman; and, crucially, upper-caste Hindus to *adivasis* (tribal), the lower castes, and Muslims. Evangelicals were influenced by a notion of a (middle-class) liberal manliness constituted by the need to educate, uplift, and "civilize" one's dependents (women, children, and colonial populations).[2] This also shaped (implicitly) the thinking of midcentury Bengali reformers, like Mukhopadhyay, who believed that (upper-caste) masculinity was constituted by a responsibility to uplift one's familial dependents, women and children, but also other, "backward" native communities.

Thus, not only were pedagogic and familial relationships hierarchically arranged, but also there was clearly a religious, cultural, and racial hierarchy of masculinities. In government normal schools, the ideal Bengali teacher or patriarch was implicitly upper caste, evidenced by the almost complete exclusion of Muslims and lower-caste Hindus in these schools. Although missionary schools trained lower-caste and tribal students, evangelicals consistently emphasized the European Christian teacher-patriarch as the dominant model that native Christian trainees had to emulate. The need to police the boundaries of enlightened masculinity can be most clearly seen in the ways that Christian, upper-caste Hindu, and government educators addressed the issue of the tribal schoolteacher. The authority of the Santhali teacher, educated in missionary institutions in the Santhal Pargannahs (an area that is today a part of the state of Jharkhandh in Eastern India), was routinely ignored by upper-caste Hindus and undermined even by the evangelicals who established the schools in the Santhali areas.

In foregrounding government and missionary normal schools, I am arguing for a rarely examined site for the construction of normative upper-caste Hindu and Christian models of masculinity. By adapting Stow's evangelical ideas, native reformers not only made the father as the center of the household (and schoolroom) but also emphasized the upper-caste Hindu teacher-patriarch as the "civilizing" force in his schoolroom, family, and ultimately society. I begin the chapter by tracing the adaptation of David Stow's theories in two distinct kinds of institutions: government normal schools to retrain the *gurumahashoy* or village schoolteacher, and missionary normal schools for educating native and tribal Christians. The Bengali training manuals written by *bhadralok* and missionary headmasters in the 1860s and 1870s gave teacher trainees explicit instructions on how to speak and carry themselves so that their students could relate to them in an affectionate but obedient manner, the putative basis of the affective bonds and intimacy in modern families. While the manuals delineate the manner in which men might be trained as teachers and fathers, I examine the reports from the Department of Public Instruction (DPI) and missionary societies to show how the abstract equation of teachers with fathers was institutionalized through racial, caste, and ethnic hierarchies in the running of government and evangelical normal schools.

DAVID STOW AND THE SIMULTANEOUS SYSTEM

One of the main apparatuses used by colonial training institutions was the "gallery," which was needed to "train the teachers to instruct a number together." The gallery was an inclined and raised platform on which children could be simultaneously taught and watched. Gallery lessons were part of the innovative teaching system developed by the Scottish Presbyterian David Stow in his Glasgow Seminary and Normal School in 1837. Stow's pedagogic theory represented an important shift in the training of teachers. Stow felt the teacher (often more reliably than the parents) should be trained to mold the everyday habits of children through continuous supervision and empathy—what he described as the "simultaneous method." Stow's simultaneous teaching technique was a direct refutation of the monitorial method popularized in the early nineteenth century by Andrew Bell and Joseph Lancaster.

The monitorial method had been based on the pedagogic principle that a single teacher could run a whole school by using older monitors to teach younger children. This system, a fairly inexpensive way to "educate" poor children, was increasingly criticized by progressive educators in metropolitan Britain and colonial India for being overly punitive and coercive, ultimately leading to rote teaching and learning. As Stow argued, "[A] monitor . . . is an imperfect substitute for the master."[3]

The literal space of the gallery reflected the effort to create a new kind of relationship between teachers and students. The teaching gallery consisted of an inclined platform, almost like bleachers, in which the students were arranged by age and ability. The teacher stood at the bottom of the platform and was able to survey the whole class at once; and in turn, everyone in the class had a clear view of the teacher. This was in contrast to the monitorial system in which students were arranged in small groups around individual monitors with the teacher serving as little more than a supervisor. The gallery was an integral part of Stow's method because it allowed the simultaneous instruction by a single teacher of a group of children "of nearly one age, learning one thing." In the gallery, the fact that the schoolteacher was visible to all of his students all of the time meant that he was able to create an environment of "gentle but remorseless surveillance,"[4] producing self-reflective, self-governing, and moral children.[5]

Educators in Britain and in colonial Bengal were drawn to Stow's training methods because of its emphasis on affection, rather than coercion, as the defining feature of relationships between teacher and student, and, by extension, adults and children. For instance, Reverend Garbett, in an 1851 speech to the Home and Colonial School Society, outlined what he considered the major difference between the monitorial schools and those run according to the Stow system. For Garbett, Stow's theory emphasized "the principle of love; taking away from its schools the influence of fear. I do not mean taking away the principle of authority . . . [nor] the principle of control which a superior intelligence will never fail to exercise over an inferior."[6]

Garbett shares the disciplinary goals of earlier forms of schooling: order, control, and hierarchy (a "superior" versus an "inferior" intelligence), but fundamentally differs on how to reach those goals. Echoing Stow, Garbett calls upon "love" (or what Stow called "sympathy") as the means to encourage mutual respect between children and teachers. Instruction based on "love" rather than "fear" encourages students to think for themselves, and to develop a personal relationship with the teacher and ultimately with God. Less obviously, Garbett's speech is an implicit critique of other societies, namely, those run by the Established Church, which continue to employ monitorial methods of teaching—methods that Garbett sees as based in fear and coercion, not unlike the methods of the Established Church itself.

Scholars of Britain have studied David Stow's training system as the pedagogic equivalent of Bentham's panopticon.[7] That is, as a popular model that was not merely used to prepare better trained teachers and students but also meant to produce new kinds of subjects. But in focusing on Stow's technique in India, I suggest a wholly different trajectory for his teacher-training theories, one that is equally ambitious in its goals. In the hands of local headmasters, missionary and native, Stow's training became nothing less than the foundation for both a native Christian and an upper-caste Hindu masculinity.

Although Stow constantly exhorted the schoolteacher to supervise and instruct children during playtime, he did not articulate an expectation that fathers should do the same. One could argue, in fact, that if "the scene of the real life of the children" occurred in the playground, then it was the school (rather than the home) where children were truly raised. The relationship assumed in Stow's theories between the school and the home was more explicitly articulated and developed in the adoption of his theories by *bhadralok* and missionary educators in mid-nineteenth-century Bengali normal schools.

THE CHRISTIAN PATRIARCH

Initially, missionaries had assumed they could employ graduates of their own education system to teach in vernacular village schools. However, by the 1850s, missionaries in Bengal recognized that teaching demanded a distinctive kind of training. Reverend James Long, one of the most important missionaries in Bengal, was struck by the achievements of the native Christian students at the Santipore Normal School (established by the Church Missionary Society [CMS] in 1855). Long saw the students as personifying "a new history in our mission . . . a step toward a time when our whole educational system may be improved and gradually a far higher standard attained among the converts generally."[8] The schoolteacher, as much as the catechist or the missionary, was responsible for the pastoral care of his community. Long's comments anticipate the wider responsibilities the native Christian teacher would be expected to take on. Missionary normal schools constantly reminded the teacher that his role was to model for his students (and their parents) that becoming a Christian was not only a matter of spiritual conversion but also a conversion to a whole new set of moral attitudes and behavior.

Evangelical teacher training was defined as much through concepts of "civilization" and "uplift" as it was through education and pedagogy. For educated native Christian men, teaching was presented as an alternative (although less prestigious) to becoming a catechist or preacher. Some mission normal schools (like the Santipore institution) were opened exclusively to train teachers, whereas others (like the Baptist Serampore College) were the result of adding teacher training to already existing institutions. Students were taught in subjects as diverse as literature, writing, arithmetic, geography, history, natural sciences, and of course religious teaching. They were also trained in giving object lessons and teaching in both the monitorial and simultaneous teaching styles. Most importantly, missionaries insisted that the teacher-training colleges be purely vernacular institutions to ensure that graduates remained in teaching.[9]

Missionary normal schools, unlike government ones, targeted and educated lower-caste and tribal native Christians, the majority of whom would not otherwise have had access to either literacy or formal schooling.[10] As James Long had suggested in the very beginning, teacher training provided an institutional opportunity to educate and "civilize" a group of native Christian men to eschew the "heathen" religious and domestic practices common to native society. Missionaries had far greater control over their students' lives than *bhadralok* headmasters and were able to closely monitor who was being trained. Native Christian schoolteachers were explicitly instructed in their training manuals on how to create both school and domestic environments that approximated those of European Christian families and classrooms. This was reinforced by the boarding school arrangement, which provided native converts proximity to (and surveillance under) a missionary family (the headmaster and his wife).

The pedagogic and patriarchal ideal to which native Christian trainees were supposed to aspire is perfectly captured in the Bengali training manual written by Reverend Gmelin, the Anglican headmaster of the CMS Krishnagur Mission School. Gmelin's text, *A Manual of Education for the Use of Vernacular Teachers*, was a rough Bengali translation of an English-language manual written by John Murdoch, *Education in India with Special Reference to Vernacular Schools*.[11] Murdoch had been trained at David Stow's institution in Glasgow, and his manual (like that of Mukhopadhyay and Bandhyopadhyay) was indebted to Stow's text and training method. Gmelin's Bengali translation stays very close to Murdoch's original (which was also translated into other Indian vernaculars).

The manual written by Gmelin shared Mukhopadhyay's assumption that the "modern" male teacher should serve as a model for the "modern" father. While Mukhopadhyay emphasized the parallels between new techniques of teaching students and raising children, Gmelin (and missionary training schools more generally) adopted a more didactic and supervisory role over his students. Not only did his manual suggest a theoretical relationship between pedagogy and parenting, but Gmelin also felt that normal schools should directly shape the domestic practices of the teacher himself.

An example of this is found toward the end of the book, where Gmelin offers a list of the "habits" that the properly trained Christian vernacular teacher should have. These include such perennial favorites as staying clean, waking early, staying physically active, and reading Scripture upon waking. But the longest section relates to how the teacher should behave in his home. Gmelin encourages the native Christian schoolteacher to eat together with his family rather than following the Indian customary practice in which the "husband [eats] first, then the children, while the remains are left to the wife." For Gmelin, eating with one's family is not merely to reproduce European dining practices, but also connected to producing different kinds of relationships within the native Christian home. "You have perhaps seen a missionary and his family at a table. Is it not much more pleasant and better than that of Hindus? If you object that there are no servants to wait on you, place the food on the table before hand. There are many thousand families of poor people in England who have no servants, yet they sit down together at meals." He further demands that the native teacher change the customary practices of his community—in fact, that the teacher "should be the first to set an example."[12]

Gmelin takes teacher training as a model for native familial patriarchy to its logical conclusion. The native Christian trainee, as part of his education, must literally be taught how to be a "good" father and husband. Like evangelical-based teaching, learning to be a good Christian father and husband involves a series of carefully cultivated behaviors and dispositions that will allow supervision and encourage closeness among family members. Eating together at the same table not only ensures that the patriarch can watch his whole (nuclear) family, but also encourages confidences and intimacies between fathers and their children, as well as husbands and their wives. Furthermore, it directly negates the tyrannical native practice that leaves women with the "remains" of a meal.

Gmelin's discussion is not only didactic but also based on a racial hierarchy in which native Christians must always look toward European Christians as their model. Thus, the "training" of native students is not only in "modern" pedagogic methods but also in European Christian models of familial behavior. After all, the many "thousand families of poor people in England" are able to lead "civilized" lives, and so it is incumbent upon Christian schoolteachers to recognize the barbarity of their own customs and be willing to be "the first to set an example." A good trainee not only learned how to be an authority in the classroom but also was given detailed instructions on how to be an authority in his home and ultimately an example for his own community.

But even as he directs his trainees to mold their "daily life" along the lines of European custom, Gmelin is aware of the hierarchy between native and missionary families. Unlike native Christian families, the majority of European missionaries had servants to give them their meals. In fact, native Christians routinely served as servants in the homes of missionaries. Rather than acknowledging that it is the labor of native Christians that makes possible the pleasant, companionate meal shared by the European family, Gmelin argues that it is "custom" that prevents native Christians from eating together. After all, even poor families in Britain are able to sit together as a loving, affectionate unit without servants.

The figure of the "civilized" European patriarch who lurks in the background of Gmelin's manual was corporeally present in normal schools in the person of the European missionary headmaster. Unlike government teacher-training institutions, Christian normal schools were all headed up by Europeans.[13] Although almost all of the inspectors in the DPI were European, it was generally accepted that *bhadralok* headmasters were better suited to educate and train teachers in the vernacular. In contrast, missionaries were convinced that physical proximity to a European was essential to train native Christian teachers who would be able to observe and (hopefully) absorb the refined sentiments and behaviors of a true Christian.

But even when missionary societies successfully employed Europeans as headmasters, the racial hierarchy of the normal school was always in tension with a rhetorical commitment to the Christian "family of man." This tension was evidenced early on when the CMS Santipore Training School was opened in 1854. The mission society decided to appoint Reverend C. Bomwetch, an Anglican missionary originally from Germany, to head up the institution. But this produced a maelstrom of protest from the local and metropolitan committees. The resistance to Bomwetch's appointment did not seem to be about his educational or evangelical credentials. Instead, after a series of elliptical exchanges, Mr. Burdwan (A CMS missionary) honestly declared, "I do not think Mr. Bomwetch will have that [good] influence over the young men if he marries a native Christian which he would with a European wife. It would therefore [b]e more advisable that he should have a trial for a year or so."[14] The controversy over the opening of the Santipore Training School, it appears, was not about Bomwetch's plans for the institution itself but rather the fear of the Home Committee and local Anglican missionaries that Bomwetch might marry a native Christian woman. While the various committees never considered giving (the future) Mrs. Bomwetch administrative or teaching responsibilities, her potential (racial) presence as the native wife of a European headmaster threatened the hierarchy and balance that missionaries tried so desperately to maintain in their institutions.

In fact, Reverend Schur argued that although the school was to be run on a largely European boarding model, the CMS would have to adjust if Bomwetch chose to marry a native Christian woman. Specifically, Schur was discomfited by the "familiar intercourse" between students and the (European) principal's family. His chief anxiety was that while such intimacy was expected in Europe, in Bengal there was the danger of native Christians "being puffed up with pride," which would inevitably lead to "the ruin of the Institution."[15]

Schur's administrative objections must be read in the light of the possibility of Bomwetch marrying a native Christian. The intimacy between headmaster and student, the patriarchal model that native trainees were meant to follow, was complicated by the fact of racial difference. Native Christians were more apt to be "puffed up with pride" should they enjoy open access to the European Christian family. But even more dangerous to the Home Committee was the possibility of the "model" of racial miscegenation presented by a European headmaster married to a native Christian. That is, while native trainees were expected to emulate European patriarchal mores and comportment, they were never meant to consider themselves actually a part of the European family. The dissemination of Christian patriarchal and familial norms was only successful, according to Schur, if both the headmaster and his wife were "English people, the latter a lady of talents, accomplishment and sterling piety.... [S]he should give them [the students] the indelible impression that Christianity is the only means of truly civilizing a nation."[16]

Schur's comments could not be more explicit. The boarding school "family" can only function if the headmaster and his wife are true moral exemplars, a position secured and indexed through their race. A non-European Christian wife would disrupt the comfortable ordering of racial and gender hierarchy upon which evangelical educational institutions were based. In the end, it was not Christianity but whiteness that ensured a "civilized" family and nation.

THE GALLERY COMES TO BENGALI NORMAL SCHOOLS

About the same time that evangelicals were formally establishing normal schools, *bhadralok* educators embarked on their own project of remaking the upper-caste Hindu man through a parallel project of teacher training. Shaping native masculine subjectivity through schooling had always been crucial to colonial educational projects from their inception in the early nineteenth century. In Thomas Macaulay's 1835 "Minute on Education," he not only argued for the inherent superiority of English over Sanskrit and Arabic, but also promised that it would create new kinds of men: "a class of persons Indian in blood and colour, but English in tastes, in opinions, in morals and in intellect." For Macaulay, an English-educated class of Indian translators would solve certain pragmatic issues of governance faced by the Empire. But the "Minute" also laid out a clear argument that the salutary effects of an English education were more than intellectual; the acquisition of English knowledge offered the possibility of transforming Indian masculine subjectivity and eventually Indian culture itself.[17]

In spite of Macaulay's grand rhetorical style, the actual institutionalization of English schooling was relatively limited and slow. Nonetheless, postcolonial theorists have tended to focus on Macaulay's "Minute" (and English education more generally) as the primary locus of contestations over colonial ideology. However, the effort to transform Indian culture through modern education was also the goal of Bengali-language schooling and, as I will show, the explicit goal of *bhadralok* headmasters of government teacher-training institutions.[18]

It was not until the 1860s that the DPI began funding normal schools for the formal training of teachers. The DPI initially set up three grades of teacher-training institutions. Although all three were meant to focus on teaching in the vernacular, the first grade normal schools also prepared students to become *pandits* in Anglo-vernacular schools that offered instruction in both English and Bengali. The second and third grade institutions were established for improving the training of the most common kind of teacher, the *gurumahashoy* or village schoolteacher. The traditional *gurumahashoy* was typically a Kayasth or Brahmin, a member of the "literary" upper castes, and his ability to read and write was the privelege of his caste status. Although upper caste, the occupational status of the village schoolteacher was quite low.

Although *bhadralok* headmasters at government schools eschewed the explicitly evangelical Christian elements of Stow's system, there were nonetheless important ways in which a Christian-inflected sensibility shaped the articulation of a "modern" Hindu schoolteacher-patriarch. *Bhadralok* headmasters perceived the formally trained village teacher as the ideal paradigm of an upper-caste masculine authority—one that could be further propagated to Bengali families. This is not that far from the expectations of missionary educators, who expected that the native Christian teacher would embody the promise of a wholly native Church, led by educated, "moral," and "civilized" patriarchs.

For instance, in an attempt to rehabilitate and inspire the *gurumahashoy* (the village schoolteacher), Bhudev Mukhopadhyay in his *Shiksha Vidyak Pustav* (1856) argues for village teaching as a crucial part of a modernist (versus an evangelical) project. Mukhopadhyay was frustrated that village schoolteachers did not understand the importance of their role in reforming society: "they [the *gurus*] have no idea of the great influence which they might exert over the mind of their pupils and they consequently neglect the highest duties which their situation would impose if they had any sense of their powers and obligations."[19] Mukhopadhyay impressed upon teaching trainees that within the modern colonial social order, they were uniquely poised to shape native society and culture and were responsible for far more than teaching literacy and basic math. Mukhopadhyay was further frustrated because there were few incentives in the colonial educational system to make him believe that vernacular teaching was a worthy and meaningful occupation.

The Hooghly Normal School, first opened by Bhudev Mukhopadhyay in 1856, not only was a first grade normal school but also served as a paradigmatic example of successful and enlightened teacher training. Reverend James Long, who had inspected the CMS Santipore School, also examined the Hooghly institution for the DPI. Long praised Mukhopadhyay's institution, which he contrasted "with the old Pundit system of nothing but books and nothing but words." Long praised Mukhopadhyay's teaching plan as a means "eminently calculated to rouse them [native *gurus*] to think," and Long was especially pleased that Mukhopadhyay had ordered that a gallery—Stow's gallery—be built by Indian workmen.[20] Long's description of the "Pundit system" as "nothing but books" references a much larger general debate about teacher training: to what degree should the training of teachers be primarily scholastic versus pedagogic (sometimes seen as a difference between a French and German system)? For Long, Mukhpadhyay's introduction of new pedagogic techniques suggests both his awareness and interest in transforming conventional teaching. But what were these techniques that "rouse [teacher trainees] to think," and how were they different from merely book learning?

Mukhopadhyay's decision to manufacture a gallery was not simply to acquire modern kinds of pedagogic equipment but also a part of his larger intent to reconfigure and reimagine upper-caste Hindu masculine authority.[21] The gallery, an inclined platform that allowed a single teacher to supervise and survey all of his students at one time was reproduced in the training of the teachers themselves. Mukhopadhyay decided to have teacher trainees in the Hooghly Normal School board rather than commute in. This made Hooghly "the first [normal] institution" to offer boarding. Mukhopadhyay felt that since the trainees were "from the interior districts," it was "greatly conducive to their improvement and the conservation of their morals" to actually live at the school.[22] Just as a gallery offered the teacher greater supervision over his students, a boarding institution offered the headmaster greater control over teacher-training candidates, especially those from poorer, rural backgrounds.

Mukhopadhyay reoriented the evangelical basis of Stow's training system. The appeal to "love" or "affection" was not seen by Mukhopadhyay as a reflection of Christianity but evidence of a more modern orientation toward gender and familial practice. As a reformer, committed to the project of rethinking his own society, Mukhopadhyay was drawn to the socially transformative possibilities of teacher training. In his manual, Mukhopadhyay considered new ways in which men and boys should interact, not only in schools but also in upper-caste Hindu households. He complained that traditional fathers "fear that it will reduce deference to their authority and so they do not want to be too close to their own sons." In contrast, Mukhopadhyay suggested that the modern *guru* "considers himself a playmate of his student [and] a lot of problems can be avoided. Playing can also be used for instruction and many of the negative tendencies in children can be controlled by watching them play."[23] Supervising and participating in "play" were far more effective means to maintain authority than distance and diffidence from one's children or one's students.

Mukhopadhyay's description of the relationship between teachers and students is curiously tautological. On the one hand, he suggests the *guru* should adopt a parental, and specifically paternal, attitude toward his students. But then he sadly concludes that Bengali fathers are actually bad models for the kind of affect-based teaching he has in mind. Although critical of traditional familial models, Mukhopadhyay sees Bengali fathers as simply misguided because they continue to believe that authority originates in distance. Mukhopadhyay distinguishes "respect" *shradhashpada,* which implies a closer and more affectionate relationship, from *shambhramayar,* a term of respect that connotes greater distance and deference, the kind of respect that Mukhopadhyay feels describes more traditional father-son relationships. I do not want to present Mukhopadhyay's approach as overly technical. Although he suggests very concrete ways in which both fathers and teachers can shape their children—through supervision of and participation in playing—the ultimate goal is not merely discipline but also a new form of familial intimacy based on "mutual affection and understanding."

Mukhopadhyay's concern, in the mid-nineteenth century, is to construct a model of teaching and a model of masculinity that are modern but not Western, and that continue to draw on traditional and customary forms of knowledge and relationships. For example, he advises his trainees that if they are able to demonstrate their knowledge of traditional subjects, they "will be respected as a father and uncle by our students, and this is no small thing, and secondly you will be able to use this knowledge to teach children other beneficial things."[24] Again, Mukhopadhyay easily collapses teachers and fathers—the respected teacher and the respected father will be able to demonstrate their mastery of both their traditions and new forms of behavior. What is surprising in Mukhopadhyay's advice is that he sees "traditional" knowledge as allowing the *gurumahashoy* to appear more like "a father and uncle." This is clearly the "respect" that comes from "mutual affection and understanding," *shradhashpada,* rather than the deference, *shambhramayar,* that Mukhopadhyay uses to describe more traditional fathers.

The crucial importance of an affective component in vernacular teaching is reiterated in the Bengali training manual written by Gopal Chunder Bandhopadhyay, the headmaster of the Calcutta Normal School. Bandhopadhyay advises training students that "it is essential that teachers are loving (affectionate) towards their students. The authors of the Shastras perceived [thought of] their teachers as fathers."[25] Bandhopadhyay suggests a rather unconvincing parallel between the *guru-shishya* or teacher-disciple relationship as enjoined in the ancient Shastras, and that of contemporary teachers and students. Brahminical authority was based on knowledge of Sanskritic texts and the transmission of that knowledge to one's students in a lineage that eventually developed into a tradition or *parampara.* That is, even if the Shastras suggest the *shishya* regard their *guru* as their father, there is little to suggest that the authority or effectiveness of ancient Brahminical teachers was related to the kind of parental love that Bandhopadhyay has in mind. Bandopadhyay's suggestion that teachers "are loving" toward their students reflects instead a very modern reconfiguration of pedagogic authority, in spite of Bandopadhyay's efforts to link the *guru* to the lineage of Shastric Brahminical authority.

The fairly intimate tone adopted in the training manuals written by *bhadralok* headmasters comes from the assumption that they share a cultural (religious and caste) background with the students they teach. Although Mukhopadhyay and Bandhopadhyay seem to posit a generalized model of paternal authority, it is implicitly based on the Hindu, upper-caste father and family. *Bhadralok* headmasters were able to comment with such confidence about the internal psychology of "traditional" fathers because they themselves came from such households and assumed that their students were from similar caste and religious (if not class) backgrounds.

Government normal schools recruited and were filled with trainees from the same ranks of the poor, rural, but genteel "literate" castes who had previously been *gurumahashoys:* Brahmans, Kayasths, and Navasiks. Thus, at least in part, there is an assumption by both native and European educational department officers that the vernacular schoolteacher's authority was also based on his caste background.

Although sharing a belief in the importance of reforming teacher-training education, government educators (especially upper-caste headmasters) were uninterested in expanding the ranks of teacher trainees. Government normal schools drew on the same group of individuals, largely poor and upper-caste Hindus, who had been village teachers in the precolonial period.[26] Mukhopadhyay and other *bhadralok* headmasters hoped the *guru* would return to his village and not only introduce new ways of teaching and new subjects into village schools but also model new ways for adults to interact with children. In this way, headmasters hoped schools and schoolteachers would indirectly shape the Bengali family.

THE TEACHER AS CULTURAL MISSIONARY

I have been focusing on the ways evangelical theories of teacher training were employed to buttress the domestic authority of the upper-caste Hindu and native Christian teacher-father. But another critical dimension of the pedagogy-inflected masculinity was the notion of the teacher as a cultural emissary and model. *Bhadralok* educators working in the DPI explicitly drew on the evangelical characteristics of missionary teachers to encourage the village teacher to see himself as an agent of cultural change and authority.

In the first chapter of Bandhopadhyay's training manual (cited above), he alludes to missionaries working among *adivasi* or tribal communities as an example of school teaching as a higher calling. Bandhyopadhyay writes that missionaries, as a part of their pedagogic commitment, willingly lived among the "ignorant and uncivilized" to educate them.[27] But once there, in the face of the "violence and anger of these uncivilized savages," certain missionaries—"great men," according to Bandhopadhyay—were killed. Yet Bandhopadhyay notes that "they do not desist from continuing to teach them. Among their sect, they generally are not paid well. They manage to live on whatever little salary they receive." Bandhopadhyay then implores the Hindu teacher trainee, "Oh *Shikhak mahashoy* (teacher)! In order to accomplish the responsibility you have taken up (to be a great teacher), and to be truly happy, you should take those exalted men as your ideal."[28]

In dramatic language, Bandhopadhyay conjures a model of evangelical selflessness and spiritual vocation as the true ideal of teaching. Rather than petty complaints about wages or status, the *guru* should recognize (like missionaries) the power they hold to transform society. Even when faced with death, missionaries believe in the transformative power of education to "civilize." Bandhopadhyay's main goal is to convince trainees that being a teacher is an important and noble profession, and to that end he asks the *guru* to identify with the missionary, who was perceived first and foremost as a teacher (there is no discussion of conversion or proselytizing). But in no way was the *guru* asked to identify with (or even identify) the "uncivilized savages" among whom the missionary works. The training manual is invested in differentiating upper-caste Bengali *gurus* from the "primitive" *adivasi,* while simultaneously maintaining their difference from missionaries. Even as missionaries established normal schools in Santhali communities in the same period that Bandhopadhyay wrote his manual, the tribal teacher remained invisible within Bandopadhyay's text.

Tribal teachers were trained almost exclusively by missionaries, and there is no evidence that they ever entered government normal schools. But as the example I used from Bandhopadhyay's manual shows, the figure of the *adivasi* made its way into the teacher-training manuals used in government schools. For Bandhopadhyay, the *adivasi* never figured as a teacher, only as a recipient of the "civilizing" ministrations of European missionaries.

"CIVILIZING" THE TRIBAL TEACHER

The use of normal schools as vehicles for theorizing and inculcating new forms of paternal behavior and familial intimacy was premised on the notion that masculine and pedagogic authority was learned. But in examining the social history of government and missionary normal schools, I have tried to show how this notion rested uncomfortably with the idea that a teacher's influence and power were inextricably tied to his race, social class, caste, or religious origins. In spite of the elaborate theoretical advances in teacher training, from the monitorial to the simultaneous system, appearing authoritative was still a fundamental feature of effective pedagogy. The tension between training authority and appearing authoritative was best exemplified in the history of normal schools for Santhali (tribal) teachers.[29]

As Bandhopadhyay suggests, one of the main fields of mission work in the late nineteenth century was among *adivasi* (tribal) communities. *Adivasi* communities were considered on the margins of upper-caste Hindu society and accordingly seen as both more "savage" and more open to evangelizing. Missionaries were encouraged by subsidies from the DPI to open schools in various tribal areas. In the Santhal Pargannahs, the American Baptist Society and the Church Missionary Society both established normal training institutions for Santhali men and women in the 1870s.[30] From the outset, the DPI and mission societies regarded the funding of Santhali schools as quite distinct from other educational efforts.

The willingness of the colonial government to fund Santhali education must be seen as part of a general policy of "subduing" tribal populations. In the Santhal Pargannahs, there had been a series of violent uprisings against Hindu merchants, colonial officials, and missionary workers that culminated in the Santhali Rebellion in 1855. Not surprisingly, Santhali education was consistently represented as a means of "civilizing" Santhals in order to domesticate the threat of insurgency and resistance they represented.

In spite of the investment of the colonial state and missionaries in tribal education, they were unsure of how to treat "educated" Santhali men and women, particularly those who had trained as teachers. Tribal communities were meant to forever remain the recipients of education and knowledge, never the producers or disseminators, and so government and mission educators were reluctant to recognize Santhali normal schools as teacher-training institutions. I will argue that this had little to do with the actual "quality" of the training institutions, and far more to do with the discomfort of missionaries and the colonial government in recognizing tribal men as figures of authority.

Missionary normal schools in the Santhal Pargannahs served multiple functions. They had initially started as elementary-level schools formally teaching reading and writing in Santhali and (sometimes) in Bengali. Eventually, these institutions added on teacher-training schools. Santhali normal schools "begin to instruct the students from the very alphabet," but very soon after the school began "sending out a supply of teachers and now 12 of 41 teachers are now employed in the Sonthali villages."[31]

In spite of the fact that the Sonthal Normal School was training and sending out teachers, the DPI never really viewed Santhali schools as "normal schools" in the same manner as government or other Christian schools. For instance, Mr. Croft, the director of public instruction, reluctantly placed the Santhali schools under the heading of normal schools, although he felt they "are not strictly normal schools. They are chiefly *civilizing institutions* for the benefit of the sonthals, promising boys being brought in from distant villages, fed and taught, and finally sent back again to their villages, some as teachers and catechists, and all as apostles of a higher civilization."[32]

There are a number of peculiar things in Croft's description. The boarding arrangements of the Santhali institutions, in which "promising boys being brought in from distant villages" are trained and then "sent back again to their villages," were a common occurrence in both government and other missionary normal schools. Yet Croft uses this as an example of the "civilizing" nature of the institution: the training of Santhalis as teachers was easily reduced to their becoming "apostles of a higher civilization."

Oddly, even as *bhadralok* headmasters suggested their trainees use the paradigm of missionaries working among tribal communities as their model, missionaries seemed to fear that educating Santhali teachers would make them like the *bhadralok*. Thus Mr. Skresfrud, the Scandinavian missionary working in the Santhali community (under the aegis of the Baptist Mission Society), warns that his pedagogical goal is "to 'raise' the people gradually, making no 'Babu [*bhadralok*]-gulf' between the instructed and the uninstructed.'"[33] Skresfrud simultaneously suggests that educated Santhali teachers should not have the hierarchal relationship to other Santhalis that *babus* (or *bhadralok*) have to Bengali peasants, and yet proudly admits they "enjoy much deference in their own villages." That is, the Santhali teacher fulfills precisely the role that *bhadralok* headmasters and mission educators want their training students to fulfill—commanding authority and respect in their communities.

It is not clear to me, in fact, that there really is any reason not to consider Santhali schools as "strictly normal schools." The schools trained boys (and men) from more remote locations in a boarding school environment. The trainees were then expected to return to their villages and teach. The only difference between these institutions and lower-level vernacular government schools or other mission schools was that the students were from *adivasi* communities. Croft's perception of them as "civilizing" institutions stemmed from his assumption that the students themselves were "savages."

The condescension and contempt toward tribal teacher trainees were equally evident in missionary institutions that were more mixed in terms of the caste and ethnicity of the students. One such school, the Serampore Baptist Training School, divided classes according to a complicated hierarchy of caste and culture, meant to reflect degrees of superior and inferior Christian character. The highest division studied the first year's course for the Government Training College (which included teaching exercise and practical instruction), and the lower two divisions took courses called the Senior and Junior Chatrobritti to become village teachers. The educational stratification mapped onto the assumed hierarchy of ethnicity and caste so that the elementary class was explicitly "intended for Kols, Garos [tribal groups] and Bengalis from backward districts."[34] These students had been sent from their respective mission stations because "the missionary of their district, being in need of teachers of the lowest grade, send[s] them as men whom he wants trained because he wants no better." The attitudes of missionary headmasters resulted in tribal and "backward" Bengalis being given the most perfunctory training, in the expectation that their communities could not appreciate and did not deserve better trained teachers. In fact, the Serampore Normal School headmaster and teachers resented having to train these young men at all. Though they recognized that "it was a duty to see to it that an elementary vernacular Christian education is provided for all the children of native converts," they felt their efforts were wasted upon these "nominal" Christian communities.[35]

As for Bandhopadhyay and other *bhadralok* educators, having *adivasi* groups connected to teaching as a profession threatened the respectability of the occupation itself. Thus, at the Serampore Normal School, the headmaster assumed that the presence of tribal students brought down the status of the school as a whole in the eyes of the government, reflected in comments that aided (that is, nongovernmental) normal schools mainly educated "Sonthals, Kols and other half civilized tribes."[36] In fact, the only school to be praised as a "true" normal school was the Krishnagur institution, which only took in students who were sons of more elite catechists and teachers and offered them an Anglo-vernacular education.[37] In the end, the CMS capitulated to the realities of the colonial economy and recognized that offering English would attract (and produce) the highest "class" of native Christian students.

Although vernacular teaching itself remained a fairly low-paying occupation, a part of its modernization was equating it with masculine authority and specialized knowledge. The reluctance to recognize tribal teacher trainees and schools as "strictly" normal schools stems from the upper-caste, government, and missionary belief that those on the margins of colonial society could never embody pedagogic respectability. At best, tribal teachers were seen as little more than conduits for the "civilizing" influence of European missionaries.

CONCLUSION

In spite of the limited expansion of teacher-training institutions in the late nineteenth century, theories of teacher training had a much larger influence on colonial modernity.[38] Methods of developing affective, disciplinary relationships between adults and children moved from the school to the family and from texts aimed at teachers to those aimed at parents. For example, Bhudev Mukhopadhyay employed many of the ideas he explored in his teacher-training manuals for a series of essays he published on the Hindu family entitled *Paribarik Prabandha* in 1882.

The repeated evocation of the necessity of a system of education for raising children, *shikha pranali* (also the title of his teacher-training manual), is the first clue that Mukhopadhyay's ideas on child-rearing (within the context of the family) have been shaped by his earlier work as an educator. Mukhopadhyay begins the section on "The Education of Children" by noting that it is said that a child (in this case, boys) must be made human (*manush*), a duty shared by all parents (mothers and fathers). Although beginning with a fairly universalistic claim, he then explains that the "English try to make their children English" and the "Chinese take great care in making their children Chinese."[39] Although all societies share in the desire to make their children fully human, the definition of what it means to be human is always nationally or culturally defined. Mukhopadhyay then continues that all people (*jatiya*) employ their own systems of education (*shikha pranali*, also the title of a teacher-training manual) to ensure the continual improvement of religion and morality (*dharma*).

In fact, in reading the list of familial obligations that Mukhopadhyay outlines, it is unclear whether he is training parents or training teachers. At the top of the list is the need to address the physical weakness of Bengali boys, an idea that reflects the growing pedagogic interest in physical education. The second issue that Mukhopadhyay raises is one that directly emerges from his readings of Pestalozzi and Stow: the importance of training children's "sense organs" so that they are better able to apprehend and understand the world. Mukhopadhyay warns that without training, Bengali children's senses will be dulled. It is therefore the duty of mothers and fathers to train their children's various senses (seeing, hearing, touching, etc.).[40] The peculiarly technical language used by Mukhopadhyay and his liberal borrowing from European pedagogic theories suggest the porous nature of teaching and parenting, and the expectation that like teaching, parenting is a skill that must be learned and practiced.

Similarly, early-twentieth-century Bengali child-rearing manuals directly drew from theories and methods of teacher training developed in the mid-nineteenth century. Pradip Kumar Bose argues that these texts instructed upper-caste Hindu mothers and fathers on techniques for raising moral, obedient, and loving children through "a pedagogy on the formation of the 'character' of children," a pedagogy that echoed the teacher-training ideas of Mukhopadhyay and Gmelin.[41] Regardless of the disparaging tone adopted by these Bengali writers toward the school, and the *pathshala gurumahashoy* in particular, becoming modern parents required the same training that *bhadralok* and missionary educators had demanded of their teacher trainees.[42]

Many of the instructions in child-rearing manuals were specifically directed at mothers: "Every mother should learn the new teaching methods for children called kindergarten."[43] The acknowledgment in child-raising manuals of the centrality of mothers to the raising of children paralleled a shift in teaching. By the early twentieth century in metropolitan Britain, primary school teaching had become completely dominated by women teachers. But this was harder to reproduce in Bengal. While child-rearing manuals could demand that mothers learn kindergarten techniques, the upper-caste practice of *pardah* made the training of "respectable" women teachers much more difficult. In the next chapter, I look at some of the similarities and important differences in efforts to train women to "mold" character and embody gendered authority and moral comportment.

CHAPTER 5

Teaching Gender in the Colony

The grand obstacle to the improvement of female schools, and to the grand extension of them, is the universal want of female teachers. Nowhere, except in mission schools, are any trained female teachers to be found.... The training to habits of neatness and order, and instruction in needlework, which are so essential to a woman in whatever position she may be placed, are necessarily neglected [when there are only male teachers].[1]

In a series of mid-nineteenth-century pamphlets, Mary Carpenter, the British social reformer, diagnosed and suggested remedies to "improve" and "extend" female education in India. Carpenter's emphasis on training women teachers resonated with what had become the common belief in Britain: women instructors were essential to model "habits of neatness and order," and other specifically gendered behavior and skills for female students.[2] Carpenter was disappointed by the limited nature of girls' schooling and teacher training in Calcutta, which "fell very far behind Madras, Bombay or even Ahmedabad."[3] This led her to press the *bhadralok* (upper-caste Hindu) reformers at the Bethune Society in Calcutta to make the training of women teachers as much of a priority as the education of their wives and daughters in the *zenana*.[4] Despite Carpenter's exhortations and the increasing popularity of female education, the effort to train larger numbers of female teachers, so necessary to instruct the *bhadramahila*, the female relatives of the *bhadralok,* in needlework and neatness, remained elusive in colonial Bengal.[5]

Carpenter's observation that only mission schools employed trained women teachers reflects the centrality of evangelicals in the development of female teacher education in Britain and India. Underlying the separate training of men and women was the evangelical conviction that one of the main purposes of education was the development of a (Christian) gendered subject. Despite the similarity in the goals underlying the project of modern teacher training, the history of women teachers in colonial Bengal offers a significant contrast to the history of male teacher education. In the previous chapter, I outlined how upper-caste educators and reformers easily adapted evangelical pedagogic models for the training of the *gurumahashoy*, the village schoolteacher, in government and mission normal schools. Moreover, the various pedagogic paradigms of good teaching introduced in the normal school informed the development of modern Hindu and Christian masculinity in the later nineteenth century.

The difficulty of training women teachers offers a striking contrast to the popularity and status of women's education more generally. By the later nineteenth century, *bhadralok* reformers took up the necessity of "modern" women's education as a means to inculcate particular upper-caste norms of gender identity in colonial Bengal, but as many scholars have noted, the education of the upper-caste woman also became crucial to the delineation of Bengali modernity itself.[6] Native reformers recognized the benefits of pedagogically inculcating values of "orderliness, thrift, cleanliness, and a personal sense of responsibility."[7] But unlike Carpenter and metropolitan British educators, *bhadra* (respectable) society rejected the idea that formal education for women might also lead to a modern career, such as teaching. Upper-caste *bhadra* society was unwilling to let their daughters teach, since teaching did not conform to the gender norms of *pardah* and the privileging of the domestic and private sphere.[8]

The notion of the teacher as a kind of model for appropriate gendered behavior, introduced by evangelicals and increasingly taken up by *bhadra* society, created a demand for both single-sex schooling and female teachers to staff such schools. Yet, as I show in this chapter, the peculiar convergence of evangelical and upper-caste gender and sexual norms effectively undermined the efforts of the Department of Public Instruction (DPI) to formally train women teachers in the nineteenth century. The various challenges faced by the DPI to educate and employ native women as teachers meant that Christian missions continued to dominate the field and also resulted in limiting the expansion of formal girls' schooling.

The first part of this chapter analyzes the failure of the Dhaka Normal School, the Bengal government's first (and only) nineteenth-century normal school for women. The women initially identified as appropriate teacher trainees by the DPI were *Bairagi* women, lower-caste Vaishnavas who were occasionally hired in the precolonial period to serve as tutors for women in Hindu households. *Bairagi* women who worked as tutors did not have to observe the *pardah,* or seclusion, rules of upper-caste society and were often widows, orphans, or mendicants and thus mobile in a way that was essential for modern teaching and still unusual in the late nineteenth century.[9] However, in choosing *Bairagi* women for teacher training, the colonial state found itself facing one of the paradoxical outcomes of upper-caste society adopting evangelical norms. Specifically, the very notions of feminine respectability that had engendered *bhadralok* enthusiasm for expanding female schooling now made *Bairagi* women—lower caste, itinerant, and thus sexually suspect—unacceptable as suitable candidates to educate their daughters and wives.

In the face of changing upper-caste sentiment, the DPI abandoned teacher training. Instead, they funded (through grants-in-aid) missionary teacher-training institutions. Like Mary Carpenter, the department recognized that evangelicals were far more successful at producing and employing native women teachers. In spite of government funding for their training, the majority of native Christian trainees eventually worked in missionary schools and as tutors in missionary-run *zenana* schools.[10] Nonetheless, some of their students (especially in and around Calcutta) were from the *bhadra* classes, and the DPI acknowledged that subsidizing the training of native Christian teachers indirectly expanded the educational options for upper-caste women.

Ultimately it was native Christian women, trained in mission schools, who came to dominate the female teaching profession well into the twentieth century. Thus, the decision to expand upper-caste women's education paradoxically created greater educational opportunities for lower-caste, non-Hindu women.[11] Although the training of women teachers was one of the more successful missionary educational endeavors, racial, caste, and class hierarchies fundamentally shaped the ways mission societies interacted with their female students.

Missionary normal schools grew out of Protestant orphan asylums and boarding schools and were attended by some of the poorest native Christians from rural and tribal areas. Their training was explicitly articulated as an opportunity to benefit from the "civilizing" influence of European missionaries who would "uplift" them from their "degraded" racial, caste, and tribal origins. Unlike the *gurumahashoy* or the native Christian male schoolteacher, who was poor but "respectable," the lower-caste *Bairagi* and native Christian woman teacher remained forever marginal to the society they were called upon to help reproduce. This marginality also extends to the histories of this period. Despite the importance of female teacher training to the extension of "modern" women's education, little historical work exists on its development. The singular focus on the *bhadramahila* and women's education as a "private acquirement" has led to the historiographical neglect of the education and training of non-elite women.[12]

THE ARGUMENT FOR SEX-SEGREGATED SCHOOLING

In mid-nineteenth-century Bengal, there was no clear precedent or demand for single-sex schooling or teaching. As the school inspector for Dhaka noticed in the 1860s, "[T]he people are not so much averse to female education as to female schools."[13] In fact, the DPI found that the conventional practice in Bengal was to send girls to the *pathshala* (village school) alongside their brothers or cousins since the *gurumahashoy* (village teacher) rarely charged any extra fees for the girls who attended.[14]

For example, in a passage in a Bengali school reader clearly aimed at girls entitled *Bala Bodh (Knowledge for Girls)*, a schoolgirl exclaims to her brother, "It is ten o'clock and the cart to take us to the *pathshala* will arrive soon, big brother!" Then, reflecting the notion of the teacher as a kind of paternal (patriarchal) authority, the young girl is told, "You must respect the *gurumahashoy* as a father and always be obedient, listen to him and do your work."[15] Of course, girls, like the young woman in this school reader, were only allowed to attend the *pathshala* until they were nine or ten, after which time they were expected to observe *pardah*—but many boys dropped out by that age as well. It is worth pointing out that although this passage in *Bala Bodh* assumes that girls went to school and learned to read alongside their brothers in the *pathshala*, the very existence of a separate reader for girls simultaneously suggests that knowledge itself was already being categorized in sex-segregated terms.

In contrast to the local Bengali practice of mixed-sex *pathshalas*, when missionaries first began establishing schools, they insisted on sex-segregated schooling. As early as 1817, the Serampore Baptist missionaries set up a woven partition between the girls and boys in their primary schools in keeping with the emerging metropolitan practice of separating children at the primary level. By the second half of the nineteenth century, the majority of missionary schools in Bengal were run as single-sex institutions. At the official level, the DPI acknowledged that single-sex schooling was preferable to the use of mixed *pathshalas*. "Wood's

Despatch" of 1854, the most important policy statement regarding vernacular education, authorized increased funding for female education and argued for the inherent benefits of sex-segregated teaching.[16] Furthermore, perhaps reflecting English norms, colonial officials believed that trained women teachers were best qualified to instruct female students in appropriate feminine skills and behavior. The fatherly *gurumahashoy* of the traditional Bengali *pathshala* was simply not an adequate model for the kinds of gendered knowledge and behavior that modern education promised.

The 1882 Hunter Commission report reiterated the Victorian belief in the benefits of single-sex schooling and teaching, recommending that mixed (girls and boys) schools (taught by the *gurumahashoy*) no longer be maintained. But in Bengal, this was resisted by the DPI, which argued that "the experience of every inspecting officer in Bengal confirms the high value which the Bengal Provincial Committee attaches to mixed schools."[17] It was far cheaper and easier to find male schoolteachers to teach in government-aided mixed schools than single-sex girls' schools. Thus, the Bengal government decided, in the face of the Hunter Commission's wishes (and the extra funding opportunities for single-sex girls' schools), to continue supporting the mixed *pathshala* and the *gurumahashoy*.[18] In fact, there were various schemes for increasing the number of girls attending the *pathshala,* including paying the *gurumahashoy* per head for each girl who attended his *pathshala.*[19]

Over time, however, the convergence of English norms of sex segregation at the primary level and increasing Hindu revivalism led to the removal of girls from mixed *pathshalas*. For instance, in the 1884 *General Report* of the DPI, the inspectors from Bengal observed a slight shift toward more girls attending single-sex schools than mixed schools.[20] By the 1890s, there was a sharper decline in the interest in mixed *pathshalas*.[21] Educational inspectors noticed that "there is a very general and marked aversion on the parts of a large proportion of the population to sending girls to school at all, not because the people are indifferent to the education of their female children, but because they do not like sending them to schools where there are male teachers, that is to say, in schools where the *pardah* is not observed."[22]

We can see further evidence of the growing popularity of single-sex schooling in a passage in a different girl's reader, *Barnabodhini* (*Knowledge of Letters*). While *Bala Bodh* had assumed that its female reader learned from a *pathshala gurumahashoy* alongside her brother, the competing text *Barnabodhini* suggested a different kind of learning environment: "Firstly, the school should be established in a good village and in a separate house. Secondly, a well-educated woman from a good lineage (*jat,* also caste) with various womanly virtues should be asked to do the work of the teacher. Thirdly, it must be insisted that every female student purchase a Bengali reader."[23] The author of *Barnabodhini* clearly assumes that girls should be taught separately not only using separate books, a rather self-serving suggestion, but also within a separate school.

In spite of their support for the mixed *pathshala,* the Bengal DPI was not immune to the ideological and moral arguments for single-sex schooling, and more importantly the need for trained women teachers. However, unlike Britain, where a number of unmarried, lower-middle-class women entered teaching, in Bengal locating teacher-training students proved difficult. Nonetheless, in the 1860s, the Bengal DPI decided to establish a teacher-training school in Dhaka. What the DPI had not counted on was that the evangelical-based norms that encouraged single-sex schooling also shaped growing *bhadralok* discomfort with particular precolonial practices—in particular, the use of lower-caste Vaishnava women as modern teachers.

THE DHAKA NORMAL SCHOOL

In 1862, the DPI opened the first women's teacher-training institution in Bengal, the Dhaka Normal School, and actively recruited *Bairagi* women (who belonged to a heterodox Vaishnavite sect) as students. The officials in the DPI perceived *Bairagi* women as appropriate teacher trainees because they were willing to be educated and work unhampered by the *pardah* restrictions of caste society. However, as I trace in this section, the changing gender and sexual norms within upper-caste society prompted various members of the *bhadra* classes to equate the *Bairagi* women's lower-caste status, mendicant lifestyle, and heterodox religious practices with "deviant" sexual behavior, ultimately complicating the DPI's effort to transform them into "respectable" women teachers.

In precolonial India, as in much of the world, the most likely place for any female literary production (especially songs and poetry) was within religious contexts. The Vaishnava mendicant women, the *Bairagi,* were exceptional because they were also literate. Vaishnavites preached a religious message of salvation through devotion, particularly for those excluded from high-caste Hinduism: the lower castes and women. As historian Tanika Sarkar points out in *Words to Win,* Vaishnavism had an ambivalent relationship to textual knowledge and literacy, exemplified in the life of Sri Caitainya, the fourteenth-century founder of the movement: "Chaitanya himself had mastered the path of knowledge, had transcended and had left it behind for simple faith and love. His devotees need not repeat the effort, they may adhere to the end product of the long process. The explicit message is, nonetheless, undercut by the medium through which it is communicated[:] a learned theological tome. This instantiates the paradoxical relationship between knowledge and unlearned faith that is forever unresolved in Vaishnavism. For we have here texts that are meant to be read—and not by pandits alone, but by the common folk."[24]

The contradictory message of Vaishnavism encouraged the growth of heterodox sects and opened up space for literacy among the popular classes. But there were significant differences in the views toward female literacy between high and low Vaishnava communities in rural Bengal.[25] While upper-caste Vaishnavites had many of the same devotional practices as the lower castes, they did not share any of the radical critique of the initial movement. High-caste Vaishnavite families were as socially orthodox as their fellow non-Vaishnavite Hindus and were reluctant to allow their wives, sisters, and daughters to read. It was commonly believed among high-caste Hindu families that literacy would lead to widowhood—that a woman could literally kill her husband by learning to read.

But the presence of lower-caste, literate *Bairagi* women in Dhaka drew the interest of the school inspector for southeastern Bengal, Mr. Martin. He felt that Dhaka, the home of many "progressive" Bengali *bhadralok,* would be a good place to set up a normal school to train teachers. In late 1864, Martin wrote to the DPI that he had located women who were willing to attend the school and be trained as teachers. Martin related the correspondence between himself and the department. "In reply [to the letter] you expressed doubts on the possibility of inducing native girls of good character and of having respectable parentage to embrace the life proposed.... If you omit the words of 'respectable parentage' from the quotation above made and substitute instead 'who would be admitted into the most respectable families as instructresses' ... I have been supplied with the names of 27 female[s] of good character, chiefly Byragynees [*Bairagi*], who have expressed their willingness to enter such a school with Rs. 4 stipends at present and prospects of Rs. 5 s[ti]pends thereafter."[26] A local *zemindar* (landowner) had supplied Martin with the names of the *Bairagi* women, some of whom were already employed as tutors in the *zenanas* of local families.[27] These women were seen as highly unusual because they were both literate and willingly engaged as teachers in and around Dhaka.

Bairagi women were quite distinct from higher-caste Vaishnavas, and Martin described them as "mix[ing] in the world more than the majority of native females." Although the willingness of the *Bairagi* to "mix in the world" accounted for them working as tutors in high-caste homes, Martin also saw such interaction as potentially improper. He went to great lengths to specify that there were two types of *Bairagi* women found in Dhaka. One group was born into the status, like any other caste community, and took vows of purity and chastity while young; they were "as well behaved as the majority of poor people." This was the group that Martin thought most appropriate to target as teachers. The second group of women voluntarily became *Bairagi*, renouncing their previous caste status. The reason for their conversion, Martin explained, was "because the world has[,] in consequence of their misconduct, renounced them."[28] Martin's implication was obvious: heterodox religious practices often attracted sexually suspect single women, individuals who would be quite unacceptable to serve as teachers or enter the homes of upper-caste families.[29]

The purpose of Martin's report was to identify a group whom the state could target for teacher training, and in Martin's description, the *Bairagi* woman became the logical female cognate for the *gurumahashoy*, the indigenous male teacher. Like the *gurumahashoy*, *Bairagi* tutors were identified as lacking the proper education needed for modern schooling but nonetheless able to fulfill an instructional role. But there were important differences between the two. The male schoolteacher had a secure position within every native village, while *Bairagi* women rarely had any institutional connection to either the village or Dhaka. Their low-caste (and sometimes mendicant) status made their teaching irregular and sporadic, and they were easily equated with sexually "heterodox" practices. While Martin was aware that the *Bairagi* women might be seen as a disruptive presence in any colonial institution, he nonetheless urged that they be trained and boarded at the Dhaka Normal School, where they would be given a small stipend to support them through their training.

Though called a normal school, the school's curriculum was not aimed at training students in pedagogy as much as simply teaching them the basic skills needed to pass an exam in a midlevel vernacular school.[30] The training was almost identical to that given the *gurumahashoy*. In spite of the DPI's rhetorical commitment to training students in "womanly" skills, the school used the same books and taught the same subjects as the various boys' vernacular schools. The one exception was a failed attempt to introduce embroidery instruction.

Although the Dhaka Normal School seemed to be serving its purpose of training teachers, it soon met with local opposition. While previously high-caste families had informally arranged to hire Vaishnava women as tutors, changing sexual and gender norms among upper-caste Hindus meant they could no longer countenance the fact that government funding should be used to educate low-caste women students. Local society accused the female students, the *Bairagi* women, of being involved in various types of nefarious activities (unnamed in the reports).[31] In a letter to a Bengali journal, *bhadra* opinion was expressed succinctly in the following manner: "There is a 'normal school' in Dhaka; but the majority of the trainees are Vaishnavites. We are not insulting them, but let us remember that people have no respect for Vaishnavite women ... if they therefore do not send their daughters to be taught by such women, we should not be surprised. Women of this type cannot educate girls who are expected to grow up to embellish their homes, provide happiness to their husbands and become ideals for their children."[32] Although the Bengali school inspector had vouched for the *Bairagi* as appropriate teacher-training candidates, the institutionalization of their training elicited strong reactions from certain *bhadralok* reformers. For the writer, the purpose of educating girls was for them to "embellish their homes," in other words, to learn the skills, habits, and comportment demanded of upper-caste mothers and wives. Low-caste *Bairagi* women, whatever their training, were inherently disreputable in the eyes of *bhadra* society. Naturally, this made them inappropriate candidates to teach or model for the daughters of the *bhadralok* how to "provide happiness to their husbands and become ideals for their children."[33]

Despite such attitudes, the teachers trained at the Dhaka Normal School occasionally managed to get teaching positions, either opening their own schools or working in ones that were already established.[34] Yet the caste Hindu complaint voiced in the newspaper and rumored about in the town eventually convinced the DPI to discontinue its efforts to train *Bairagi* women in government-funded schools, and the Dhaka Normal School closed after nine years.

Ostensibly, the reason for the closure was financial. The *Bairagi* women who trained at the Dhaka Normal School felt that since it was an institution funded by the colonial state, they could demand higher salaries for their teaching services. The deputy inspector complained that the women's salary demands were too excessive for the community. Others felt that the relatively high cost of running a normal school, Rs. 1800, could be better spent to extend women's education by opening primary schools. But it is clear that equally problematic was the low-caste and marginal status of the *Bairagi* women themselves.

In 1873, after the Dhaka Normal School closed, an unnamed colonial administrator bemoaned the folly of their efforts to train teachers. He complained that the women in the Dhaka Normal School had been "leading lives of gross immorality" of which the local English officers had remained blissfully ignorant. The educational inspector succinctly made the normal school an object lesson in the impossibility of women being "honorably" trained as workers for the colonial state. "Some serious scandal has recently been caused by the discovery, in a normal school for the training of schoolmistresses, that the women admitted to the institution had been leading lives of gross immorality. . . . It is plain that considerable responsibility implying need of great vigilance and caution is incurred by any official employment of adult women in the profession of teaching, whenever the system necessitates their disregarding and dispensing with the safeguards by which they are surrounded."[35] The concern about the Dhaka Normal School, the official suggested, was not merely who was chosen to be teachers, but also how they were educated. The school had cavalierly "dispens[ed] with the safeguards" of home, village, or caste by having adult women live together in an urban environment.

The adult *Bairagi* woman's relative freedom from the structures of home, village, and caste made her a "problem" for both the colonial administration and local caste society. The DPI had misjudged and incompletely understood the complexity of the social and religious system in Dhaka: the relationship between high and low castes, between heterodox and orthodox Hinduism, and the shifting perceptions of lower-caste Vaishnava women in the late nineteenth century.

But the DPI, and by extension the colonial government in Bengal, had learned their lesson, and the later ethnographic records of caste groups in Bengal instantiated the orthodox Hindu perception of low-caste Vaishnavas as sources of instability and immorality. For instance, H. H. Risley's 1892 book, *The Tribes and Castes of Bengal,* described the *Bairagi* as the source of disorder and criminality in the rural countryside. Risley's observations reflected a more general colonial view of the problems that "deviant" sects posed to the state's functioning. "The mendicant members of the *Vaishnava* community . . . are of evil repute[,] their ranks being recruited by those who have no relatives, by widows, by individuals too idle or depraved to lead a steady working life, and by prostitutes.... The habits of these beggars are very unsettled. They wander from village to village, and from one akhara to another[,] fleecing the frugal and industrious peasantry on the plea of religion and singing songs in praise of Hari (Krishna) beneath the village tree or shrine."[36]

Risley's description of the *Bairagi* emphasizes the characteristics deemed most disruptive for a stable village society, echoing Martin's characterization of those women who became *Bairagi* as adults. Mendicant *Bairagi* men and women were not tied down by familial obligations, and their peripatetic existence subverted the industriousness, stability, and hard work of the peasant society, ultimately threatening the respectability of native culture itself.

The government of Bengal's perception of the "perilous" nature of employing lower-caste women reinforced the gender hierarchy of native society. It was no longer enough for teacher trainees to be literate (as the *Bairagi* women had been). By the later nineteenth century, it was far more important (as the Bengali letter writer had implied) that women teachers be "respectable" or *bhadra* in order to conform to definitions of "modern" women's education that demanded teachers modeling bourgeois feminine behavior for their students. To return to the passage in the girls' primer, *Barnabodhini,* the writer explicitly notes that "a woman who is well-educated, from a good *jat* (alternately caste, lineage, family)," is essential to furthering female education. In describing the appropriate teacher, the schoolbook writer emphasizes the importance of the teacher's *jat*—a capacious term that most narrowly means caste and more broadly (in this instance) suggests social respectability. This double meaning is not accidental and is critical in understanding the rejection of the Dhaka Normal School and *Bairagi* teachers.

In the colonial period, as much as in the precolonial period, definitions of respectability were inextricably tied to caste and, crucially in the case of women, sexuality. Heterodox religious practices, such as those of the *Bairagi* women, had always been looked upon askance by upper-caste Hindus; however, some distinction had been made between those deemed respectable and nonrespectable. This difference seemed to disappear under the increased expectation that modern female education be tied to the progress and uplift of the upper-caste family. Vaishnava women had been employed previously because of their knowledge and skills, but now the woman teacher's primary attribute had to be her respectability. By the later nineteenth century, it seemed that heterodox religiosity was collapsed into heterodox femininity. In spite of Martin's efforts to maintain some kind of distinction in individuals who might be appropriate teacher-training candidates, larger colonial society apparently felt that this work could no longer be entrusted to lower-caste Vaishnavas. The expense as well as the failure of the Dhaka Normal School led the DPI to withdraw from directly running teacher-training institutions in Bengal. Instead, the department chose to fund private institutions, mainly missionary schools, to increase the ranks of trained women teachers.

THE CHRISTIAN WOMAN TEACHER

From Barrackpore, the Bengali Christian *Didi-moni* (teachers) used to come in horse-drawn carts to teach us. The doors and windows of the horse cart were closed. Every day four Christian Bengali teachers used to come. Two of their names were Prathibha and Shushila. I don't remember the names of the other two. From Barrackpore, the European teacher used to come on Saturdays and teach us. Her name was Miss Graham. The main European teacher used to come every one or two months.[37]

In 1991, *Nagaropantha*, a local Bengali magazine printed in the suburbs of Calcutta, published a series of oral histories about the Kharaday Mission Girls' School, which was one of the first formal schools established in the area at the turn of the twentieth century. Manorama Manna, who had attended the school in the 1920s, spoke fondly of her school days. Though Mrs. Manna was clearly aware of the hierarchy in the administration of the mission schools, she knew very little about her Bengali schoolteachers, since they were not from her neighborhood and, being Christian, not from her social class.

The issue of *Nagarpantha* is filled with stories like Mrs. Manna's, stories from older women who had attended the mission schools as girls and who treasured those memories even as the neighborhood around them changed and the mission school was replaced by a government school. But none of the oral histories was written by or explicitly about the women who taught the girls, the Christian teachers. In this section, I want to trace the histories of those women Christian schoolteachers, individuals who, like Mrs. Manna's teachers, remained shadowy figures going to and from the school in their horse-drawn cart.

By the 1920s it was commonplace to find trained Christian women teachers, but missionary organizations had only adopted normal school curricular and instructional methods in the 1860s, roughly the same time that the DPI established the Dhaka Normal School. However, unlike the Dhaka Normal School, missionary normal schools developed out of already existing evangelical institutions, namely, the orphanage and boarding establishments for urban and rural Bengali and tribal (*adivasi*) Christians and Anglo-Indians. Native Christian students, unlike *Bairagi* women, lived, trained, and worked under the supervision of European headmistresses.[38] In spite of the low-caste status of most native Christian students, the Bengal DPI and evangelical societies were convinced that their conversion and education in a more European Christian environment precluded any accusations of sexual impropriety.

Missionaries saw the training of native Christian teachers as a means to "civilize" Bengali Christian girls away from their natal homes, families, and communities in order to teach the beliefs, work, and comportment expected of a true Christian. Thus, the schools employed a mix of racial, caste, and ethnic hierarchies that determined the degree and level to which Anglo-Indian, lower-caste, and tribal Christian girls were educable. While the idea of training teachers might evoke a process of professionalization and rigorous instruction, in fact missionary normal schools saw themselves as merely extending the work that had been done by their orphanages and boarding schools.

Like upper-caste, *bhadra* society, missionaries felt that formally educating native Christian girls as teachers and Bible women would make them more attractive marriage partners. But while the education of the *bhadramahila* continued to be defined as a "private acquirement," missionary normal schools made no distinction between producing good wives and good workers. A young woman trained in a boarding school or orphanage might end up being a wife, a servant, a teacher, or any combination of the three.

Christian missionaries became involved in women's education for practical and theological reasons: the desire to reach potential women converts and the belief in the connection between literacy and conversion. Just as the Vaishnava movement (in fourteenth-century Bengal) had created new forms of worship that opened up the possibility for women (like the *Bairagi*) to read, nineteenth-century Christian evangelicalism also made literacy (and the extension of literacy) a fundamental part of religious practice and piety.[39] By the early nineteenth century, larger numbers of British women became involved in the educational mission of the church, particularly the Dissenting churches.

The other equally important component of nineteenth-century Christian identity was the desire and support for proselytizing to the world. Initially, missionary wives took up the work, but by the late nineteenth century many single women teachers made their way to India to educate native Christians and non-Christians.[40] But the need for more trained female teachers in Christian girls' schools and *zenana* missions led European missionaries to look to their native female students as potential instructors. The first orphanages and boarding schools in early-nineteenth-century Bengal were established as charitable institutions for Anglo-Indian children.[41] But by the mid-nineteenth century, Bengali Christian students and native orphans (the victims of the frequent famine and cholera epidemics of nineteenth-century Bengal) began to form the majority of boarders. Historian Michael Laird has argued that a new emphasis by Protestant missionaries on boarding schools (and away from day schools) was evident as early as the 1830s. "This work [opening boarding schools] expanded greatly in 1833, a year of storms, widespread flooding, and disease in lower Bengal."[42]

Boarding schools and orphanages presented their primary goal as raising young native girls in a purely Christian environment, but the schools tended to emphasize industriousness and work as the central aspects of a good Christian education. This is vividly illustrated in the 1840 memoirs of Mary Weitbrecht, one of the most prominent missionaries sent to Bengal by the Church Missionary Society (CMS). Weitbrecht chose promising native Christian girls from the CMS boarding school and orphanage in Burdwan (an institution with over 35 students) to serve as domestic servants in her home, insisting that by "training these dear girls, both morally and religiously ... at the same time they become more active in domestic concerns turn[s] out the best wives and mothers of the whole number."[43]

Weitbrecht implied that learning to serve the European family would ideally train native girls to learn to serve their own families. By blurring the line between labor and education, Weitbrecht was able to justify the racial and class hierarchy in which Indian (and sometimes Anglo-Indian) Christians were meant to serve, and European Christians were meant to be served. For Weitbrecht, the close proximity to a missionary family and the opportunity to observe the familial relationships in a European household (while simultaneously cleaning up after them) were the best "training" that the young women in the boarding schools and orphanages could hope for.

While Weitbrecht was satisfied with training (and using) native Christian girls to become domestic servants, in the 1860s other missionary boarding schools and orphanages consciously transitioned away from training for domestic service to training for teaching. The need for more women teachers, the higher status accorded teaching, and the desires of native Christian families converged around this effort. Although most educational historians focus only on the Central School in Cornwallis Square (Calcutta) when discussing teacher training, there were equally successful (and more numerous) missionary training institutions run by the Scottish Free Church and the Baptist Missionary Society, organizations that entered the field of teacher training almost as early as the Anglicans. The Free Church ran a relatively successful (as measured by the number of students) orphanage and normal school in Calcutta. The Baptists, meanwhile, had three boarding and orphanage institutions that were used as normal schools, in Calcutta, Entally (on the outskirts of Calcutta), and Barisal (in southeastern Bengal).

The shift away from education for domestic service can be seen in the letters from Frances Hebron, the headmistress of the Scottish Free Church Orphanage in Calcutta. Hebron clearly saw a higher calling for her students than serving in the homes of Europeans. She was particularly committed to seeing her charges married to promising young Christian men since it would help extend the Christian community and reflect well on the mission itself. "We have had several applications to allow the girls to go out as servants, but Mr. Herdman and I do not approve of it; for that is not the object of this institution, but to prepare them as useful wives and mothers."[44]

Hebron measured the success of her institution by her ability to get her students married and save them from working as domestic servants (although the training for both kinds of work might be the same). However, as I discuss later in the chapter, "respectably" marrying did not preclude the students of the Free Church Orphanage from seeking (and needing) paid employment as teachers, *zenana* tutors, or Bible women. In fact, by marrying a reader, teacher, or catechist, these students were able to find work in day schools attached to the churches or boys' schools where their husbands worked.

Native Christian families seem to have shared the conviction that teaching was more "respectable" than being a servant. Native Christians did not observe the same rules of *pardah* that precluded even poorer upper-caste Hindus and urban Muslim families from sending their daughters to be trained as teachers. In fact, for most native Christians, teaching was far more respectable than the other employment possibilities open to their children, such as becoming domestic servants or *ayahs* (nursemaids). In a report in 1877, the London Missionary Society (which got involved in female teacher training quite late) recognized, "We are losing girls connected with our mission who might be trained as teachers. Some of our people[,] wishing that their daughters should have such a training[,] have placed them with other missions which might have schools of the kind we need."[45] Although the Protestant organizations in India were basically ecumenical, Methodist girls trained by the Church of England would often end up teaching in Anglican schools instead of Methodist ones.

In spite of denominational differences, missionaries who ran the orphanages and boarding schools shared a basic belief that educating native Christians away from their natal families and communities was critical to developing the right kind of Christian community in India. The missionary boarding school, like the orphanage, functioned as a surrogate family for those Christians who came from poorer rural backgrounds. The poverty and "backwardness" of most native Christian communities meant that children were raised "lack[ing] the greatest blessing the young can enjoy—the protecting care, the supporting strength, the enabling inspiration of a lively Christian home."[46] In some sense, it did not matter if a student had "natural" parents: native Christian mothers and fathers could not be trusted to properly raise their own children.

Although the ideological basis of orphanages and boarding schools run by various missionary societies was similar (that supervision and guidance by Europeans were inherently beneficial for native students), the ultimate goals of the Baptist and Free Church institutions were quite distinct. The Baptists viewed their schools as a means to "civilize" the daughters of local, rural Christians, in the hopes that these young women would return and "uplift" their respective communities. The Baptist boarding school in Entally (opened in 1855), for instance, was closely linked with the 24 Parganas Church that sent the children of the poorer members of its congregation to the school. The school seemed a particularly good example of the possibilities offered by boarding schools, not only to civilize native Christian girls but also to then "export" that influence (through the girls) to more distant and rural Christian populations. "The children [at Entally] are almost entirely drawn from the villages, whither they return on the completion of their education, carrying with them the piety and instruction they have received."[47]

Like the Entally school, the town of Barisal, where the other Baptist girls' boarding school was located, also had a substantial native Christian population. The majorities of native Christians were agricultural laborers and widely dispersed throughout the delta region, the *beels*. The Baptist population as well as the presence of other educational institutions in Barisal, including the Barisal *zillah* (district) school, made the town an ideal place to start a boarding school, and most missionaries concluded that educating "the daughters of the native Christians of the Barisal district" would have a greater "influence for good."[48]

Unlike the Baptist boarding schools, orphanages located in Calcutta did not have such close ties to a particular community or congregation. They tended to be more elite institutions, educating students in English and Bengali and finding them husbands and work in more urban areas or even abroad. For instance, the Scottish Free Church orphanage in Calcutta (which shifted from Lower Circular Road to the more central Bow Bazar in 1877) was not directly connected to a particular Christian community. Frances Hebron, the headmistress of the Scottish orphanage, preferred taking in infants and girls who had been abandoned. As Miss Hebron, the headmistress of the Free Church Orphanage, reported to the Home Committee, "We could get a great many children who have parents, but that is not the object of this Institution. Our orphans do not leave us till they marry, but children who have friends may be removed at anytime; so we wish to make it purely an Orphanage."[49] Although the missionary boarding schools set strict parameters on the involvement of native parents in their children's lives, training orphans ensured that no one could make a claim on a student except the teachers and the mission.

CIVILIZING THE NATIVE TEACHER

Regardless of whether they were located in (or served) urban or rural areas, the various missionary normal schools shared a system of education and training that demonstrated a clear continuum between the skills for domestic service, marriage, and teaching. At the Entally Boarding School, Baptist missionaries described the "training" received by their female students in the following manner: "The education is such as fits them for the station of life which they will hereafter fill, as wives and mothers, and as teachers. They receive careful instruction in their own language, in grammar, arithmetic, in geography, in needlework ... [and] in domestic cookery."[50]

Echoing Frances Hebron's desire to produce better mothers and wives, the Entally Baptists also lauded the benefits of a training that not merely prepared their students for their "future stations" but also would be immediately useful since the girls were expected to grow their own food, cook, and clean. It was rhetorically important for the missionaries to distinguish the education offered in their schools from the traditional manner in which girls learned the domestic arts from their mothers and grandmothers; "geography" had to have a place alongside "cookery."

A typical normal school curriculum from the 1860s on included geography, grammar, reading, writing, dictation, translation, arithmetic, natural history, and object lessons and drawing.[51] A large number of the training pupils were preparing for *zenana* teaching, so the normal school did not emphasize the infant-training techniques that were becoming popular on the European continent for training primary school teachers. Protestant normal schools were also concerned to teach Christian values of humility and submission in addition to a basic vernacular education and pedagogic training. Though intellectual subjects were not completely disregarded, apprentice-teachers were expected to devote as much time to their personal prayers and introspection as to teaching practice.

Initially, "practical" teacher training came from having older students teach lower-level classes in the orphanages and boarding schools. In the Scottish Free Orphanage, for instance, Frances Hebron reluctantly decided against making one of her students, Bolaki (who had married a local catechist, Jadorib Ghosal), a permanent teacher: "I make use of her sometimes. I should like to make her a permanent teacher; but yet I like the elder girls to teach a class."[52] Various informal means of giving students teaching experience were eventually replaced by more formal efforts at practical instruction. The Baptist Normal School (opened in 1881), for instance, made sure that there was a day school on the mission grounds that "served the purpose of a practicing school for the normal school pupils."[53]

Although I have been emphasizing the curricular and pedagogic aspects of teacher education, it is critical to remember that one of the main goals of missionary normal schools was to "civilize" native Christian girls into appropriate feminine behavior. But this gender training, aimed at producing "good wives and mothers," was institutionalized through an explicitly racial, caste, and ethnic hierarchy in these various institutions.

Perhaps the earliest racial distinctions made between normal school students were the divisions between racially mixed and native Christian girls. In the Free Church Orphanage and Normal School, Frances Hebron decided to sartorially divide her students. Referring to Ellen Lawson, a "very nice East Indian child," Hebron decided that she "should like her always to dress different from the others, I mean in frocks, and not in petticoats and vest."[54] Hebron's desire to sartorially mark Ellen as distinct because she is mixed speaks to the peculiar racial hierarchy and anxiety at the orphanage. A frock indicated to the rest of the world (and, one would presume, to the child) that she was different from her native Christian schoolmates.

Anglo-Indian and native were not the only ethnic-racial distinctions made. Normal schools were just as concerned to separate out *adivasi* children from other "higher-status" native girls. Missionaries believed that tribal and rural Christian girls needed more training than their urban Bengali counterparts since their respective communities were seen to be morally and spiritually more "backward" than others. At the Barisal boarding school, it was observed, "The new girls from the Beels (ricegrowing delta districts) are, as a rule, so ignorant, dull and unaccustomed to control that anyone who had not already seen the four a few week[s] earlier would almost be ready to despair. . . . The Rev. R. Spurgeon says that one could scarcely find greater ignorance in the wilds of Africa, than that which exists among the Beels."[55] There was a clear hierarchy of Christian civilizational attainment, and it is interesting to note that larger imperial hierarchies, in which Africa lay behind India, were easily transposed onto the rural and urban split within the Indian Christian community. Rural and tribal Christian communities, like those from the marshy *beel* areas, were in particular need of native teachers. In keeping with missionary ideology, this education should be provided by one "from among themselves," whose own simplicity would allow her to tolerate otherwise "ignorant" and "uncontrollable" populations.

Thus, a few years after the girls from the *beel* had come to the Barisal boarding school, two of them were sent to study at the Calcutta Normal School, the higher-status urban institution run by the Baptists. The girls were sent to the normal school in the hopes that they would return to work in the rural *beel* areas, where most of the other trained native Christian teachers refused to go. In fact, Christian girls from the *beels* were thought incapable of teaching anyone other than members of their own community. As late as 1919, missionaries at the Entally Normal School insisted that "these women are never to be used except in the class of schools indicated and are never to do more than lower primary teaching."[56]

It appears that one of the most common ways of finding employment for teacher-training students was to set up individual schools for girls. The Church of England Zenana Missionary Society (CEZMS) journal, *India's Women,* noted that normal school students, after taking both a mission and government exam, often rented out a small room or verandah from which they ran a school. Not surprisingly, these tended to be makeshift and temporary, and these teachers depended on hiring a male Hindu pundit or widow to help with some of the secular teaching.[57] This practice is statistically borne out by the dubious distinction held by Bengal, which had the largest total number of girls' schools but one of the lowest retention rates among the colonial presidencies (only 2 percent of female pupils made it to Class IV, meant for children between 10 and 12). The single-sex girls' schools, many run by native Christian teachers, rarely lasted more than a few years and had little institutional or local support to sustain them. In contrast, the government and native boys' schools had far more prestige and permanence in Bengal.

By the 1890s, the DPI in Bengal brought the missionary normal schools more directly under their supervision by offering junior and senior teachership certificates. Though inspectors in the department complained about the limited training that mission students received in secular subjects, they recognized that almost all of the trained women teachers in Bengal had come out of missionary institutions. Mission societies in Bengal continued to train far larger numbers of teachers than any other private or public body.

CONCLUSION

The history of teacher training demonstrates the importance of gender in understanding the ways evangelical norms were adapted in the context of colonial Bengal. The changing norms of respectability that animated upper-caste Bengali society ultimately precluded *Bairagi* women, who had informally served as tutors, from stepping into the role of the modern woman teacher. The new definition of teaching, one that emphasized gendered respectability, meant that *Bairagi* women, no matter their education, were excluded. Although mission normal schools were ostensibly based on the notion of Christianity and teaching as a set of learned behaviors, inculcated through proximity to Europeans, education, and domestic work, there was a simultaneous conviction (shared with *bhadralok* educators) of respectability as an inherent quality based on gender, caste, and race.

The women recruited as teachers, *Bairagi* and native Christian women, had very different experiences and successes. By the early twentieth century, *Bairagi* women were infrequently mentioned in teacher-training reports. Although teacher training had initially offered them a place within the new colonial economy and culture, the specter of sexual "disrepute" continued to haunt their efforts to be trained and find work. Native Christians, on the other hand, seemed best able to take advantage of the limited autonomy and employment afforded them by a normal school education. Even mission societies recognized that one of their great "successes" in Bengal was training and educating women teachers. By 1897, there were 450 native Christian women being trained in eight different normal schools, in contrast to just 282 native Christian men.[58] Native Christian teachers taught in missionary schools, attended largely by native Christians, and *zenana* missions, where they tutored upper-caste women students in their homes. But native Christians were never fully accepted by upper-caste Hindu society, and by the early twentieth century, upper-caste Hindu widows were being seen as more appropriate trainees and tutors.[59]

The prejudice against women teachers in Bengal precluded any significant state or native investment in more formal normal schools until the twentieth century. The paradox of teaching respectability through nonrespectable teachers helps explain how, in spite of multiple traditions of female literacy, women's education remained relatively limited in colonial Bengal. Although the Department of Public Instruction barely funded primary education, boys (especially those of the upper castes) still had the possibility of attending the *pathshala* or the few government and district schools. Bengali girls, meanwhile, were left learning to read in temporary and poorly funded verandah schools.

CHAPTER 6

Mission Schools and Qur'an Schools

> The difficulties that beset Muhammadan education are of two kinds—one arising from their poverty and the other from their religious prejudices. Both alike operate to prevent Muhammadans from gaining full advantage of the educational facilities.[1]

Abdul Karim was appointed in 1889 as the first Muslim school inspector in Bengal's Department of Public Instruction (DPI), and the quote above appears in his subsequent book on the status of Muslim education in Bengal. Karim's appointment to the DPI reflected the new visibility of the Bengali Muslim community after the 1870s. Scholars of South Asia have pointed to the crucial role of the 1872 census, along with other forms of "enumerative" governmental technologies, in constructing and giving material reality to various collective religious identities in the later nineteenth century. In Bengal, the census revealed that almost half of the population of the province was Muslim, a finding that greatly surprised the colonial state, which had assumed that the province was largely Hindu. Moreover, the data collected from the census also revealed that the newly enumerated Muslim community was grossly underrepresented in government employment and educational institutions in Bengal.

In order to explain this disparity, the colonial state and urban Muslim leaders, the *ashraf*, emphasized two issues: the "conspiracy" of upper-caste Hindus, the *bhadralok*, to dominate educational resources and marginalize the *ashraf*, and the inherent religious prejudices (alluded to by Karim) that kept poorer Muslims from taking full advantage of Western education.[2] While the low levels of Muslim participation in schools and government employment could be partially explained by the social class of most Muslim Bengalis (who were rural peasants), religious identity became the privileged means to explain the differences between Hindu and Muslim educational achievement.

As Peter Hardy, and more recently Sanjay Seth, have argued, what emerged from the census data and the publication of the book *The Indian Musalmans* by W. W. Hunter was the figure of the "backward" Muslim who was unable or unwilling to modernize. The "backward" Muslim as a trope not only circulated in state discourse but also was important in the reformist rhetoric of the urban Muslim elite, the *ashraf*.[3] Thus Abdul Karim, as both a Muslim leader and an official for the colonial state, claims that poverty, a problem shared by the majority of the population in colonial Bengal, is in fact a defining characteristic of the Muslim community. Karim also assumes that Muslims, rich and poor alike, share an inherent "religious prejudice" that precludes them from taking adequate advantage of formal schooling.

Historians have tended to understand the trope of "backwardness" in the way that Karim highlights in this quote—as referencing the supposed aversion of Muslims to Western education. But I suggest that the trope of "backwardness" had two quite distinct meanings. On the one hand, it was used to describe the attitude of those *ashraf* families who refused to send their sons to colonial schools, suggesting their highly ambivalent attitude toward modern, colonial institutions.[4] But increasingly for those leaders, as well as for the colonial state, the problem of "backwardness" was used to describe what they perceived as the degraded and un-Islamic practices of poorer, rural Muslims.

In this chapter, I argue that the state and urban Muslim elite in Bengal came to see rural Bengali Muslims as backward not only because they were poor and prejudiced against Western schooling but also because they were not properly Muslim. That is, the rural Bengali population was thought to not fully understand what it meant to be authentically Muslim, as evidenced by their religious practices, which shared many similarities with their rural Hindu counterparts; Muslim Bengalis, it seemed, were religiously "backward."

The two connected issues of "conspiracy" and religious "backwardness" fundamentally shaped the history of Bengali Muslim education in ways that diverged from the history of upper-caste Hindu and missionary schooling I have thus far been tracing. As I have shown, mid-nineteenth-century Hindu and missionary educators were granted significant autonomy to develop primary, Bengali-language schooling because the colonial state remained largely uninterested in vernacular education. The state's diffidence was reflected in the privatized nature of vernacular school funding (through grants-in-aid) and an explicit commitment to religious neutrality.

By the 1870s, the rhetoric and actions of the colonial state and colonial society resulted in the privileging of religious and sectarian identity. This meant that the *ashraf* articulated their economic and educational interests through their religious identity as Muslims, and in opposition to the interests of Hindus. The *ashraf* petitioned for, and were often granted, increased funding for higher-level urban educational institutions and placement in colonial jobs. But the state and Muslim leaders pursued something quite different for the rural Muslim masses: the extension of modern, state-supervised primary-level *religious* schooling.

This chapter focuses on how the colonial state and *ashraf* leaders' plans for expanding basic education for the Muslim masses were inextricably connected to their efforts to more clearly delineate a modern Muslim subjectivity and Muslim community.[5] By arguing that rural Bengali Muslim peasants, referred to as *atrap*, were religiously backward, the DPI and Muslim educators were able to dictate a new educational curriculum that emphasized religious knowledge and practice. In fact, the effort to prepare a modern, primary-level religious education allowed *ashraf* leaders to express their vision of authentic religiosity and intervene in the religious practices of rural Muslims.

I see the creation of a separate system of modern Muslim religious education as modeled, paradoxically, on the Christian mission day school. The state and *ashraf* educators reformulated the place of the primary school in the Muslim community so that, like the mission school, it was meant to inculcate new forms of religiosity and offer a corrective to familial or community norms. In fact, the late-nineteenth-century rhetoric of the "backward" Bengali Muslim was parallel to the rhetoric around the "nominal" Bengali Christian, both of whom were perceived by the state and religious reformers as always on the verge of "lapsing" back into Hinduism. This prompted the state and Muslim leaders to demand that modern Qur'an schools and *maktabs* emphasize textual literacy and the teaching of "authentically" Muslim stories and ritual texts. The ultimate purpose of these pedagogic interventions was to battle the "conspiracy" of Hindu culture, and demarcate and standardize the particular religious practices and beliefs that would ensure the creation of a separate and distinct Bengali Muslim community.

I begin my discussion by looking at the publication of W. W. Hunter's *The Indian Musalmans* in 1871, a text that was critical in formulating both the problem and solution for Muslim "backwardness" and Hindu dominance in education. My reading of this text provides the background for understanding how "backwardness," as a trait ascribed to religious culture, became a way for the colonial state and *ashraf* leaders to pass judgment on and justify their interference with the religious culture of their poorer co-religionists. In fact, as a member of the 1882 Education Commission, Hunter and the DPI successfully reframed the expansion of education in wholly religious terms and effectively precluded the possibility of a secular village-level system of schooling.

In the second part of the chapter, I shift my historical lens to explore how Muslim *ashraf* leaders took up the issue of primary-level religious education for their poorer, rural counterparts in part to claim their status as the spokesmen for a homogeneous Muslim community—one that was in fact still in the process of being created. One of the central critiques of *ashraf* leaders was that the existing system of government-aided village schools, the *pathshala,* was never "secular" but actually reproduced upper-caste Hindu culture at the level of both administration and curriculum. The accusation of a Hindu "conspiracy" to marginalize and denigrate Bengali Muslim culture allowed *ashraf* leaders to petition the colonial state for separate funding for religiously oriented Muslim schooling since the colonial state was increasingly wary of *bhadralok* aspirations.

The history of how Muslim education came to be defined by assumptions of upper-caste Hindu "conspiracy" and religious "backwardness" is critical in understanding its eventual connection to nationalism and communalism. By the early twentieth century, debates over Bengali-language schooling came to stand in for debates over Bengali culture itself, and particularly the degree to which it was possible to imagine an India that incorporated both Hindus and Muslims. That is, the development of separate Hindu and Muslim schooling both helped create and also became a metaphor for the possibility of separate Hindu and Muslim nations.

CONSPIRACY AND BACKWARDNESS IN *THE INDIAN MUSALMANS*

The issues of Muslim "backwardness," upper-caste conspiracy, and colonial governance were given a distinctly imperial reframing in the work of Sir William Wilson Hunter, a British civil servant whose very influential book, *The Indian Musalmans: Are They Bound in Conscience to Rebel against the Queen?* was published in 1871. Hunter's book was written in response to a question posed by Lord Mayo (contained in the subtitle) and spoke to a growing perception among British colonial officials of a "conspiracy" among Muslims to overthrow British rule. The 1857 Mutiny and Rebellion, various armed insurgencies on the Northwest frontier, religious peasant movements in Eastern and Western Bengal (the "Wahhabi trials"), and finally the assassinations of high-profile British officials prompted a more general enquiry into the potential insurgency of the Muslim community.[6] Recent scholars have read Hunter's book as primarily a text of counterinsurgency, but one that suggested a more humane colonial policy. Rather than merely detailing the military efforts to quell peasant and Muslim "insurgents," Hunter acknowledged that the colonial state needed to provide greater services for Muslims themselves.

Hunter's text became equally known for the explicit connection it drew between religious backwardness and educational backwardness. This homology effectively displaced an older economic understanding of Muslim underrepresentation in schooling. In 1835, the Protestant missionary William Adam conducted a large-scale study of indigenous schooling in Bengal and ascribed the problem of low enrollment of Muslims in higher education to their class position. Like their lower-caste Hindu counterparts, the vast majority of Muslims in Bengal were *raiyats* (peasants) and had little incentive to attend, or practice in attending, the village school, the *pathshala*. *The Indian Musalmans* reformulated the problem as one of a more general Muslim apathy to modern education—implying that both *ashraf* leaders and rural peasants shared the same interests and prejudices. Poor Muslims did not go to school because they were poor (as Adam had suggested), but rather they did not go to school because of a general religious predisposition against modern schooling. Thus, *The Indian Musalmans* managed to rewrite an issue of social class and political disenfranchisement into a problem of religious character.

Hunter felt his goal was to inform the British of the "grievances of the Muhammadans under English Rule; to point out their real wrongs, and the means of remedying them." The alienation and rebellious nature of the Muslim community, Hunter argued, resulted from Muslims holding "aloof from our system, and the changes in which the more flexible Hindus have cheerfully acquiesced, are regarded by them as deep personal wrongs."[7] Ostensibly as a means to legitimate particular Muslim grievances, Hunter points out to the colonial state the danger of a situation in which Muslim reluctance to take advantage of Western education meant they remained outside of the reach of colonial institutions. It was necessary for the state to ensure that Muslims were brought into the fold, but the question remained: how?

It is at this point that Hunter suggests that the relatively low participation of Muslims, all Muslims, in school could be solved in two ways: by reapportioning educational funding for urban Muslims and by expanding primary religious schooling among rural Muslims. While the first plan would cultivate elite Muslim loyalty, the second would check the "fanatical" and insurgent tendencies of rural Muslims. He suggested that "fifty cheap schools, with low-paid Musalman teachers," funded mainly by the government would transform "the popular tone of Eastern Bengal."[8] Hunter explicitly connected the ideological goal of creating a docile colonial population with religious schooling, indicated by his singling out of the need for "Musalman" teachers.

Ultimately Hunter's solution, particularly for rural Muslim Bengalis, is counterintuitive. Although he poses the problem of the poor Indian Muslim as one of religion (that is, the hyperreligiosity of Muslims makes them a potential threat), he saw the solution to the problem as lying in a *religious* education. Hunter claimed that "a system of purely secular education is adapted to very few nations. In the opinion of many deeply thinking men, it has signally failed in Ireland, and it is certainly altogether unsuited to the illiterate and fanatical peasantry of Muhammadan Bengal."[9] The "failure" of secular education in Ireland had resulted in nationalist insurgency, and Hunter was determined that a similar situation would not repeat itself in Bengal. It was thus incumbent on a Protestant Empire to ensure that it provided modern religious schooling for its Muslim subjects.[10] Moreover, by setting up the problem of the "backward" Muslim, both the urban *ashraf* and the rural *atrap*, in this manner, Hunter creates a space for the colonial government to weigh in on what might constitute the proper knowledge and training required for a "forward"-thinking Muslim—a modern Muslim.

There is little evidence to suggest that mass religious school was ever a feature of precolonial Bengali society. In earlier periods, there were multiple types of religious education patronized by local Muslim elite and funded through mosques: from high-level Persian and Urdu *madrassahs* to lower-level *maktabs* and village Qu'ran schools. The *madrassahs* offered a more specialized curriculum of rigorous religious training, but *maktabs* and Qu'ran schools were primarily concerned to teach reading, writing, and occasionally some Arabic. Such schools were never compulsory, their curricula were never standardized, and they were never meant to be mass institutions. The development of religious education for the Bengali masses was thus a distinctly modern endeavor.

But it was not only Muslim "backwardness" that prompted Hunter's emphasis on religious schooling. He also deployed the trope of Hindu "conspiracy" and effectively reframed the whole issue of mass education in religious terms. Hunter argued that the 1854 "Wood's Despatch" that had established grants-in-aid for vernacular education had been quickly taken up by "the astute Hindu," who successfully extended schools that were "adapted to the wants of his own community, but wholly unsuited to the requirements of the Muhammadans." Hunter was referring to the success of the grant-in-aid policy in encouraging *bhadralok* educators to open their own schools so that there was a greater ratio of "aided" (privately funded) to departmental (state-funded) schools: 1:5 at the secondary level and 1:10 at the primary level. Hindu educators tended to open Anglo-vernacular schools—where a modern education in both English and Bengali was offered. Although these schools successfully educated the children of upper-caste Hindus, the grants were largely unsuccessful in inculcating any sense of obligation among the *bhadralok* to expand vernacular education among other Bengali groups—especially lower-caste and Muslim communities. Instead, as I have shown in previous chapters, upper-caste reformers created institutions that served the cultural, educational, and commercial needs of their own community.[11]

For Hunter, the success of upper-caste Hindus in opening aided schools was nothing short of a conspiracy to monopolize all of the educational, political, and economic posts of the government in hopes of eventually usurping the British. The relative success of the *bhadralok* in education and employment had made them demanding rather than grateful to the colonial state, as evidenced by their participation in the nationalist *swadeshi* movements and restlessness in light of the limited employment opportunities in the colonial economy. Faced with a putative upper-caste Hindu conspiracy, Hunter argued that it was incumbent on the colonial state to directly intervene on behalf of their Muslim subjects and cultivate the loyalist sympathies of Muslim leaders by reapportioning both educational and employment opportunities. Perhaps the real conspiracy afoot was the effort of the colonial state to foment competition and acrimony between Hindu and Muslim communities.

In 1882, 12 years after the publication of *The Indian Musalmans*, William Hunter was appointed the head of a major education commission and given the opportunity to formalize and more clearly flesh out some of his observations (prejudices) about religion, education, and politics from his 1871 book. The Hunter Commission interviewed a wide range of colonial constituencies, from missionaries to leading native reformers and leaders, and used this qualitative data alongside statistical information in order to address education at all levels in India.

The section of the report entitled "Reasons Alleged by the Muhammadans for Holding Aloof from the Education Offered in Government Schools" laid out a wide range of grievances that precluded Muslim participation in government schools. The list contained a whole set of reasons that ranged from the putatively antimodern and anti-English stance of the Muslim community ("the injurious effects of English education in creating a disbelief in religion") to complaints about the bias within government and government-aided schools *against* Muslims ("the small proportion of Muhammadan teachers in Government institutions ... the use in Government schools of books whose tone was hostile or scornful towards the Muhammadan religion"). However, the commission concluded that "a candid Muhammadan would probably admit that the most powerful factors are to be found in pride of race, a memory of bygone superiority, religious fears and a not unnatural attachment to the learning of Islam."[12]

Hunter's report went to great lengths to describe the inherent and insurmountable differences between Hindu and Muslim orientations toward education. In the section entitled "The Democratic Nature of Elementary Indigenous Schools," the report argued that in Hindu schools, even where a religious prayer was recited, "secular subjects are the chief part of the course." But the democratic nature of the Hindu school was constrained by the fact of its "sacerdotal class" of Brahmins invested in maintaining exclusive literacy. The Muslim elementary school, in contrast, was seen as inherently more democratic and more religious: "'Government and religion are twins,' is a common saying of the Muhammadans; and their schools for the masses are hardly less religious than their madrasas."[13] In lieu of providing empirical evidence, the commission relied upon a priori ideas about Hinduism and Islam as religious traditions to describe the kind of education offered in a Hindu or Muslim elementary school. While there was little evidence that *ashraf* leaders were any more interested in education as a means to equalize internal status differentiation than their *bhadralok* counterparts, the Hunter Commission perpetuated this notion to emphasize fundamental religious differences between the two communities.

The 1882 Education Commission was influential insofar as it articulated, in policy terms, what Hunter had argued in counterinsurgency terms: that it was incumbent upon the colonial state to address and treat its Muslim subjects differently than its Hindu subjects. That religious affiliation eclipsed other markers of identity in the subcontinent—linguistic, regional, or class. But, as I will show in the next section, in Bengal, the colonial state demonstrated far more ambiguity in its efforts to educate its Bengali Muslim subjects. The ambiguity, I would suggest, was the result precisely of the fact that religious identity could not be so easily separated from regional, linguistic, and class markers.

BENGALI, MUSLIM, AND HINDU

Although Hunter was quite clear about the need for separate provisions for Muslim education in Bengal, at the provincial level and within the DPI, there was a fundamental ambivalence about the "real" identity of the Bengali Muslim. Was this person basically a Bengali peasant—that is, no different from his or her Hindu peasant neighbor? Or was she or he first and foremost a Muslim, whose Bengali identity was only incidental? In articulating a policy relating to Muslim education, the colonial state appointed itself judge of what constituted authentic Muslim identity. The correspondence among colonial officials, ostensibly related to education, is equally instructive in revealing colonial views on the relationship between social class, linguistic affinity, and religious identity. In fact, I would argue that the tension between these multiple identities would remain unresolved for the Bengali Muslim community itself and constitute the crucial question for Bengali politics in the face of two major nationalist movements—in 1947 and 1971.

The policy to target the Muslim community was in part a response to census statistics that revealed significant underrepresentation of Muslim children in schools in the Bengal Presidency. Muslims, who in the 1871 census were seen to make up 32 percent of the population in Bengal and Assam, made up only 14 percent of the students in schools. This discrepancy was even more pronounced at the college level, where Muslim students comprised only 4 percent of the college population.[14]

The statistical findings and Hunter's influential book led the colonial state to acknowledge the need to pay special attention to the educational needs of its Muslim subjects. Yet the state was reluctant to spend any extra money toward that effort and instead wanted to rely on the paltry sums set aside in the grant-in-aid system. In 1871, the Government of India sent a resolution to local governments (no. 300) that "assistance might just be given to Muhammadans by grants-in-aid to create schools of their own.... That greater encouragement should be given to the creation of a vernacular literature of the Muhammadans."[15] In the resolution, the government of India is purposefully ambiguous as to what the term "schools of their own" connotes: wholly separate schools opened only for Muslims, or vernacular schools (like *pathshalas*) that also educate Hindus? The ambiguity within the 1871 resolution was carried forward into the various efforts in the 1880s to determine the most appropriate way to educate Bengal's Muslim population.

Wary of any increased expenditure, the state first noted that "the almost unanimous opinions of those consulted was that, with the schools already in existence, there was no sufficient justification for expending State funds in this direction."[16] The government of Bengal chose to initially encourage "the schools already in existence"—the village *pathshalas*—which they believed would be adequate for the educational needs of Bengal's Muslim community. In doing so, the government of Bengal privileged linguistic affinity over other identities: "the vernacular of the mass of Musalmans in Bengal was known to be Bengali, the ordinary pathsalas of the country [could] supply the proper means of elementary education." The government of Bengal reiterated this view in 1884, arguing that in Bengal there was little reason to make separate provisions for Muslim schooling since "the vast majority of the Musalmans being cultivators speaking the Bengali vernacular of their Hindu neighbors."[17] These observations seem to contradict the very anti-insurgency strategy that Hunter had suggested in his text: the need for the state to distinguish between its Hindu and Muslim subjects.

In my reading of the correspondence related to Muslim schooling, there appears to be a deep ambivalence about how to understand rural Muslim Bengalis. I see this ambivalence as rooted in the state's acceptance of the shared linguistic world of Bengali Hindus and Muslims and its concomitant skepticism of the degree to which Bengali Muslims were properly Muslim. The colonial state more easily accepted the funding of higher-level schools offering Persian, Urdu, or Arabic as a part of an authentic religious education, since North India was still perceived as the home of classical Islamic culture. However, even as they continued to support Bengali as the major vernacular of the province, the Department of Public Instruction was less sanguine about the degree to which it (or its speakers) was part of that same classical culture.[18]

For instance, the Bengal government noted the particular challenges faced by Muslim students in a system that was dominated by upper-caste Hindus: "a want of consideration between Hindu teachers and

Musalman pupils [and] a want of consideration in the arrangements of the Education Department." Yet, the real issue, the official concludes in the same paragraph, is "the depressed condition of the bulk of Bengali Musalmans—*Musalmans in the first instance by conversion only and not by descent.*"[19] While the division between "converted" and "descent" Muslims was (and is) an important marker of status within the Muslim community, here it is worth asking why the colonial state should be invested, at this point, in making such distinctions.

I would suggest that the state's concern must be seen in the context of the late-nineteenth-century political culture, which had become increasingly sectarian, deploying religious symbols and rituals in newly public and social ways. There was an energy around proselytizing and enumerating since determining who was or was not a Muslim, or a Hindu, or an Untouchable became essential for political mobilization. While Protestant missionaries had directed their proselytizing efforts at non-Christians, by the late nineteenth century all religious communities (including Christians) wanted to ensure that they had drawn in (and, if needed, uplifted) those they considered "their own."

It is in this historical juncture that we begin to see a departure in the educational policy directed toward Bengali Muslims. Although the state initially expressed its desire to see an expansion in the vernacular *pathshala* system, it soon began emphasizing the need to extend, and improve, vernacular religious schools. The government of Bengal decided that "the maktabs might be gradually moulded into true primary schools." The lower-level *maktab* tended to be village- and town-level institutions that were funded through local landowners and often attached to a local mosque. The Bengal government decided that it would focus on introducing into the *maktab* "certain subjects of instruction which should bring the schools so aided into some relation, more or less close, with the general system of education in the Province."[20]

The proposal, unimaginatively called "the Bengal system," was a departure from previous grant-in-aid efforts, as evidenced by the Bengal government's insistence that "the religious character of the schools *should be no bar to its receiving aid, provided that it introduced a certain amount of secular instruction into the course.*"[21] This statement allowed the state to maintain its religious neutrality (and its noninterference policy toward Indian religions) while justifying its support for a religious school.

The Bengal system of giving grants-in-aid to primary religious schools represented the kind of policy that Hunter's 1882 Education

Commission had outlined. In fact, the Education Commission had gone to great lengths to demonstrate the continuity between the precolonial and colonial notions of religious education. But, Sanjay Seth argues, premodern education "was not predicated upon a conception of society as a horizontal field, as a population, but rather as a series of segmented and hierarchically organized domains."[22] Thus, historians of precolonial education history point out the relative scarcity of any institution that resembled modern mass education in Bengal, let alone mass *religious* education.

The informal and mixed nature of indigenous elementary schooling was not easily translatable into the kinds of elementary religious schooling imagined by officers of the education department or the Hunter Commission. While the lower-level *maktab* did not offer the same specialized training that a Persian or Arabic *madrassah* or Sanskrit *tol* did, it was nonetheless never meant to educate the large majority of Muslims. Apart from its limited reach, what distinguished the precolonial *maktab* from the religious primary school envisioned by the colonial state was that it was never meant to teach children how to be good Muslims. This was a concept that very much came out of the Sunday school paradigm.

The decision to "count" *maktabs* (or "mosque schools," as colonial officials labeled them) as primary schools then allowed the government of Bengal to claim that the proportion of Muslims in primary education had risen from 14 percent in 1871 to 24 percent in 1880. The reports asserted that the lower-level *maktab* not only was being counted by the state but also had actually been transformed in the process—they had been "brought into a relationship to the indigenous primary school system without interfering with their religious side."[23]

The confidence with which higher-level officials professed success was belied by reports from educational inspectors. Abdul Karim, in his address to the Muhammadan Education Conference, decried the level of schooling he observed in the *maktabs*. He dismissed out of hand the lowest-level *maktab,* the Qur'an school, before criticizing the higher-level Urdu and Bengali *maktabs*. Karim was convinced that the *maktab* was not providing Bengali Muslim boys with a satisfactory education and was impeding rather than supporting their material aspirations. He noted that "the average pupil after years of study [in the *maktab*] fails to write letters or keep accounts correctly, the pupils of the *pathshalas* after going through the second and third Bengali primers in about two years are able to write letters and keep accounts satisfactorily."[24] Karim's observations belie the success claimed by the government of Bengal: it seems that the *maktab* had not been magically transformed. Karim saw few of the pedagogic practices or materials he expected in a modern school: no language primers, and no instruction in writing or arithmetic. Moreover, the traditional *maktab* instructor, the *mianji,* was unlikely to have had any professional teacher training; as Karim humorously observes, "[F]ew of the mianjis of our maktabs are likely to learn and teach clay-modeling."[25]

In spite of Karim's distress at the low level of education offered in the *maktab,* he was nonetheless convinced that it was essential that Bengali Muslim children receive a religious education. He bemoaned the fact that boys educated in the *pathshala* were less knowledgeable and committed to their religious tradition. "If once boys be thoroughly well-grounded in the principles of Islam, their faith is not likely to be easily shaken by the education they may afterwards receive in institutions meant for higher education of all classes." Karim was adamantly opposed to middle or higher schools that were separate but felt the primary schools must be "separately organized and supported."[26]

Karim's observations demonstrate the conundrum facing Muslim leaders in Bengal: a scorn for lower-level religious teachers (the *mianji*) who lacked basic pedagogic training but a simultaneous belief that religious education was crucial for rural Muslims who were not adequately committed to (or knowledgeable of) their faith. This led Abdul Karim to continue to argue for separate religious schooling. The insistence on separate Muslim schooling at the primary level—schooling that incorporated reading primers and clay modeling—reflected the successful incorporation of a particular model of religious education by colonial officials and Muslim leaders. Not surprisingly, Karim's views echoed those of other colonial educational officials who felt that addressing Muslim "backwardness" demanded a model of separate religious instruction. But this educational strategy must to be seen in the larger context of growing nationalism and increasing communal sentiment between Hindus and Muslims. The familiar accusation of colonial efforts to "divide and conquer" was no doubt a part of the ways Hunter and the rest of the DPI articulated the question of Muslim religious schooling.

Not surprisingly, by the 1880s, vernacular education had become intimately connected to the issue of equity between Hindus and Muslims and the articulation of separate religious and caste identities. There was considerable manipulation by the colonial state to both ensure Muslim loyalty and also charge Hindu "bias" in all areas. *Ashraf* leaders were promised increased funding and placement in urban colleges and jobs, and the state also accepted the need to offer basic religious education to their *atrap* co-religionists. These various efforts would balance the ascendancy and power of upper-caste Hindus in colonial society and also ensure that poor Muslims were given the opportunity to attend schools taught by Muslims, not the village *pathshalas,* which were seen as "Hindu" schools.

TEXTUAL LITERACY AND MUSLIM SUBJECTIVITY

While Karim had focused on the need for *maktabs* to incorporate modern pedagogic practices, he had largely ignored the religious instruction offered in the schools. However, in looking closely at the educational policies of the Department of Public Instruction, my study suggests that the unstated goal of formalizing Muslim religious education was to modernize the nature of Muslim religious identity and subjectivity itself. In order to receive state funds, religious primary schools had to meet certain requirements for their secular curriculum, but the divisions between the secular and religious components of a primary education were constantly blurred. This meant that the colonial government was able to demand, in the name of higher secular standards, changes in the modes of religious instruction at the primary Qur'an schools and *maktabs.*

My argument challenges the conventional ways scholars understand the changes enacted by the DPI. In Sufia Ahmed's important book, *Muslim Community in Bengal, 1884–1912,* she accepts at face value that the main objective of the DPI was merely to increase the secular instruction at Muslim religious primary schools by encouraging greater Bengali literacy and the teaching of mathematics. While it is convenient to demarcate a purely "secular" or "religious" (or Islamic) orientation to education, in fact, as Muhammad Qasim Zaman reminds us, the two "major intellectual and religiopolitical trends that have successively emerged in the Muslim world since the late nineteenth-century—modernism and Islamism—have both been largely rooted in modern, Westernized institutions of education."[27]

Thus, in scrutinizing the standards used by the DPI to measure the secular and religious pedagogy of Muslims schools, I argue that they were shaped by a distinctly Protestant orientation toward learning and subjectivity. Teaching by rote, for example, was an accusation constantly leveled against native education, particularly Hindu education. It was a part of the evangelical view that natives were incapable of independent, creative thought in part because of their religious background. This view, which I have explored in previous chapters, was based on the perception that the tendency to memorize unthinkingly by rote was particularly acute in South Asia because of the influence of Hinduism, Islam, and Buddhism, religions that he perceived to be based wholly upon repetition. An anonymous 1854 article in the *Calcutta Review* warned missionaries that the Bible should "not to operate as a mere mantra or charm, independent of the use of our faculties in Indian Christian schools."[28] The fear was that even within a Christian school, the Indian proclivity toward "unthinking" repetition—here glossed as "mantra"—threatened to overwhelm the pedagogic efforts at intellectual and moral cultivation. That is, the Bible had to be approached through "the use of our faculties," rather than as a charmed object.

The evangelical fear that, in colonial Indian schools, religious knowledge would become nothing more than a "mantra" anticipated the colonial state's critique of Indian Muslim schooling. The DPI began criticizing native Muslim teachers for instructing their students in Qur'an schools to learn unimaginatively by rote. The state willingly funded the *maktab*, the higher-level Muslim school, but it hesitated in providing funding for the lower-grade Qur'an schools, questioning the worth of their instruction. These schools were private institutions that provided instruction in reading the Qur'an in Urdu and seemed to reach a larger number of people than the *maktab*. Though the colonial state was committed to extending primary education, it was perennially uneasy about the status of Qur'an schools as "modern" learning institutions.[29]

In 1892, the government of Bengal actually decided to stop funding Qur'an schools, in spite of their promise to encourage Muslim education. They defended their action by asserting that the schools were too traditional in their methods of teaching Islam and thus were inherently at a disadvantage in their ability to offer secular instruction. The deputy inspector commented that in Qur'an schools "the course of instruction does not go beyond *the mere mechanical repetition of the Koran* and that they can scarcely be regarded as imparting any real practical education."[30] Though ostensibly about the need for practical education, the report highlighted the manner in which religious education was being conducted.

In spite of this criticism, significant numbers of students attended the Qur'an schools in India and the government of Bengal received warnings from other parts of the country criticizing their hasty decision to end government subsidies for these kinds of institutions. The DPI in the Bombay Presidency argued that excluding Qur'an schools "would be contrary to the special policy which has been adopted by the Educational Department towards Mahomedan indigenous schools owing to the obstacles which beset the education of Mahomedans, and that Koran schools can be utilized for the purposes of secular instruction as well as for religious."[31]

The Bombay government suggested that it could categorize and hierarchize the Qur'an schools and fund them accordingly. That is, the higher-level Qur'an schools, where some kind of secular and practical education could be imparted, should be better funded. The Bengal government conceded that "if they [the Koran schools] were excluded it would not be possible to ascertain the degree to which the Education Department has succeeded in bringing them within the system of useful instruction, and what scope still remains for extending efforts in this direction."[32]

On the surface, this exchange between the Bombay Presidency and the government of Bengal seems to be about little more than the most efficacious way to encourage Muslim education while maintaining certain modern standards. In spite of the constant evocation of secular instruction as the primary determinant of state funding, the real criterion for determining this school's efficacy was the nature of its religious instruction. The Bengal government wanted to exclude Qur'an schools because Muslim students did not go beyond "mechanical repetition of the Qur'an," and thus the department assumed that the students did not understand the deeper meaning of the text. This could be ascertained, claimed the DPI, merely by observing how Muslim children learned: unimaginatively and unthinkingly.

When the inspector from the Bombay Presidency wrote the criteria for judging the schools, he explicitly argued that how a school taught religion determined its ability to teach secular subjects. He observed that in the Bombay Presidency, there were three kinds of Qur'an schools that represented three stages of instruction, "(1) where the Koran is merely chanted; (2) where it is read in a printed book in the Arabic Urdu characters and (3) where reading and writing Urdu in Persian characters are practiced with the instruction in the Koran."[33] The education department determined which schools offered the highest level of secular teaching not by examining the presence of mathematics training or general literacy but by judging the ways in which the Qur'an was taught. Thus, the most backward kind of school was one where the Qur'an was merely orally repeated, a pedagogic method dismissed out of hand as leading to neither the learning nor the understanding of the text. Moreover, if students were memorizing Qur'anic passages, the DPI assumed that they were not able to think or act independently, skills that were critical in a modern world. On the other hand, the best kind of Qur'an schools used textual reading, writing, and instruction in the Qur'an. The DPI, even as it insisted that its aim was to not disturb the religious basis of native schools, judged the form of religious instruction within the school to index its authenticity as a Muslim institution. Educational hierarchies were constructed on the basis of an evolutionary model that privileged literacy over orality so that the "three stages of instruction," I contend, represented the "three stages" of religious development.

In fact, as Francis Robinson points out, "[O]ral transmission of the Qu'ran has been the backbone of Muslim education. Learning the Qur'an by heart and then reciting it aloud has been traditionally the first task of young Muslim boys and girls."[34] The notion of *reading* the Qur'an, argues Robinson, is a relatively modern notion, and even today early instruction is conducted orally. Yet the most basic expectation of school inspectors was that religious primary schools base their instruction on the analysis of *texts*, criticizing the native propensity for transmission through oral memorization. I would argue that this reflects a very modern Protestant orientation toward a particular religious subjectivity produced through reading. Individual reading, which allowed reflection, was crucial to the inner transformation at the heart of evangelical Christianity.

Thus, the funding of only those Qur'an schools that made texts and reading the center of their pedagogy was as much about a particular definition of religious subjectivity as it was about rationality or secular learning. Ultimately, reading and understanding the Qur'an, the Bible, or the Gita (which was perceived as the standard Hindu text) became more important in defining religious affiliation than the actual and varied practices of Indian Christians, Muslims, and Hindus. Practice, as the *ashraf* elite, missionaries, *bhadralok,* and colonial state realized, could not be so easily delineated and supervised.

The deputy inspectors' evaluations reflected the imperial common sense that the highest level of religious development was the religious traditions that replicated the evangelical-inflected pedagogic centrality of reading. The Qur'an schools that received the most funding were the ones that most functioned like Christian schools: teachers used texts to instruct students in both reading and writing. The DPI completely discounted other forms of pedagogy, oral traditions that emphasized memorization for instance, as a legitimate means for cultural transmission within the Muslim community.

The department's attempts to modernize the Qur'an schools coincided with attempts on the part of Muslim elite and rural reform movements to create a pan-Islamic identity based on text rather than practice. Ironically, the dismissal of repetition as a means to communicate knowledge in Qur'an schools resonated with the attempts by rural reformers to privilege textual understanding of the Qur'an over the syncretic religious practices of Bengali Muslims: practices that had previously blurred the lines between rural Hindus and Muslims. A religious education based on a single book, the Qur'an or the Bible, would solve the dual purpose of convincing the DPI that students were receiving a modern education and allow *ashraf* leaders to standardize religious knowledge within Muslim communities. Here, Muslim educators were closer to missionary educators in the place they saw for education in the reproduction of religious community—education would uplift both the nominal Christian convert and the "backward" rural Bengali Muslim.

SCHOOLS AND THE PROBLEM OF MUSLIM RELIGIOUS BACKWARDNESS

Education as a means to modernize religious ideas and practice was an effort enthusiastically taken up by Muslim leaders themselves, but they were initially less concerned with the need to extend primary-level religious education among their rural brethren. Instead, two of the best-known institutional efforts to educate and create a modern Muslim identity were focused on higher-level schooling. The Deobandi *madrassah,* located outside of Delhi, provided reformist religious training for the Indian *ulema* (religious scholars), while the Aligarh Anglo-Oriental College offered a Western education that emphasized science and English training. These two institutions represented very different answers to the question of what it meant to be a Muslim under colonial rule. Barbara Metcalf has argued that for the Deobandis, scriptural knowledge and tradition were crucial to the survival and flourishing of the Muslim community and possible only by maintaining a separation from the colonial state. Autonomy in religious education was considered central to autonomy in religious community. In contrast, Syed Ahmed Khan, the founder of Aligarh College, was convinced that the real challenge faced by the Muslim community was to acquire a modern education appropriate for the new colonial economy and culture. To those ends, he modeled the Aligarh Anglo-Oriental College on Cambridge in the hopes of producing a class of educated Muslim leaders in India who would be loyal subjects of the British Raj.

Both Sayid Ahmed Khan and the Deobandi School established contacts with Muslim leaders and reformist movements in Bengal. But the large numbers of rural peasants among the Bengali Muslim population meant that any effort to modernize the community had to address the question of basic primary schooling in the village. Moreover the publication and popularity of Hunter's *The Indian Musalmans* effectively put basic Muslim schooling at the center of educational debates in Bengal.[35]

To understand the relationship between the Muslim leadership, the *ashraf*, and the larger rural population in Bengal, the *atrap*, it is worth briefly considering the social history of Islam in Bengal. One of the most crucial differences between the *ashraf* and the *atrap* was language. The *ashraf* in Bengal routinely spoke, read, and wrote Urdu, the language of North Indian Muslim reform and connected (within colonial discourse) with Islamic classicism. In spite of the recognition by the *ashraf* of Urdu as representing Muslim high culture—connected to the Perso-Arabic traditions of North India—many Bengali Muslim leaders nonetheless "refused to replace Bengali with Urdu in the interests of a common Muslim nationhood."[36] Although committed to Bengali as a Muslim language (and Bengalis as Muslims), the *ashraf* were nonetheless anxious that the Muslim peasantry continued to participate in Bengali practices that were actually Hindu. To stop this possibility, Muslim leaders turned to modern religious schooling as a means to reinforce Muslim religious practices and community identity among the rural population.

The rural population of Muslims in Bengal largely resided in the eastern parts of the province, in some of the more unnavigable delta regions. Many Bengali Muslims shared far more, linguistically and culturally, with their Hindu neighbors than they did with their Urdu-speaking *ashraf* co-religionists—a fact that was in no way specific to Bengal. Nonetheless, the particular forms of Bengali Muslim practice encouraged nineteenth-century religious leaders (often from outside Bengal) to insist on the need to further Islamicize the customs of the Bengali Muslim masses. These religious reform efforts were often connected to various antilandlord and anti-British political movements. It was precisely the political content of these critiques that not only led to their violent repression by the colonial state but also prompted William Hunter to insist upon the inherently "fanatical" tendencies of the Bengali peasantry. Equally important in the reform of nineteenth-century *atrap* religious practices was the propagation of cheaply printed pamphlets and tracts, *punthis,* which focused on changing religious practice and belief. In his seminal book on Bengali Muslim identity, Raifuddin Ahmed emphasizes the importance of the *punthis* in propagating the notion that the customs of Bengali Muslims had to be purified. Religious reformers targeted the continued use by Bengali Muslims of devotional traditions and charms, astrological beliefs, and stories of their Hindu neighbors.

Rural religious reformers, *maulavis,* used a variety of informal means to spread their message—but it was always directed toward the rural masses. In contrast, the various Muslim organizations established by the *ashraf* in Bengal, individuals who were socially, economically, and politically distant from the rural peasantry, were addressed toward the colonial state. Urdu-speaking *ashraf,* who were educated and lived in Calcutta or Dhaka, recognized the wide social chasm between themselves and the majority of Bengali *atrap,* who lived in the delta areas of eastern Bengal (present-day Bangladesh).[37] Thus, the concern for the rural Bengali masses may have been largely rhetorical, but it was constituted by the colonial state's expectation that Muslim leaders be prepared to speak for their "community." The realities of late-nineteenth-century mass politics meant that in spite of the social distance, the political power of the *ashraf* vis-à-vis the colonial state depended on their ability to represent the whole of the Muslim community.

The *ashraf* initially turned to mass religious education for Bengalis as a means to speak for and address the issues of the rural masses. Paradoxically, it was in the process of delineating a "proper" religious education for all Bengali Muslims that the community itself was constituted, as was the crucial question of how modern religious subjectivity should be defined. This was a process in which the colonial state, *ashraf* elite, and eventually the emerging Bengali Muslim middle class were invested. In the next two sections, I will look at the different ways that the state and the Muslim *ashraf* defined what constituted modern religious education and subjectivity.

MAKING THE MODERN MUSLIM

While Muslim *ashraf* discourse in Bengal drew upon the North Indian Muslim reformist debates, it also paralleled discussions of religious identity among missionaries and Indian Christians. Schools had long been seen as a constitutive element of evangelical Christianity from its very beginning, but the expansion of Christianity among lower-caste, *dalit* (untouchable), and *adivasi* (tribal) peoples in the late nineteenth century prompted European missionaries to demand greater funding for educating their own rural congregations. Missionary committees became anxious about the "nominal" status of recent converts and felt that religious education was crucial to incorporate the new communities into the Church.

Pastoral care, protecting and being responsible for the spiritual care of one's congregation much as one would a flock of sheep, was a concept that Protestant Christians constantly touted as a practice that differentiated them from Hindus and Muslims.[38] A significant part of the pastoral duties of missionaries in a colonial setting revolved around "civilizing" native Christians and ensuring that they did not "lapse" back into heathen behavior or practices. Recognizing that a Scottish Christian might be different from a Bengali Christian, the missions nonetheless wanted to make sure that a Bengali Christian would not be confused with a Bengali Hindu or Muslim. The policing of cultural practices was a tension inherent in missionary work, especially as more tribal and low-caste populations were brought in through mass conversion movements. Missionaries felt that the religious life of native Christians from low-caste and tribal areas reflected their former "heathen" habits and practices. As early as 1859, the Baptists complained that "our nominal Christian community, for the most part, is very ignorant and have apparently received but little education. What is bad amongst us has nearly wholly arisen from their cause. Ignorance is our worst foe." The recent converts were pejoratively referred to as "rice" Christians, the implication being that they converted for the sake of material gain alone. In particular, "rice" Christians were brought into the Church during famines and were ignorant of most Western Christian traditions.[39] The reproduction of the Christian community depended on schools as much as churches since pastoral duties did not end in the chapel.

The pastoral imperative of Protestant missionaries paralleled Muslim *ashraf* rhetorical demands for a separate system of schooling to educate their "backward" Bengali brethren. In a largely illiterate society, primary schools clearly had never been the way most Bengali *atrap* learned their religious tradition, but in the context of late-nineteenth-century colonialism, the primary religious school had become one of the preeminent means to both centralize and reproduce a modern religious identity and counter the effects of the larger Hindu influence on rural society.

Initially, the *ashraf* embraced a nineteenth-century pan-Islamic identity that sought to link Bengali Muslims with their North Indian co-religionists.

Late-nineteenth-century Urdu and Bengali language newspapers reflected the interests and opinions of this urban *ashraf* class, many of whom tended to be politically loyal to the colonial government. Newspapers carried stories of Muslim world politics, critiques of Hindu dominance and machinations, literary production, and of course discussions on education.[40] The urban print world of the *ashraf* was paralleled by the growth of various voluntary organizations called *anjuman,* which, as Peter Hardy notes, were established in the 1880s "to promote Muslim culture and/or the diffusion of Western knowledge among Muslims."[41] A number of these *anjuman* were established to discuss a variety of political, social, and religious issues relating to cultural reform. Organizations like the Mohamedan Educational Conference and the Mohamedan Literary Society regularly held meetings in Calcutta and Dhaka and published speeches and pamphlets arguing for funding for Muslim higher education and an expansion of instruction for peasants and women.[42] By adopting a public role in educational gatherings, David Gilmartin suggests local Muslim leaders "sought to establish themselves as rational, independent, morally responsible spokesmen for the Muslim community as a whole."[43] That is, by adapting the argument initially developed by missionaries about schooling and religious identity, *ashraf* leaders (and the colonial state) placed themselves as the guardians and spokesmen for Muslims in Bengal.

In spite of the fact that the colonial state emphasized that it was Muslim fears of a loss of faith engendered by modernity or excessive pride in their culture that kept Muslim children from attending school, *ashraf* leaders argued that the real issue was that of representation. That is, Muslim leaders were less concerned with village education as a means to ameliorate the economic or social conditions of their coreligionists than as an occasion to demonstrate the inherent bias against Muslims and Muslim culture by upper-caste Hindus. The expected outcome of such a critique was to not merely increase the number of Muslim schools in villages, but also increase the number of Muslims in the educational service to balance the power of upper-caste Hindus.

When Syed Nawab Ali Choudury, a prominent *ashraf* leader and politician, took up the question of primary-level Muslim education, he first observed that the majority of *pathshalas* (village schools) were in predominantly Hindu villages or centers, even in northern and eastern Bengal, where Muslims were up to 75 percent of the population. He pointed out that this meant that large sections of the Muslim community had no access whatsoever to a state-funded *pathshala*—although, of course, this was equally true of the majority of poor Hindus who lived in Bengal. But Choudury felt that this was not simply a question of class—that the real reason for *pathshalas* being in predominantly Hindu areas was that the majority of inspectors employed by the DPI were upper-caste Hindu.[44] This meant that "their religion do not allow them, when on tour, to pass a night or take a meal in the house of a Mussalman. For their personal comfort . . . [they] establish schools in Hindu localities."[45] The ritual and caste practices of Hindu school inspectors meant that they could not stay in a Muslim's home, and thus predominantly Muslim areas rarely got visits from inspectors and thus no funding from the state for a *pathshala* or any other primary school.

Choudury's complaint simplified the much larger problem of the lack of schooling for the majority of Bengal's villages because his real goal was to uncover, for the state, what he perceived as the systematic bias of Hindus in governmental services. Choudury implied that increasing the number of Muslims in government service, in this case in the DPI, would inevitably lead to an extension of Muslim schooling.[46] Critiques like Choudury's eventually prompted the state to address the lack of Muslim representation by appointing Abdul Karim, with whom I began this chapter, as the first Muslim inspector of schools in Bengal in 1889. Like Choudury, Karim also complained that upper-caste Hindu dominance in government service continued to plague the DPI and diplomatically described the "family influence" that clearly favored the employment of Hindus. The difficulties faced by *ashraf* trying to find government employment were not only the result of Hindu nepotism but also the result of the attitudes of European officials, who "naturally prefer connections of Government servants to strangers."[47] Since the majority of government servants were Hindu, this created a vicious cycle in which it was difficult for any other individual or group to be hired.

While Choudury or Karim may have been initially concerned with government jobs for urban-educated Muslims, their concerns were not wholly self-interested. While the *ashraf* certainly did not see primary schooling as a means to erase the distinctions (cultural and economic) between themselves and rural Muslims, they nonetheless wanted more Bengali villagers to have access to formal religious schooling. Arguments about rural education, then, can be seen as a means for the *ashraf* to proselytize to their "own" community through the agency of the school. Like the Sunday school, the village school was meant to teach the *atrap* to be properly Muslim.

In government and *ashraf* discussions of primary-level education, one of the main issues that had to be decided was the question of language. While many Muslim leaders in Bengal identified more strongly with the Urdu-based culture of northern India, the majority of rural school goers and the teachers available to teach them were almost exclusively familiar with Bengali. But the Bengali taught in Muslim schools had to be an appropriately Islamicized language, *dobhashi* Bangla—a language that incorporated more Persianized vocabulary. Although recognizing the importance of teaching in the vernacular, Muslim leaders were concerned that the Bengali education most available in the *pathshala* or village school was incompatible with their larger goals.

In fact, *ashraf* leaders felt that equally insidious as the Hindu dominance of the DPI were the ways in which Muslims and Muslim culture were marginalized within the established Bengali schools. It is here that the complaints of the Muslim *ashraf* were most closely aligned with the statements of the Hunter Commission. That is, like the Hunter Commission, the Muslim *ashraf* dismissed the traditional village school or *pathshala* as wholly unsuitable for their purposes. For example, when Choudury spoke to the All-India Muhammedan Educational Conference in 1900, he bemoaned the consequences of a *pathshala* education for young Muslims. He noted that if young Muslims were asked "to recite the first principles of his faith in which he was born, the formalities of ablution, bathing and of burying the dead, he is simply nonplussed." But if he is asked about Hindu epics or Puranic stories, such as "how many Apsaras the love-god Krishna dallied with," the Muslim student is easily able to answer.[48]

Implicit in Choudury's criticism is the concern that the *pathshala* functions as a Hindu school, not merely a vernacular institution. In the *pathshala*, according to Choudury, Muslims are taught stories of gods and characters from the Hindu epics along with their lessons in Bengali reading and writing. For the Muslim children who attend the *pathshala*, the Hindu orientation of the schools only further distances them from their religious heritage. That is, they are effectively taught how to be a Hindu rather than a Muslim. In a curious way, Choudury seems to suggest that the traditional *pathshala* education actually poses a greater threat to Muslim identity than the English schooling offered by the colonial state. Unlike himself, rural Bengalis, fed on a steady diet of idolatrous, polytheistic stories, are unaware of their Islamic roots and heritage, and the colonial government's long-standing support of the *pathshala* is in fact de facto support for Hindu religious traditions.

For Choudury, discussions of village schooling become occasions to amplify continued Hindu cultural dominance and assert a narrower definition of what constitutes "authentic" Muslim knowledge. Choudury neither believes nor wants to argue for secularizing the *pathshala* curriculum, since he is committed to a parallel and separate system of religious education. Choudury feels that rural Bengali Muslims should be educated through modern Muslim primary schools like the Qur'an school and the *maktab,* assuming that the true purpose of modern schooling should be to teach poor Muslim children the principles and rituals of their faith.

Azizul Huque, in his *History and Problems of Modern Education in Bengal,* similarly laments that the great days of Islamic culture had given way to the present state of degradation. Huque complains that the Muslim youth "remain[s] more of a Hindu in dress, customs, inclinations, prejudices and predilections, save perhaps the outward veneer of religion, which but sits loosely on him." Like Choudury, he sees only one solution to the problem of the "loose" religious identity of his fellow Muslims: an education, which alone could "bring us back joy, hope and prosperity in our midst."[49] For Huque and other Muslim leaders, increased educational opportunities for themselves and their children would eventually mean more jobs in the colonial economy and greater prosperity for the Muslim leadership. But extending the benefits of primary-level religious schooling to rural Bengalis was less about immediate material benefits or greater mobility, but rather to ensure that Muslim villagers had a religious alternative to a *pathshala* education.

Abdul Karim had earlier suggested that "only primary schools . . . should be separately organized and supported."[50] That is, rather than the traditional ways in which religious education was structured (emphasizing the study of Arabic and Urdu at the higher levels), it was now most crucial to reach Muslims through schooling at the primary level. He felt that "once boys are thoroughly well-grounded in the principles of Islam, their faith is not likely to be easily shaken by the education they may afterwards receive in institutions meant for the higher education of all classes."[51] Thus, a primary education actually allowed Muslim students to continue their schooling in mixed institutions alongside Hindus and be taught secular subjects without jeopardizing their religious identity.

Karim, in his post as school inspector, felt that any primary Muslim school must deliver a religious education through the most modern pedagogic techniques and schoolbooks (as employed in Anglo-vernacular schools). His efforts, like those of the DPI, argued for modern pedagogic techniques to improve the instruction offered at the schools, but in the process Karim was redefining the meanings of Muslim religious identity. For example, Karim was critical of the use of the popular text *Miftah-ul-Janna* (*The Key to Paradise*) by Karamat Ali in Qur'an schools and *maktabs* to teach the basic rules and tenets of Islam. According to Karim, the problem with Ali's text was that it delineated all the rules related to rituals of the body, including rules about bathing, menstruation, child birth, and so on. This knowledge, which had previously been understood to be a part of general ritual knowledge, was now perceived as "demoralizing" and inappropriate for the education of the modern Muslim boy. Instead, Karim encouraged Bengali schools to adopt translated versions of the schoolbooks being published by the Anjumani Hemayet Islam in Lahore—schoolbooks that offered an education that would be appropriate for each sex. The need to segregate ritual knowledge, I would suggest, reflected a distinctly modern notion of religious respectability.

CONCLUSION

I began this chapter with a section of a speech from the first Muslim Bengali school inspector, Abdul Karim. Karim's appointment and extensive critique of Bengali education reflected a new common sense among Muslim leaders—that there was a need for a separate system of religiously inflected primary education. This demand, as I have tried to show, did not reflect the "backward-looking" and obscurantist traditions of Muslims, as Western contemporary media constantly argue. Instead, it was the colonial efforts to modernize the putatively "backward" and potentially insurgent Muslim community that prompted the funding of primary-level religious schooling. Religion and religious identity, rather than secularism, became constitutive of the expansion of modern education.

This is seen most directly in the ways that the content and curriculum of Muslim primary schools were developed. The colonial state, as much as Muslim *ashraf* leaders, was invested in how Muslim boys would be taught their religion since it was assumed that their own families and communities could only reproduce a "backward" and "Hinduized" version of Islamic practice. Through choosing the language of instruction, the insistence on the reading of the Qur'an, and the policing of boundaries of Hindu and Muslim knowledge, the everyday definitions of what it meant to be a Bengali Muslim were transformed.

The demand for separate religious schools was a manifestation of and fed back into the growing perception of difference among religious groups. Debates over language, religious education, and the Hindu dominance of educational facilities became increasingly acrimonious in the twentieth century. There were important differences in the perceptions and experience of educational change by the various religious and caste communities in Bengal. Education, positioned at the juncture of politics and culture, was critical to the nascent nationalist imaginings of Bengali Hindu and Muslim elite. The reluctance of the colonial state to adequately finance any centralized system of mass education, even as compulsory state education was introduced in Britain, ensured its highly privatized nature. The historical paradox is that the demand for separate systems of primary schooling happened even as the definitions of religious instruction (and thus religion itself) were being standardized.

Ultimately, the desire of Muslim leaders for equal representation in schooling was closely connected to their desire for equal access and representation in politics. In 1906, the year after the Bengal Presidency experienced its first partition into eastern (with Dhaka as its capital) and western (with Calcutta as its capital) halves, Choudury's organization also went through a transformation. It became the All-India Muslim League. The shift, from an organization that addressed various issues of Muslim educational and economic access to a political organization, is not accidental. It speaks to the fact that educational disenfranchisement had become a central component of Muslim political rhetoric and nationalism.

Conclusion

Pedagogy for Tolerance

The global circulation of pedagogic theory in the nineteenth and twentieth centuries successfully propagated the notion that primary schools were an essential site for the production and dissemination of modern cultural forms. An example of this idea is a manual that figures prominently in this book, David Stow's 1859 text, *The Training System of Education*. Stow's text was widely distributed all over the British Empire and translated into multiple vernaculars, including Bengali. The highly practical nature of the text, describing a training system, belied Stow's philosophical aspiration, which was to create a universal theory of subjectivity and cognition that helped explain cultural difference and change. *The Training System of Education* repeatedly associates the early education of children with the production of cultural identity. Stow rhetorically asks that "if habit is not so strong as almost to be a second nature, why the difficulty of changing the manners of the Hottentot, the Turk, and the Indian?" His conclusion, one that might have surprised many of his contemporaries, is that neither "climate or religion, or laws" helped explain the difficulty of changing ("civilizing") these different groups, but rather "the power of early impressions and habits that presents the greatest barrier to any change."[1] For Stow, both cultural difference and cultural transformation could be reduced to the education of children and habits of child rearing. The teacher trained in Stow's simultaneous method is not a mere pedagogue, but a cultural missionary.

An Argument for Religion has focused specifically on how Stow's belief in the constitutive role of schooling in the formation of cultural and religious "habits" was taken up by the very people he had hoped to convert and mold: "the Hottentot, the Turk and the Indian." In Bengal, the breadth of Stow's intellectual ambitions resonated with the cultural aspirations of mid-nineteenth-century upper-caste (*bhadralok*) educators and Muslim reformers.

The previous chapter highlighted one of the critical outcomes of this process—the conviction that religion was not merely an abstract form of belonging but also something within that children (in this case, rural Bengali children) had to be taught to locate themselves. To be modern was to be religious; Bengali Muslims, like Bengali Hindus and Christians, had to learn to possess and inhabit their religiosity in recognizable and acceptable ways. By the 1880s, this politically manifested in a push for separate educational systems for Hindus and Muslims—a dynamic that only amplified the perception of difference between the two communities.

Yet what is striking in the development of twentieth-century Bengali education is how, in the midst of an increasingly religiously divided politics and growing nationalist agitation, Muslim reformers continued to try to rethink the relationship between modern education, religious diversity, and national identity. This "rethinking" did not challenge any of the fundamental definitions of modern education that I have been tracing—the privileging of written over oral instruction, a demand for moral and religious education, or separate male and female curricula. But two educational reports produced by Muslim leaders in 1935 and 1942 reflect a pragmatic and serious effort to create a single system of schooling that directly addressed the differing needs of religious communities. Bengali Muslim educators offered a surprising and at times radical perspective from which to rethink cultural pluralism from the perspective of the "minority" community.

In this, the reports manage to trouble the powerful binary that continues to mark the historiography of modern South Asia in which there is a clear division and set of assumptions that undergird the distinction between the secular and the communal. Instead, they offer us, the modern reader, a surprising and even radical example of how an ostensibly "communal" suggestion—the necessity of religious education within the modern school—was simultaneously one that reflected a far more flexible and plural approach to the question of religion and community than any of the ostensibly "secular" approaches. As one scholar has suggested, Bengali Muslim politics were based "quite firmly within a Muslim religious and Bengali regional political discourse."[2] But in looking toward education as a place in which to understand the political alternative being offered by Bengali Muslim leadership, we can also see that the question of what constituted both the "Muslim religious" and its relationship to the "Bengali regional," that is, the relationship between language, religion, and nation, was hardly self-evident. The educational reports suggest that the creation of a plan for mass schooling was precisely where these questions could be worked out within and between communities.

By exploring issues of representation, culture, nation, and schooling from another time and place, this conclusion asks how we might reframe our own discussions about the place of religion in modern society. The mid-twentieth-century Bengali educational reports never lose sight of the larger fact of nationalist politics. In oblique and sometimes direct ways, they demand to be read as an effort to imagine how separate religious curricula (and religious communities) could be folded into a single school system or nation. In many ways, the double minority status of Bengali Muslims—as Muslims in colonial India and as Bengali speakers among the larger Urdu-language-dominated Muslim leadership—offered them a unique perspective. They were finely attuned to the multiple vectors of identity—linguistic, cultural, and religious—that made any separation of schools along purely religious lines untenable. The two partitions faced by those in Bengal, in 1947 and 1971, only underline their farsighted vision in the 1930s and 1940s in trying to preempt such a simplistic division.

The two reports that I examine in this chapter are unique in that they both diagnose and suggest a solution for the very tricky question of religion and schooling—a solution that comes out of a minority perspective and that understands the national stakes of the discussion. In the reports, one sees the frustrations of Bengali Muslim leaders like Azizul Haq (chancellor of Calcutta University) and A. K. Fazlul Haq (the chief minister of Bengal between 1937 and 1942) over "the Hindu domination over the system of education."[3] To address the disparities over access to formal schooling and the cultural bias they perceived in governmental and nongovernmental institutions, they produced a series of reports that argued for a more pluralist model for Bengali-language education. I am interested in these texts less for what they tell us about literacy or the new administrative practices around schooling than for the ways they function as cultural and political documents. The reports should be read in much the way that I have thus far been analyzing nineteenth-century pedagogy—as an effort to theorize and transform the religious and social values of Indian society. Even more explicitly than nineteenth-century pedagogic texts, the discourse about modern Muslim education functioned as parallel (and surrogate) discussions about the relationship between religious identity and national identity in India.

The efforts by Muslim educators to think through a practical solution to the question of religious diversity and national schooling, coupled with their skepticism about any possibility of a culturally "unmarked" schooling system, lie at the heart of Bengali attempts to think pragmatically about what it means to live in a multicultural society. This is the core question that continues to haunt modern education as a whole, and in this conclusion I will suggest that the solutions posed by mid-twentieth-century Bengali Muslim educators offer us a new perspective from which to approach this very contemporary issue.

SEPARATE AND SPECIAL SCHOOLING

The two educational reports on Muslim education, *Report of the Moslem Education Advisory Committee* (1935) and *Report of the Kamal Yar Jung Education Committee* (1942), articulate a set of much broader questions than simply those of Indian schooling. Through the reports, Bengali Muslim leaders express their particular anxieties about the need to preserve cultural autonomy, retain their distinctiveness vis-à-vis the larger Hindu population, and grapple with the inequity of institutional structures segregated by religion. The reports were prompted by the introduction of the Bengal (Rural) Primary Education Act in 1930.[4] The Primary Education Act, similar to ones being enacted in other colonial provinces, increased Indian autonomy over education and also aimed to create a system of compulsory mass schooling. Muslim leaders, like leaders of other "minority" communities, felt the need to vigorously defend (and lobby) for the distinctive needs of their community.

In the larger context of colonial India, Bengal's primary education system stood out in some distressing ways that explained the low levels of literacy in the province and also exposed the structural issues that ensured the underperformance of Muslim schools in particular. The typical Bengali primary school had only three classes, with an untrained, badly paid single teacher and little inspection or supervision. Yet all these were "counted" by the Department of Public Instruction (DPI), and so Bengal had the dubious distinction of having the largest number of primary schools in India.⁵ The same peculiarities of general primary schooling in Bengal were also true for Bengali Muslim schools. Bengal had a series of "special" (versus separate) schools, which were "traditional" religious institutions: *madrassahs, maktabs,* and Qur'an schools. While the commission recognized that separate schooling meant that larger numbers of Muslims were now reached by formal education, they also noted that on the whole these institutions delivered a lower level of education.⁶

Although the 1935 and 1942 Muslim education reports purport to represent the interests of an already constituted community, their production should also be seen as part of the process of creating an all-India Muslim identity. For instance, in the 1935 *Report of the Moslem Education Advisory Committee,* the committee members described their effort to identify, and thus grant authority to, certain individuals who could then address the educational and social conditions of their respective communities. These individuals—local officials, *maulavis,* local landowners, and so on—effectively became the spokesmen for Muslims as a whole. Perhaps more humorously (and poignantly), the 1942 *Report of the Kamal Yar Jung Education Committee* "noted that commission members were unable to keep up with the hospitality extended to them by Muslim communities and families or to stand the varieties of rich food from the Malabar coast to the Frontier day after day."⁷ The identification of a particular set of spokesmen and the geographic articulation of a Muslim community that stretched from the southern coast to the northwestern frontier helped constitute the "imagined" community of Muslims in colonial India—an identity that was presented within the reports as already self-evident.

The major themes that I earlier discussed as salient among Muslim reformers were consistently reiterated in the reports from the 1930s and 1940s. For instance, in the 1935 report, the writers criticized the putative "secularity" of the village schooling by comparing the curriculum of the *maktab* (an explicitly religious school) with that of the *pathshala*. They note that while "maktab readers are not acceptable to non-Moslems, the readers now in use *in ordinary primary schools* abound in stories drawn mainly from Hindu mythology which are repugnant to Islam."⁸ Although *pathshalas* or government schools are not explicitly religious institutions and do not impart religious training, they nonetheless impart a culturally Hindu curriculum. For the committee members, this is exemplified by the content of the respective language readers (now generally accepted as an index of cultural values) employed in the two types of schools. I would argue that in drawing a comparison between the religious orientation of *maktab* and *pathshala* readers, the reports implicitly challenge the claim that colonial educational institutions are in any way culturally neutral or unmarked.

It is not difficult to see a parallel between the Muslim educational critique of the (Hindu) *pathshala* and its claims to secularity and the broader political critique of Indian politics being made by people like Fazlul Haq. Many twentieth-century Muslim leaders were frustrated with the Indian National Congress' claims to be a purely national and secular party while charging every other political party, notably the Muslim League, with narrow sectarian and religious interests. But if we draw out the analogy suggested by the *Moslem Education Advisory Committee Report,* it would seem that although it is easy to categorize the Muslim League (like the *maktab*) as a religious party, it is no more culturally or religiously based than the Indian National Congress (or the *pathshala*).

While critical of the Hinduized nature of the *pathshala* curriculum, Muslim educators were not advocating for the creation of a purely secular form of schooling. Quite to the contrary, the committee members were adamant that in the Primary Education Act, "religious instruction should form part of the curriculum of primary schools and that due provision should be made for the teaching of the subject. The Moslem boys should learn to read the Quoran and also the rituals of Islam through the medium of vernacular."[9] There is a clear distinction being made between the ways a curriculum was culturally religious versus the need for religious schooling. As I argued in chapter 6, Muslim educators continued to point out the various ways that Hindu cultural bias informed the writing of schoolbooks and the like, but distinguished this as a separate problem from the issue of religious education. In many ways, the *pathshala* might have proved less objectionable if it had offered explicit religious instruction rather than (what Muslim reformers perceived as) covert cultural instruction. But the persistence of a "Hinduized" curriculum threatened to further alienate Muslim children from their own religious traditions.

An equally important reason for separate Bengali Muslim schools was the need to ensure that some part of the school day be set aside for explicit religious instruction, something rarely done within the *pathshala* and certainly not offered in government schools. The committee felt that this was necessary for every community, who could use the same period for "learning such subjects as will suit their own religious requirements."[10] The argument made by Muslim leaders to treat religion as a separate subject, echoing mid-nineteenth-century evangelical debates, represented the more general process of separating out religion from politics or economics or language as subjects. In a more concretized way, this reflects what Talal Asad underscores in more abstract terms as a result of the European historical experience: "[the] construction of religion ensures that it is part of what is *inessential* to our common politics, economy, science and morality."[11] Thus, the articulation of a separate (modern) religious curriculum was a part of a much larger process through which religion, as a category, was being defined in colonial India. Moreover, in making religion a separate and compulsory primary school subject, Muslim leaders used the opportunity to outline the content of appropriate Muslim religious knowledge and practice.

Alongside the process of making religion, in this case Islam, separate from other forms of knowledge, the modern Bengali *maktab*'s religious curriculum also reflected a democratization of Muslim religious knowledge and authority under the colonial state. In fact, the religious expertise expected from every Muslim child was so elaborate and specialized that it was only in the school, with a trained teacher, that they might actually learn it. The knowledge meant to be imparted to Muslim children had previously been restricted to religious authorities and urban Muslim culture. But now, the Bengali Muslim peasant child was also expected to have a basic understanding of legal learning and rules for personal maintenance. This also resulted in a curriculum that further standardized and narrowed what could be defined as "religious."[12]

The report reflects the process I have been tracing in this book: the new expectation that the modern Muslim learned to be a Muslim through formal schooling, not just in the home or through informal lessons at the *masjid*. That is, if being a modern Muslim was now defined through familiarity with legal texts and the ability to decipher Arabic and memorize rules of ablution, then the Bengali Muslim child had to go to a *maktab*. Muslim primary schools and *maktabs* were the only solutions to such a "demussalmanising" since they would ensure that "the rituals and broad outlines of the essentials of Islam "were being taught to the next generation."[13]

While there is a constructive aspect of developing a separate Muslim religious curriculum, I would also note the more defensive aspect of these efforts. Running through the reports is an anxiety around the "preservation" of Muslim culture that is repeatedly glossed in the texts as a "demussalmanising tendency" among Muslim students. The term echoes the late-nineteenth-century fears that attendance at *pathshalas* was making the Muslim child more familiar with the stories of Krishna than the history of Muhammad. Separate schools would counteract the threat posed by a highly Hinduized curriculum for the Muslim boy or girl and ensure that Muslim students, who stood in for the community as a whole, retain their distinctive "culture and social order."

But even as Muslim leaders recognize the need for religious instruction, they are aware of the pitfalls of having separate religious schools for Muslims. The 1935 report notes that "the strong religious tendency of the maktabs" meant that they were less easily assimilated into the DPI than the *pathshalas*. Moreover, "while the pathshalas lost their religious significance in the course of time, the *maktabs* continued to be more or less religious in character."[14] The report notes that the religious nature of the *maktab* automatically predisposes the DPI to be skeptical of any secular instruction found in the school and thus less likely to fund the institution. Moreover, Muslim leaders doubt that children who attend the *maktab* are really prepared for higher education or employment in the colonial economy. Muslim leaders and educators are wary of any kind of religious identity that does not conform to the demands and needs of a modern society and economy. What is needed is a *maktab* that will successfully meet the DPI's definitions of modern religious schooling.[15]

The 1935 and 1942 educational reports testify to the frustration and struggle of Muslim educators to determine how best to protect the needs and cultural identity of Muslims, even as they recognize the political, social, and educational problems associated with a segregated school system. This remains a paradox and struggle for minority community leaders in India. From language readers to teacher training, Muslim educators were frustrated with the consistent bias they observed in ostensibly "secular" institutions—like government schools dominated by upper-caste Hindus. At the same time, Bengali leaders were well aware that any separate school system would never be fully supported in the ways that government schools were. That is, schools meant only for "minority" children would always be underfunded and marginalized; the presence of majority children (in this case, caste Hindus) was one of the few ways to ensure any real educational and social equity.

This highly productive conundrum led Muslim educators to propose a solution that would both meet the needs of the various communities in Bengal and maintain a single educational system. Referring to the texts used in primary schools, the Muslim Education Committee suggests that textbooks "contain nothing objectionable to any community ... [and] that books and the standards prescribed for secular subjects should be the same for children of all communities."[16] If the recommendations for the creation of appropriate textbooks and separate provisions for religious instruction during some part of the day are met, then Muslim leaders feel that "it will not be necessary, when the Primary Education Act is brought into force, to maintain maktabs as separate institutions."[17] Thus, at the end of the report, the model for an effective primary school that emerges from Muslim leaders is a single institution that educates all Bengali children together, but sets aside some part of the day for separate religious instruction for each community.

Even as Muslim leaders, particularly Bengali Muslim reformers, argue for the need to maintain (and reproduce) the distinctive nature of the Muslim community through separate education, they remain committed to the possibility of a single school system and a single nation. In fact, the discussion of schools is nothing if not an occasion to contemplate what lies ahead. In a long section toward the end of the *Report of the Kamal Yar Jung Education Committee,* Azizul Haq (the chancellor of Calcutta University) pointedly remarks that there are two possible alternatives for Indian education. Either the schools have "syllabuses and themes that the Hindus, the Muslims and all other creeds and communities can meet on an essentially common platform with no influence tendency or bias in favour of the one or the other"; or, if this is not possible, then "India must be a federation of two more distinct types of educational organizations, each trying to develop its own culture and heredity, but in a spirit of catholicity and good will to others."[18] It is impossible to escape the highly political metaphors that Azizul Haq employs. If a "common platform" on education (or nationalist politics) cannot be found, then India must consider a "federation" of educational systems (or nation-states) that would reflect separate cultures but not necessarily be antagonistic toward one another. Even in his federated scheme, Azizul Haq is at pains to insist upon "catholicity" that each community should adopt toward one another.

The proposed educational plan attempts to outline a successful schooling system that would meet the needs of a religiously pluralist society. Although the committee members were by no means radicals, there are some radical implications in their plan. For instance, Azizul Haq does not make the state the arbitrator of claims between communities. This is in part because education has now devolved toward provincial legislatures, so that the colonial state no longer has full jurisdiction (or interest) in such issues. But it is also because Haq remains skeptical of the ability of a colonial or national state to remain neutral. Instead, he wants the communities themselves (through their representatives) to negotiate a workable system.

Second, the report consistently points out the various ways that putatively nonreligious institutions and texts, like village schools or language readers, represent the culture and cultural habits of high-caste Hindus. In doing this, Muslim educators reject any claim that an institution or artifact can remain culturally unmarked. If this is true, the only solution lies in *all* communities, including the upper-caste Hindu community, negotiating with other groups to develop schooling materials and methods that are acceptable to everyone. While an imperfect solution, it nonetheless offers an interesting way to think through the nature of Indian secularism. Bengali Muslim leaders had greater faith in the ability of communities to successfully negotiate with one another and produce a pluralist model than they did in any state-defined system, which they believed would always represent the cultural interests of the dominant group. Implicitly, the plan also suggests the ways that the actual process of developing a "common platform" is itself an exercise in pluralist thinking and imagination.

What is most instructive in the plan for mass primary education laid out in the two reports by Muslim leaders is that they offer a compelling model of cultural pluralism—the kind of pluralism that the political theorist William Connolly champions in his work. Connolly argues, "When you see how faith commitments vary in intensity, content, and imperiousness, you set the stage to explore what it takes to engender modesty in the relations between faiths co-existing on the same territory. And when you include yourself and your faith in the equation, rather than pretending to float above the fray, you place yourself in a better position to commend the ethos to others."[19] Here Connolly is speaking to the necessity of twenty-first-century secular (or nominally Christian) Europeans to no longer place themselves "above the fray" but to be self-conscious about their own cultural practices even as they critique the practices of other Europeans, particularly Muslims.

Muslim educators in Bengal demanded that upper-caste Hindus not "float above the fray" but instead see themselves as representing a particular community, not the "nation," as they modestly negotiated with others who share "the same territory"—Christians, Muslims, and so on. Of course, while Connolly insists upon what he describes as multidimensional pluralism (that is, along many different identity vectors), Muslim leaders privileged religion and religious community. But, as I suggested before, Bengali Muslims are also keenly aware of other identity vectors, especially those of language (Bengali versus Urdu) and region (Western versus Eastern India).

The *Report of the Kamal Yar Jung Education Committee* ends with a rather poignant expression of the necessity of this kind of pluralism. Azizul Haq asks of his own community—and also of the nascent Indian nation—if "Muslim India [will] rise to the height of the occasion in the name of Islam and take up a new life in the new shape of things existing and yet to come?"[20] Unfortunately, it was precisely the constraints of the "things existing"—colonial power, religious and caste bias, segregated instruction, and the form of the modern school itself—that made it difficult to imagine a "new shape" for things to come for either the Bengali school or the Indian nation.

CONCLUSION

Although this book began with the history of the mission school and ends with the debates over Qur'an schools, I am not advocating a model of historical predetermination. That is, it was never inevitable that an increased emphasis on religion in schooling would lead to a partitioned and antagonistic school system and nation. Nor do I want to suggest any nostalgia for a premodern "indigenous" educational system in which everyone happily participated. After all, formal Bengali-language schooling extended, in a very modest way, the promises of modernity to a much larger group of individuals, from lower-caste Christian teachers to Bengali Muslim peasants. Moreover, I see the demands of Muslim leaders for formal, separate schooling reflecting a determination to harness the promise of colonial modernity, in all its slipperiness and contestability, for their own community.

It is hardly surprising, then, that education globally remains one of the critical spaces for public debates over religion and culture. But, as this conclusion suggests, schools can also serve as metaphors for rethinking what it means to live in a pluralistic society. The modern Bengali school became a laboratory in which Muslim leaders tried to work out a solution to the two-school and two-nation problem. Working within the framework of a modern conception of religion and an increasingly politicized notion of religious identity, they nonetheless attempted to apprehend the possibilities for teaching, learning, and living in a truly pluralist society.

Notes

INTRODUCTION

1. Niall Ferguson, *Empire: The Rise and Demise of the British World Order and the Lessons for Global Power* (New York: Basic Books, 2003), xxvii.

2. The theoretical work on the formative influence of Protestant paradigms in the definition of religion includes Talal Asad, *Genealogies of Religion: Discipline and Reasons of Power in Christianity and Islam* (Baltimore: Johns Hopkins University Press, 1993); Tomoko Masuzawa, *The Invention of World Religions* (Chicago: University of Chicago Press, 2005); Peter van der Veer, *Imperial Encounters: Religion and Modernity in India and Britain* (Princeton, N.J.: Princeton University Press, 2001); and S.J. Balagangadhara, *The Heathen in His Blindness: Asia and the West and the Dynamic of Religion* (Leiden: Brill, 1994).

3. Peter Hardy, *The Muslims of British India* (Cambridge: Cambridge University Press, 1972), 85. Mayo was assassinated in 1872 when Hunter's text was published, and soon after Hunter published an educational minute to encourage the state to increase Muslim participation in government colleges and schools.

4. William Hunter, *The Indian Musalamans: Are They Bound in Conscience to Rebel against the Queen?* (London: Trubner and Company, 1871), 179.

5. *Sketch of the official career of the Hon'ble Ashley Eden: with an appendix containing the hon'ble Ashley Eden's evidence before the indigo commissission, the Treaty with Sikhim, and Sir Charles Wood's Despatch to the Government of India*. 1877. Calcutta: Kally Prosono Dey.

6. My study diverges from the recent book by Hayden Bellenoit, who sees schooling in binary terms of missionary and Indian, thus never challenging the upper-caste Hindu claims that their norms constituted what was seen as Indian "secular" schooling. Hayden Bellenoit, *Missionary Education and*

Empire in Late Colonial India, 1860–1920 (London: Pickering and Chatto, 2007), 127.

7. Sanjay Seth, *Subject Lessons: The Western Education of Colonial India* (Durham, N.C.: Duke University Press, 2007).

8. For example, Michael Mawema, "British and Portuguese Colonialism in Central African Education" (Ph.D. diss., Teacher's College, Columbia University, 1981). One of the best examples of this in the Indian context is B.T. McCully, *English Education and the Rise of Indian Nationalism* (New York: Columbia University Press, 1963). An interesting fictional account of this process in Sri Lanka is Shyam Selvudurai, *Cinnamon Gardens* (New York: Hyperion Press, 1999).

9. For some recent examples, see Janaki Bakhle, *Two Men and Music: Nationalism in the Making of an Indian Classical Tradition* (New York: Oxford University Press, 2005); Prachi Deshpande, *Creative Pasts: Historical Memory and Identity in Western India, 1700–1960* (New York: Columbia University Press, 2007); Andrew Sartori, *Bengal in Global Concept History: Culturalism in the Age of Capital* (Chicago: Chicago University Press, 2008); Rochona Majumdar, *Marriage and Modernity: Family Values in Colonial Bengal* (Durham, N.C.: Duke University Press, 2009); and Ritu Birla, *Stages of Capital: Law, Market and Governance in Late Colonial India* (Durham, N.C.: Duke University Press, 2009).

10. For a discussion of nineteenth- and twentieth-century language politics, see Vasudha Dalmia, *The Nationalization of Hindu Traditions: Bharatendu Harischandra and Nineteenth Century Banaras* (Delhi: Oxford University Press, 1997); David Lelyveld, "Talking the National Language: Hindi/Urdu/Hindustani in Indian Broadcasting and Cinema," in *Thinking Social Science in India: Essays in Honor of Alice Thorner*, ed. Sujata Patel (New Delhi: Sage, 2002); Sumathi Ramaswamy, *Passions of the Tongue: Language Devotion in Tamil India, 1871–1900* (Berkeley: University of California Press, 1997); Veena Naregal, *Language Politics, Elites and the Public Sphere: Western India under Colonialism* (New Delhi: Permanent Black, 2001); and Farina Mir, *The Social Space of Language: Vernacular Culture in British Colonial Punjab* (Berkeley: University of California Press, 2010).

11. This is true even in the writing on colonial schooling in Bengal; see Brian Hatcher, *Idioms of Improvement: Vidyasagar and Cultural Encounter in Bengal* (Calcutta: Oxford University Press, 1996); Sumit Sarkar, "Vidyasagar and Brahminical Society," in Sumit Sarkar, *Writing Social History* (Delhi: Oxford University Press, 1998); Asok Sen, *Vidyasagar and His Elusive Milestones* (Calcutta: Riddhi—India, 1977); and Poromesh Acharya, "Is Macaualay Still Our Guru?" *Economic Political Weekly*, May 28, 1988, 1124–30. For a Foucauldian analysis of "discipline" within Vidyasagar's colonial pedagogy, see Sibaji Bandhopadhyay, *Gopal-Rakhal Dwandasamas: Uponibeshbad O Bangla Sishu-Sahitya* (Calcutta: Papyrus, 2001).

12. See, for example, Vicente Rafael, *Contracting Colonialism: Translation and Christian Conversion in Tagalog Society under Early Spanish Rule* (Ithaca, N.Y.: Cornell University Press, 1988); Gauri Viswanathan, *Outside the Fold: Conversion, Modernity, Belief* (Princeton, N.J.: Princeton University Press, 1998);

Peter Van der Veer, ed., *Conversion to Modernities: The Globalization of Christianity* (New York: Routledge, 1996); Saurabh Dube, *Stitches on Time: Colonial Textures and Postcolonial Thought* (Durham, N.C.: Duke University Press, 2004); and Webb Keane, *Christian Moderns: Freedom and Fetish in the Mission Encounter* (Berkeley: University of California Press, 2007).

13. Some of the most important and most recent work on the historical role of missionaries in Indian history has been based in South India. These include Eliza Kent, *Converting Women: Gender and Protestant Christianity in Colonial South India* (New York: Oxford University Press, 2004); Ines Zupanoav, *Disputed Missions: Jesuit Experiments and Brahmanical Knowledge in Seventeenth-Century India* (New Delhi: Oxford University Press, 1999); Susan Bayly, *Saints, Goddesses and Kings: Muslims and Christians in South Indian Society, 1700–1900* (Cambridge: Cambridge University Press, 1989): and Koji Kawashima, *Missionaries and a Hindu State: Travancore, 1858–1936* (Delhi: Oxford University Press, 1998).

14. Some recent work that seems to be framed in this manner includes Robert Frykenberg and Judith Brown, eds., *Christians, Cultural Interaction and India's Religious Traditions* (London: Routledge Curzon, 2002); Jeffrey Cox, *Imperial Fault Lines: Christianity and Colonial Power in India, 1818–1940* (Stanford, Calif.: Stanford University Press, 2002); and Anthony Copley, *Religions in Conflict: Ideology, Cultural Contact and Conversion in Late Colonial India* (Delhi: Oxford University Press, 1997). One of the most interesting new books on Christianity and colonialism is Rowena Robinson and Sathianathan Clarke, eds., *Religious Conversion in India: Modes, Motivations and Meanings* (New Delhi: Oxford University Press, 2003). Some of the earlier and most important work on missionaries includes G.A. Oddie, *Social Protest in India* (New Delhi: Viking Press, 1979); and Daniel Potts, *British Baptist Missionaries in India* (Cambridge: Cambridge University of India, 1967). For a discussion of the relationship of missionaries to caste, see Duncan Forrester, *Caste and Christianity* (Calcutta: Firma KLM, 1980).

15. Andrew Porter, *Religion versus Empire? British Protestant Missionaries and Overseas Expansion, 1700–1914* (Manchester, UK: Manchester University Press, 2004); and Catherine Hall, *Metropole and Colony in the English Imagination, 1830–1867* (Oxford: Polity, 2002).

16. Porter, *Religion versus Empire?* 317, emphasis mine.

17. Studies on the role of evangelicalism in the making of the British middle classes include John and Jean Comaroff, *Of Revelation and Revolution: Christianity, Colonialism and Connsciousness* (Chicago: University of Chicago Press, 1991); and Susan Thorne, *Congregational Missions and the Making of an Imperial Culture in Nineteenth-Century England* (Stanford, Calif.: Stanford University Press, 1999).

18. Norman Etherington, "Introduction," in *Missions and Empire*, ed. Norman Etherington (Oxford: Oxford University Press), 107.

19. Gauri Viswanathan, *Masks of Conquest: Literary Study and British Rule in India* (Delhi: Oxford University Press, 1998), 3.

20. For one of the best theoretical analyses of colonial and postcolonial education, see Krishna Kumar, *Political Agenda of Education: A Study of Colonialist*

and Nationalist Ideas (New Delhi: Sage, 1991). An important precursor to this book is Michael A. Laird, *Missionaries and Education in Bengal, 1793–1897* (Oxford: Clarendon Press, 1972). However, Laird's study ends in the first half of the nineteenth century, and thus does not examine the important conjuncture of nationalist, mission. and colonial government interests in the field of mass primary education.

21. William Carey, *An Enquiry into the Obligations of Christians to Use Means for the Conversion of the Heathen*, new facsimile ed. (London: Carey Kingsgate Press Ltd., 1961), 11–12.

22. This does not mean that the company wanted missionaries in the new colony; in fact, the reason why Carey went to Serampore was that the Dutch were willing to "host" Protestant evangelicals, whereas the East India Company would not. It was not until 1813, with the passage of the Pious Clause, that Parliament forced the East India Company to allow missionaries onto its Indian territories.

23. Homi Bhabha, *The Location of Culture* (New York: Routledge, 1994), 87.

24. Bengal District Administration Committee, 1913–1914 (Calcutta: Bengal Secretariat Press, 1915), 165.

25. Bengal District Administration Committee, 165.

26. See Anindita Ghosh, *Power in Print: Popular Publishing and the Politics of Language and Culture in a Colonial Society* (New Delhi: Oxford University Press, 2006). Ghosh argues that after the 1857 Mutiny, the colonial government began scrutinizing vernacular publishing because of fears that natives were printing seditious or anticolonial publications.

27. The seminal text for this argument is Partha Chatterjee, *The Nation and Its Fragments: Colonial and Postcolonial Histories* (Princeton, N.J.: Princeton University Press, 1993).

28. John Murdoch, *Letter to Babu Ishwar Chandra Bidyasagar on Bengali Typography* (1865), 4.

29. Dipesh Chakrabarty, *Provincializing Europe: Postcolonial Thought and Historical Difference* (Princeton, N.J.: Princeton University Press, 2000), 17.

30. There is considerable debate about the precise caste and class composition of the *bhadralok*. For a longer discussion, see J. H. Broomfield, *Elite Conflict in a Plural Society: Twentieth Century Bengal* (Berkeley: University of California Press, 1968); John McGuire, *The Making of a Colonial Mind: A Quantitative Study of the Bhadralok in Calcutta, 1857–1885* (Canberra: Australian National University Press, 1983). The most recent discussions can be found in Tithi Bhattacharya, *The Sentinels of Culture* (New Delhi: Oxford University Press, 2005); and Andrew Sartori, *Bengali in Global Concept History* (Chicago: Chicago University Press, 2008).

31. For a longer discussion of the making of a Bengali Muslim identity, see Sufia Ahmed, *Muslim Community in Bengal, 1884–1912* (Bangladesh: Oxford University Press, 1974); Tazeen Murshid, *The Sacred and the Secular: Bengal Muslim Discourses, 1871–1977* (Calcutta: Oxford University Press, 1995); and Rafiuddin Ahmed, *The Bengal Muslims, 1871–1906: A Quest for Identity* (Delhi: Oxford University Press, 1996). For a study of the Namasudra move-

ment in Bengal, see Sekhar Bandyopadhay, *Caste, Protest and Identity: The Namasudras of Bengal, 1872-1947* (Surrey: Curzon, 1997).

32. Sufia Uddin, *Constructing Bangladesh: Religion, Ethnicity, and Language in an Islamic Nation* (Chapel Hill: University of North Carolina Press, 2006), 11.

33. M.P. Western, "Problems regarding Female Education in N. India," in *The East and the West* (January 1911): 26, Education Miscellaneous File 59, 1890-1914, London Institute of Education, London.

34. David Ludden, "Territorial Politics, Spatial Inequality, and Economic Development: The Case of the Province of Eastern Bengal and Assam," unpublished paper, 4.

1. THE MOLDING OF NATIVE CHARACTER

1. For a discussion of the place of Adam's reports in Bengal educational policy see Joseph DiBona, ed., *One Teacher, One School: The Adam Reports on Indigenous Education in 19th Century India* (New Delhi: Sita Ram Goel, 1983).

2. Ashok Sen, *Iswarchandra Vidyasagar and His Elusive Milestones* (Calcutta: Riddhi, 1977), 41.

3. Lal Dena, *Christian Missions and Colonialism* (Sillong, 1988), 13.

4. Victor Kiernan, "Evangelicalism and the French Revolution," *Past and Present*, no. 1 (February 1952): 46.

5. David Owen, *English Philanthropy: 1600-1960* (Cambridge: Belknap Press, 1964), 74.

6. The historiography of British primary education is very rich. There are works that posit larger theoretical arguments as well as works that look closely at regional difference. For a wonderful discussion of the Sunday School movement, see Thomas Laqueur, *Religion and Respectability* (New Haven, Conn.: Yale University Press, 1976). Comprehensive histories include H.C. Barnard, *A Short History of English Education* (London: University of London Press, 1947); and Stanley J. Curtis, *History of Education in Great Britain* (London: University Tutorial Press, 1948). I have been especially influenced by Carolyn Steedman, *Childhood and Culture in Britain: Margaret McMillan, 1860-1931* (New Brunswick, N.J.: Rutgers University Press, 1990), as a model of doing educational history.

7. Eric J. Hobsbawm, *The Age of Revolution 1789-1848* (New York: New American Library, 1962), 270.

8. Daniel E. Potts, *British Baptist Missionaries in India, 1793-1897* (Cambridge: Cambridge University Press, 1967), 7-8.

9. M.A. Laird, *Missionaries and Education in Bengal, 1793-1837* (Oxford: Clarendon Press, 1972), 55.

10. *Christian Observer*, February 1808, p. 117, emphasis mine.

11. Kazi Shahidullah, *Pathshalas into Schools* (Calcutta: Firma KLM, 1987), 14.

12. There is actually some debate about how open the *pathshala* was to other castes. Hriteshranjan Sanyal argues that many different castes and religions (that

is, Muslim boys as well) attended the *pathshala*; see Hriteshranjan Sanyal, "British Purba Athihagoth Shikkhababastha," *Yogasutra* (January–March 1992). Poromesh Acharachya, in his study of *pathshalas* in precolonial Bengal, rejects the romanticization of *pathshala* education, which was largely confined to higher-caste, Hindu males (since the majority of Muslims in Bengal were peasants), and not vehicles for the education of the peasant masses. See Poromesh Acharaya, *Banglar Deshaj Shikhaguru* (Calcutta: Anushoopapookashani, 1989).

13. Laird, *Missionaries*, 71.

14. Laird, *Missionaries*, 74.

15. For a longer discussion of the various debates over the parish school model, see R.D. Anderson, "Education and the State in Nineteenth Century Scotland," *The Economic History Review* 36, no. 4 (November 1983): 518–34.

16. Alexander Duff, born in Scotland in 1806, was a product of Scotland's elite educational system and soon became a renowned theologian and missionary of the Scottish Presbyterian Church. He was prompted to go to India after reading an article in the *Edinburgh Encyclopedia* while at university.

17. Gauri Viswanathan, *Masks of Conquest: Literary Study and British Rule in India* (Delhi: Oxford University Press, 1998).

18. Alexander Duff, *India and Indian Missions* (New Delhi: Swati Publications, 1988), 331.

19. Scottish educational tradition can be traced back to John Knox and the Calvinist reformation in the mid-seventeenth century that set up parish schools so that all Christians could be instructed in the elements of faith and reading the Bible. The 1696 Act remained the legal foundation of parish schools until 1872 (there was no new legislation until 1803). The parish school system demanded that each landowner of the parish appoint a schoolmaster and give him a schoolhouse and small salary (paid for by rate on landed property), and that parents pay a certain fee to bring a schoolmaster's wage up to a living wage. R.D. Anderson, *Education and the Scottish People, 1750–1918* (Oxford: Clarendon Press, 1995).

20. As Thomas Metcalf has argued, after the Mutiny, the colonial state receded from intervening in any way that might be considered hostile to native religions. Thus, many of the social reform projects of the first half of the nineteenth century were curtailed, and the colonial state took great pains to assure native elite that they were in no way trying to "Christianize" the country. Thomas Metcalf, *The Aftermath of Revolt: India, 1857–1870* (Princeton, N.J.: Princeton University Press, 1964).

21. *Sketch of the official career of the Hon'ble Ashley Eden : with an appendix containing the hon'ble Ashley Eden's evidence before the indigo commissission, the Treaty with Sikhim, and Sir Charles Wood's Despatch to the Government of India*. 1877. Calcutta: Kally Prosono Dey.

22. "Vernacular Education for Bengal," *Calcutta Review* 22, no. 44 (1854): 306.

23. *General Report on Public Instruction, 1868–69* (Calcutta: Baptist Mission Press, 1869), 49.

24. *General Report on Public Instruction, 1864–5* (Calcutta: Baptist Mission Press, 1865), 72.

25. Edward Storrow, Letter to the Directors of the London Missionary Society, October 18, 1854, London Missionary Society 1852–1857, N. India, Bengal, Incoming Correspondence, box no. 9.

26. *Reports of the Baptist Missionary Society, 1855–58* (London: Haddon Bros. and Co., 1855), 35.

27. In regard to the larger amount of money spent in the North West Provinces, one historian has pointed out, "[A] ryotwari [based on taxing the peasant directly] rather a zamindari system [in Bengal] of land tenure obtained in these provinces so that a larger number of peasants and bureaucrats were engaged in rendering and receiving land revenue. Therefore, the inspiration of Government efforts for schooling was also different." Sureshachandra Shulka, "Introduction," in Dibona, *One Teacher, One School*, xiv.

28. "Wood's Education Despatch," quoted in J.P. Naik and Syed Nurullah, *A History of Education in India* (Bombay: Macmillan & Co., 1951), 206.

29. *General Report on Public Instruction, 1863–64* (Calcutta: Baptist Mission Press, 1865), 58.

30. *General Report on Public Instruction in the Lower Provinces of the Bengal Presidency, 1856–57* (Calcutta: John Gray, 1857), 120–1.

31. Baboo Rajendra Lall Mitra, letter to the secretary of the government of Bengal, April 29, 1868, in *Correspondence Relative to the Expediency of Raising an Educational Cess in Bengal* (Simla, India: Government Central Press, 1870), 58.

32. Certain individuals, like Baboo Joykishen Mookerjee, suggested that government employees should bear the cost of educating the masses, since they also took advantage of the English-based system of schools in Calcutta and the *mofussil* towns. This was never seriously considered.

33. Thakurdas Chakrabarty, *Popular Education in Bengal* (Calcutta: Banders, Cones and Co., 1873), 11.

34. Reverend James Long is best known for his support of the publication of *Nil Darpan*, the play that dramatized the oppressive conditions and exploitation in the indigo plantations.

35. Reverend J. Long, "Letter to the Secretary of the Government of Bengal," *Correspondence Relative to the Expediency of Raising an Educational Cess in Bengal*, 10.

36. One of the most famous images in the nineteenth-century antislavery movement was that of a black man kneeling on one knee and beseeching his white audience, "Am I not a man and a brother?" The image was credited to an antislavery medallion designed by Josiah Wedgewood in 1787.

37. Rev. Lal Behari De, *Primary Education in Bengal: A Lecture Delivered at the Bethune Society* (Calcutta: Barham, Hill & Co., 1869), 27.

38. "Vernacular Education for Bengal."

2. A CURRICULUM FOR RELIGION

1. The few manuscript texts included the *Saraswati Bandana* ("Praise for Goddess Saraswati") or *Ganga Bandana* ("Praise for Ganga") and *Chanakya Slokas*. Initially, students wrote with a stick in the dirt, then they moved up to

writing on palm leaf (usually compound letters or vowel-consonant combinations) before the plantain leaf stage and finally the paper stage (although, by that point, many students had already left the *pathshala*). Kazi Shahidullah, *Pathshalas into Schools* (Calcutta: Firma KLM, 1987),, 17.

2. The history (and transformation) of the Calcutta School Book Society is detailed in Brian Hatcher, *Idioms of Improvement: Vidyasagar and Cultural Encounter in Bengal*. (Calcutta: Oxford University Press, 1996).

3. Sumit Sarkar, "Vidyasagar and Brahminical Society," in Sumit Sarkar, *Writing Social History* (Delhi: Oxford University Press, 1998); Asok Sen, *Vidyasagar and His Elusive Milestones* (Calcutta: Riddhi—India, 1977); and Sibaji Bandhopadhyay, *Gopal-Rakhal Dwandasamas: Uponibeshbad O Bangla Sishu-Sahitya* (Kolkata: Papyrus, 2001).

4. There was less consensus among Muslim educators, but by the late nineteenth century, both the Department of Public Instruction and many urban Muslim leaders were behind primary-level vernacular schooling. See chapter 6.

5. "This literary form of prose became the standard and the growth of the printing press established the grammar and orthography: the latter the work of Sanskritists ignorant of the history and phonetic tendencies of the language, threw overboard the meager traditions of spelling for the *tadbhava* words that obtained in Middle language." In Suniti Kumar Chaterji, *The Origin and Development of the Bengali Language* (Calcutta: Calcutta University Press, 1926), 134.

6. John Murdoch, *Education as a Missionary Agent in India* (Madras: Forster Press, 1872), 23, emphasis in original.

7. J.M. Goldstrom, "The Content of Education and the Socialization of the Working-Class Child 1830–1860," in *Popular Education and Socialization in the Nineteenth Century*, ed. Phillip McCann (London: Methuen and Co. Ltd., 1977), 94.

8. "Any other set of readers was discouraged or forbidden, thus the only additional printed material to find its way into the classroom would be Bibles, religious tracts and moralizing tales." In Goldstrom, "The Content of Education," 94.

9. These less sectarian books were based on the "set of non-denomination readers financed by the English government ... in Ireland by Irish Commissioners ... because they were both cheap and completely non-sectarian they found a ready market in English schools." In ibid., 94.

10. Michael A. Laird, *Missionaries and Education in Bengal, 1793–1897* (Oxford: Clarendon Press, 1972), 14.

11. Christian publishers in Bengal included the Bible Translation Society, Baptist Missionary Society, Baptist Missionary Press, Bengal Sunday School Union, Society for the Propagation for Christian Knowledge, Calcutta Tract and Book Society, Christian Literature Society, and Christian Endeavor Union. For a complete list, see James Long, *A Descriptive and Classified Catalogue of Bengali Christian Literature Published up to 1917* (Calcutta: Council of Missions, 1918).

12. Hatcher, *Idioms of Improvement*, 169.

13. See Anindita Ghosh, *Power in Print: Popular Publishing and the Politics of Language and Culture in a Colonial Society* (New Delhi: Oxford University Press, 2006), 132, table 3.

14. *General Report on Public Instruction, 1871–72* (Calcutta: Bengal Military Orphan Press, 1872), 81.

15. In the readers aimed at upper-caste girls, the debt to Vidyasagar was explicitly acknowledged. For example, in the introductions to both *Bala Bodh* and *Balika Bodhika*, the authors suggest that parents use the readers as supplements to Vidyasagar's hugely popular primer, *Barnaparichoy*.

16. *Bala Bodh* (Dhaka: Sri Mathlabkra Printers, 1874), preface.

17. The Normal Seminary trained Christian teachers in modern pedagogic method, mainly preparing them for positions in Scottish parish and missionary schools. Stow's school was the foremost institution for teacher training and pedagogic methods in nineteenth-century Britain.

18. John Murdoch, quoted in Henry Morris, *The Life of John Murdoch: The Literary Evangelist of India* (London: Christian Literature Society for India, 1906), 38.

19. James Brown, *The Missionary Record of the United Presbyterian Church* (Edinburgh: Crawford and M'Cabe Printers, 1881), 265.

20. This proved to be the common pattern, and the majority of vernacular schoolbooks and teacher-training manuals were written by individuals who had connections to the Department of Public Instruction.

21. "Literary Bengali of prose, during the greater part of the 19th century, was thus a doubly artificial language; and, with its form belonging to Middle Bengali and its vocabulary highly Sanskritised, it could only be compared to a 'Modern English' with a Chaucerian grammar and a super-Johnsonian vocabulary, if such a thing could be conceived." Suniti Kumar Chatterji, *The Origin and Development of the Bengali Language* (London: Allen and Unwin, 1972), 134.

22. Suniti Kumar Chatterji takes Vidyasagar and his fellow pandits to task for their orthography. He argues that such "Sanskritists" were ignorant of the history of the Bengali language and instead "standardized" the orthography by arbitrarily applying rules of Sanskrit to non-Sanskrit words, the *tatbhava* words. Chatterji, 140.

23. The problems with Bengali orthography are the suppression of the inherent vowel is not always indicated, several of the vowel combinations have double forms, and there is too great a variety of compound letters. Murdoch uses English to demonstrate the orthographic problem. See John Murdoch, *Letter to Babu Ishwar Chandra Bidyasagar on Bengali Typography* (1865), 4.

24. Murdoch, *Letter*, 3.

25. Ibid., 7.

26. Ibid., 4. Murdoch also felt that simplifying the alphabet would lead to cheaper books since much smaller fonts could be cut.

27. *Bengali Primer (Parts I and II): Barnamala* (Calcutta: Baptist Mission Press, 1872).

28. James Long, "Vernacular Education for Bengal," in Hatcher, *Idioms of Improvement*, 101.

29. Wesleyan Methodist Missionary Society, 1893 Report, Box 360, no. 126, Archive in School of Oriental and African Studies, London.

30. "The triumph of his [Vidyasagar's] chaste Bengali (the so-called sadhubhasa) closed off avenues of vernacularization that might have reached deeper into popular life. This issue remains vital even today, when it is recognized that to teach village children through the school-book literature of authors like Vidyasagar carries significant socio-economic implications." Hatcher, *Idioms of Improvement*, 17.

31. *Third Annual Report of the S. India Christian School Book Society, 1856* (Madras: LC Graves, 1857), 6.

32. John Murdoch, *Education as a Missionary Agent in India* (Madras: Forster Press, 1872), 16.

33. Murdoch, *Education as a Missionary Agent*, 28.

34. A.F. Lacroix, letter to London Missionary Society, January 1859, N. India—Bengal Incoming Correspondence 1858-92, box 10, Council for World Mission Archives, School of Oriental and African Studies, London.

35. For a list of published Bengali schoolbooks, see Reverend James Long, *Handbook of Bengal Missions in Connexion with the Church of England* (London: John Farquhar Shaw, 1848).

36. *Prachin Kahini* (The Old, Old Story) was a short, 15-page pamphlet that combined various Old and New Testament Stories. Murdoch, *Education as a Missionary Agent*, 4.

37. *Barnamala*, 9.

38. Reverend C. Bomwetch, *Nutan Barnamala* (Calcutta: Bengal Press, 1877), 11. One of the striking aspects of *Nutan Barnamala* is that it is filled with orphaned children, perhaps reflecting the native converts who came to Christianity through missionary orphanages and boarding schools.

39. "Reply of the Church Missionary Conference to the Pamphlet of Dr. Murdoch on the Reading Books Chiefly Used in Mission Schools in Bengal" (Calcutta: Baptist Mission Press, 1872), found in Reports and Papers, Calcutta Corresponding Committee of the CMS, CI 1/04/5/1, Church Mission Society Archives, Birmingham, UK.

40. The CVES Bengali School-book Series published several Christian schoolbooks, but circulation had declined to 246 (although 11,985 students attended mission schools). *6th Annual Report of the Christian Vernacular Education Society for India* (London: WM Watts, 1864).

41. Whenever Murdoch went to London, he "visited educational museums, and, after careful examination of the best school-books, prepared new editions of the series of reading books, which had already obtained an extensive circulation in India and Ceylon. The books were stereotyped—the first as far as I am aware ever subjected to this process for use in India." On his visits to Britain, Murdoch would go to the British Museum Library, pore over nearly 30,000 books, and make a list of 250 that were suitable for translation. Henry Morris, *The Life of John Murdoch: The Literary Evangelist of India* (London: Christian Literature Society for India, 1906), 118.

42. Murdoch, *Education as a Missionary Agent*, 1.

43. Simon Frith asserts that the common narrative of the replacement of a moral by a secular curriculum is misinterpreted. "There is counter evidence that the primary purpose of these [National] schools continued to be 'the greatest blessings, a sound religious education' and one of the effects of the lack of local patrons was, in fact, to increase the importance of the local clergy in the National schools." In Simon Frith, "Socialization and Rational School: Elementary Education in Leeds before 1870," in McCann, *Popular Education and Socialization*, 78.

44. Murdoch, *Education as a Missionary Agent*, 2.

45. "Reply of the Church," 23.

46. Dobhashi Bangla began appearing in a variety of printed materials in the late nineteenth century, but was rarely used in educational texts or language primers. Initially, it appeared in a variety of *nasihat namahs*, or Muslim religious manuals. For a description of various kinds of *dobhashi* literature, see Ghosh, *Power in Print*, 260; and Ahmed, *The Bengal Muslims*, 25.

3. AN OBJECT LESSON IN COLONIAL PEDAGOGY

1. Thomas Morrison and David Stow, "Oral Lessons on Common Things," in *Object Teaching and Oral Lessons on Social Science and Common Things*, ed. Henry Barnard (New York: F. C. Brownell, 1860), 46.

2. See E. L. McCallum, *Object Theory: How to Do Things with Fetishism* (Albany: State University of New York Press, 1999).

3. Kaushik Ghosh, "A Market for Aboriginality: Primitivism and Race Classification in the Indentured Labour Market of Colonial India," in *Subaltern Studies X*, ed. Gautam Bhadra (Delhi: Oxford University Press, 1999). Prathama Banerjee's recent book analyzes the emergence of new temporal forms and the notion of the primitive *adivasi* among upper-caste middle-class Bengalis. Prathama Banerjee, *Politics of Time: "Primitives" and History—Writing in a Colonial Society* (Delhi: Oxford University Press, 2006).

4. Object lesson theory does find its way into some of the work on imperial exhibitions and museums, but again the pedagogic origins of it are neglected. George Stocking, *Objects and Others: Essays on Museums and Material Culture* (Madison: University of Wisconsin Press, 1985); and David Jenkins "Object Lessons and Ethnographic Displays: Museum Exhibitions and the Making of American Anthropology," *Comparative Studies in Society and History* 36, no. 2 (1994): 242–70.

5. The British modifications to Pestalozzi's technique (making three-dimensional objects into two-dimensional images) also suggests another future of the object lesson: the development of the ethnographic museum and exhibition. Jenkins, "Object Lessons," 248.

6. Kate Sibler, the most prominent English biographer of Pestalozzi, argues that "How Gertrude Teaches Her Children" vacillates between idealist conceptions of self-activity of the human mind and the notion of life as organically ordered. Kate Sibler, *Pestalozzi: The Man and His Work* (New York: Schocken Books, 1973), 140.

7. Allen Richardson, *Literature, Education and Romanticism: Reading as Social Practice, 1780–1832* (Cambridge: Cambridge University Press, 1994).

8. Jacqueline Rose, "State and Language: Peter Pan as Written for the Child," in *Language, Gender and Childhood*, ed. Carolyn Steedman, Cathy Urwin, and Valerie Wakerdine (Boston: Routledge and Kegan Paul, 1985), 97.

9. Rose, "State and Language," 97–98.

10. Elizabeth Mayo, *Lessons on Objects, as Given to Children Between the Ages of Five and Eight, in a Pestalozzian School, At Cheam,, Surrey*, 3d ed. (London: R. B. Seeley and W. Burnside, 1832), 114.

11. J. Walker, *The Handy Book of Object Lessons from a Teacher's Note Book* (London: Jarrold & Sons, 1876), 41.

12. By the 1840s, it was clear that there were increasing numbers of schools for the middle classes that offered more practical education, but they were separate from the elementary and missionary schools for the working and lower classes. "The list of schools founded for the growing middle class market tells its own story of educational innovation. . . . Across the whole sector of education in Britain the census conducted in 1851 revealed that of the nation's 46,042 schools, 22,214 had been created since 1840." David McLean, *Education and Empire: Naval Tradition and England's Elite Schooling* (London: British Academic Press, 1991), 22.

13. It is worth noting, again, that unlike Pestalozzi's continental method, the Perkins used pictures of objects rather than the objects themselves. This seems to have been quite common in Britain (Stow also used object lesson cards). Reverend James Long, *Handbook of Bengal Missions in Connexion with the Church of England* (London: John Farquhar Shaw, 1848), 407.

14. Frances Brockway, "Dusky Darling's School, 1909," London Missionary Society, N. India Annual Reports, Box 4 (1907–1909).

15. My discussion of the place of objects in Christianity is heavily influenced by William Pietz's work. Pietz traces the development of "fetishism" from its earliest uses among Portuguese traders on the African coast to its popularity in religious studies and psychoanalysis. Arguing against any "universalist" understanding of fetishism, he sees the fetish emerging in the new cultural space created in the trade between Europe, West Africa, and mercantile capital. William Pietz, "The Problem of the Fetish, I," *Res* 9 (Spring 1985): 5–17; William Pietz, "The Problem of the Fetish, II" *Res* 13 (Spring 1987): 23–45; and William Pietz, "The Problem of the Fetish, IIIa" *Res* 16 (Autumn 1988): 105–23.

16. Pietz, "The Problem of the Fetish, I," 7.

17. In fact, Tomoko Masuzawa speculates that fetishism, as a "third category," helped to clarify the distinction between illegitimate and legitimate uses of material objects in religious practice. Tomoko Masuzawa, "The Ghost of Fetishism in the Nineteenth Century," *Comparative Studies in Society and History* 42, no. 2 (April 2000): 248. For an extended discussion of the relationship between fetishism and the notion of agentive speech within Christianity, see Webb Keane, "From Fetishism to Sincerity: On Agency, the Speaking Subject, and Historicity in the Context of Religious Conversion," *Comparative Studies in Society and History* 39, no. 4: 674–93.

18. Pietz suggests that African fetishism was putatively arbitrary and fanciful. In some ways, Pestalozzi's theory of *anschauung*, or sense perception, arising spontaneously and directly from the objects, seems to parallel this.

19. Richard Davis, in his book *Lives of Indian Images,* emphasizes the centrality of context in looking at objects, particularly religious objects. "Admittedly there are better and worse places to read, but generally location do not enter profoundly into the dynamic relationship established between the reader and the text during the moment of reading. The location of an object, by contrast, plays a constitutive role in the act of looking." In Richard Davis, *Lives of Indian Images* (Princeton, N.J.: Princeton University Press, 1999).

20. Ella N. Wood, *Object Lessons for Junior Work* (New York: Fleming H. Revell Company, 1897), 3–4.

21. *64th Annual Report of the Society for Promoting Female Education in the East* (London: Suter and Alexander, 1898), 15.

22. Miss Budden, "1901 Report to LMS Home Committee from Almora, North India," Reports 1898–1901, Box 2, Council for World Mission Archives, School of Oriental and African Studies, London.

23. Idolatry was consistently criticized by various Hindu reform movements. Both the Brahmo Samaj (from the 1830s) and the late-nineteenth-century Arya Samaj were highly critical of and eschewed idol worship. Similarly, in the early twentieth century Swami Vivekananda distanced himself from the mysticism of Ramakrishna and conceived of Vedanta philosophy in monistic and nonidolatrous terms.

24. I do not want to suggest that there weren't many festivals that were shared between Bengali Hindus and Muslims, but the evocation of a household altar to Lokhi is clearly reflecting Hindu religious practice. Bhudev Mukhopadhyay, *Sikhavidhyaka Pastava: An Introduction to the Art of Teaching* (Calcutta, 1856), 59.

25. In addition to Mukhopadhyay, other Bengali training manuals include Gopal Chunder Bandhyopadhyay, *Shiksha Pranali,* 3rd ed. (Calcutta, 1872); and Somnath Mukhopadhyay, *Shiksha Paddhati,* 3rd ed. (Dhaka, 1870).

26. Joel Schwartz, "Robert Chambers and Thomas Henry Huxley, Science Correspondents: The Popularization and Dissemination of Nineteenth Century Natural Science," *Journal of the History of Biology* 32 (1999): 344.

27. Robert Chambers and William Chambers, *Rudiments of Knowledge,* new ed. (Edinburgh: William and Robert Chambers, 1860), 6.

28. Iswar Chandra Vidyasagar, *Bodhodoy,* 33rd ed. (Calcutta: Sanskrit Press, 1868), 20.

29. Chambers and Chambers, *Rudiments of Knowledge,* 11.

30. Vidyasagar, *Bodhodoy,* 24.

31. Murdoch, *Hints on Education in India,* 6–7.

32. Akshay Kumar Dutta, *Charupath: Entertaining Lessons in Science and Literature, Part I* (Calcutta: New Sanskrit Press, 1878).

33. *Ratnashar* was clearly a popular object lesson schoolbook, since it had gone into at least eight editions by 1878.

34. Kamakhacharan Ghosh, *Ratnasar: First Part* (Calcutta, 1870), 7.

35. Stow, "Stow's Gallery Training Lessons," 46.

36. *General Report on Public Instruction in the Lower Provinces of Bengal, for 1905–06* (Calcutta: Bengal Secretariat Press, 1906), 23–24.

37. Charles Mayo had hoped to sponsor a few Swiss boys and girls as teachers in Pestalozzi's schools. He expected that these students, after their training, would come to England and teach the poor in the schools started by his organization. See Sibler, *Pestalozzi*, 302.

4. THE SCHOOLTEACHER AS MODERN FATHER

1. Bhudev Mukhopadhyay, *Sikhavidhyaka Pastava: An Introduction to the Art of Teaching* (Calcutta, 1856), 21.

2. The best account of competing masculinities in mid-nineteenth-century Britain is Catherine Hall's *White Male and Middle-Class: Explorations in Feminism and History* (Cambridge: Polity Press, 1992); for India, see Mrinalini Sinha, *Colonial Masculinities* (Manchester, UK: Manchester University Press, 1995); and Subho Basu and Sikata Banerjee, "The Quest for Manhood: Masculine Hinduism and Nation in Bengal," *Comparative Studies of South Asia, Africa and the Middle East* 26, no. 3 (2006): 476–90.

3. Stow's pedagogic ideas grew out of the evangelical conviction in the importance of pastoral guidance for developing moral character. He felt that the authoritarianism of the monitorial system spoke to the authoritarianism of the Established Church itself. Rather than encouraging individual thought (and individual relationships to God), the monitorial system set up a hierarchy that paralleled the religious hierarchy within the Established Church.

4. Ian Hunter, *Rethinking the School: Subjectivity, Bureaucracy, Criticism* (Sydney: Allen & Unwin Private Ltd, 1994), xxi.

5. Theorists of British pedagogy see Stow's "simultaneous method" as prefiguring the emergence of Foucault's pastoral state: the teacher (like the state) caring for and disciplining (through the inculcation of habits) his students (subjects). Ian Hunter describes Stow's evangelical-inflected theories as "a specific pedagogical technology, a special site of 'spiritual disciplines'—a particular practice of relating to and governing the self—embodied in the pastoral relation between teacher and student . . . a distinctive articulation of surveillance and self-examination, obedience and self-regulation." In Hunter, *Rethinking the School*, xxi.

6. Reverend Edward Garbett, *Reprint of Speech to the Home and Colonial School Society, 1851* (London: Home and Colonial School Society, 1881), 5. As early as 1836, the Home and Colonial Society broke with the monitorial system for Stow's simultaneous method. In contrast, as late as 1843, the British and Foreign School Society continued to rely on training monitors for Bell's system. Asher Tropp, *The School Teachers: The Growth of the Teaching Profession in England and Wales from 1800 to the Present* (London: William Heinemann Ltd., 1957), 16.

7. In addition to Hunter's *Rethinking the School*, see James Donald, *Sentimental Education* (London: Verso, 1992).

8. "Report of Santipore Training Institution by S. Hassel and Rev. J. Long," Calcutta Corresponding Committee Reports and Papers, November 1855, 1/079/431, Church Missionary Society Archive, Birmingham, UK.

9. The full certification at the missionary teacher colleges was usually five years, but it was recognized that students who needed to leave earlier could easily find work (though on a lower scale) in the mission schools. The boys entering had to be at least 12 years old, and were all trained together. Eventually the mission decided that teachers and theologians should be taught separately from the divinity students, who formed a "distinct class" and should receive better treatment and more advanced training. Reverend C. Bomwetch, Suggestions on Santipore Training College, 1855, Calcutta, Corresponding Committee, 1/079/514-22. Church Missionary Society Archives, Birmingham, UK.

10. Although missionaries trained fewer male teachers, considering the small number of government institutions the mission effort was still significant. In 1897, there were nine missionary schools with at least 300 students.

11. The Bengali title of Gmelin's book is *Adhapan Padhathi Bangla Shishookdigayr Babobhartha*. Frederic Gmelin, *A Manual of Education for the Use of Vernacular Teachers* (Bowanipore: BM Bose Publishers, 1872).

12. Gmelin, *A Manual of Education,* 237. Like the rest of the book, this section is almost a direct translation of Murdoch's *Hints on Education*. An important difference, however, is that Murdoch refers to the "people of this country" as "heathen" and their customs as "barbarous." Gmelin's translation of Murdoch's text is far more sympathetic to his audience of native Christian teachers, their families, and "their" society. John Murdoch, *The Indian Teacher's Manual: With Hints on the Management of Vernacular Schools* (Madras: Christian Vernacular Education Society, 1885).

13. Nonetheless, it is worth noting that Lal Behari De left European institutions in part to escape the condescension and humiliation of serving under less qualified European educators.

14. Mr. Geidt Burdwan, letter regarding Santipore Training College, September 16, 1854, Calcutta Corresponding Committee, 1/079/514-22. Church Missionary Society Archives, Birmingham, UK.

15. Rev. Schur, Letter regarding Santipore Training College, July 1, 1854, Calcutta Corresponding Committee, 1/079/514-22. Church Missionary Society Archives, Birmingham, UK.

16. Rev. Schur, Letter regarding Santipore Training College, July 1, 1854, Calcutta Corresponding Committee, 1/079/514-22. Church Missionary Society Archives, Birmingham, UK

17. The now classic take on Macaulay's "Minute" is Homi Bhabha's trenchant essay on the "mimic men" of colonial discourse. Homi Bhabha, "Of Mimicry and Man: The Ambivalence of Colonial Discourse," in Homi Bhabha, *The Location of Culture* (London: Routledge, 1990), 121–31.

18. Historians note a shift in the 1870s toward a more conservative social discourse and the rise of an aggressively masculine Hindu identity among Bengali upper-caste men. This was in part a response to the colonial government's increasing racism and derision of educated native men as overly "effeminate." The imperial dialectic of the "manly Englishman" and the "effeminate babu" mirrored the self-perception of upper-caste men, who saw the daily humiliation and alienation of colonial society as emasculating the (upper-caste) Hindu male

body. In late-nineteenth-century Bengal, for instance, the notion of *chakri* referred not only to low-level clerical work but also more generally to the degradation faced by upper-caste men who were forced to move to urban areas and take up the "discipline of work regulated by clock time." This particular masculine degradation is detailed by Sumit Sarkar in "Kaliyuga, Chakri and Bhakti," in Sumit Sarkar, *Writing Social History* (Delhi: Oxford University Press, 1997), 309. Sumit Sarkar and Partha Chatterjee have also discussed how alongside this "manly" Hindu identity was a competing ideal of the highly feminized religious figure Ramkrishna Parahamsa. Ashish Nandy also examines competing models of Kshatriya manliness and Gandhian androgyny in various nationalist movements. See Ashish Nandy, *The Intimate Enemy: Loss and Recovery of Self under Colonialism* (Delhi: Oxford University Press, 1983).

19. *General Report on Public Instruction, 1870–71* (Calcutta: Bengal Military Orphan Press, 1871), 142.

20. "Report of the Reverend J. Long on the Normal School at Hooghly," in *General Report on Public Instruction in the Lower Provinces of the Bengal Presidency, 1856–7* (Calcutta: John Gray, 1857), app. A, 159.

21. Most who write on Bhudev Mukhopadhyay focus on his historical writings, especially his utopian history, *Svapnalabdha Bharatbarser Itihas* (*The History of India as Revealed in a Dream*). He is seen as "the most brilliant defender of 'orthodox' tradition," against the reformist zeal of some of his contemporaries. See Partha Chatterjee, "A Religion of Urban Domesticity," in *Subaltern Studies VII: Writings on South Asian History and Society,* ed. Partha Chatterjee and Gyanendra Pandey (Delhi: Oxford University Press, 1993), 46. Tapan Ray Chaudhuri suggests that Mukhopadhyay was most at home "in the social world of the orthodox Bengali Brahmin." Ray Chaudhuri is uninterested in Bhudev's educational writing, merely commenting that he "noted with regret the lack of affection between fathers and sons, which in his view, was a characteristic failing of Indian society." Tapan Ray Chaudhuri, *Europe Reconsidered: Perceptions of the West in Nineteenth-Century Bengal* (Delhi: Oxford University Press, 1988), 27. But Mukhopadhyay was also committed to self-examination and critique in the hopes of rectifying the aspects of native society that allowed it to be colonized in the first place. Although, as Sudipta Kaviraj argues, it was beyond Mukhopadhyay's historical horizon to imagine removing the British (that is, to have a truly "nationalist" vision), his writing and his educational work speak to his desire to bring together in a "rational" manner the best parts of both native and British science. See Sudipta Kaviraj, *The Unhappy Consciousness* (New York: Oxford University Press, 1995).

22. *General Report on Public Instruction, 1882–1883* (Calcutta: Bengal Military Orphan Press, 1883), 84.

23. Mukhopadhyay, *Shikha Vidyak Prastav,* 32.

24. Ibid., 16.

25. Gopal Chunder Bandhopadhyay, *Shikha Pranali,* 3rd ed. (Calcutta: 1872), .3.

26. For instance, in the Dhaka Normal Schools, there was not a single Muslim student and very few lower-caste students.

27. Gopal Chunder Bandhopadhyay, *Shikha Pranali,* 3rd ed. (Calcutta: 1872).

28. Bandhopadhyay, *Shikha Pranali,* 11.

29. The Santhals are an *adivasi* group who speak a language of the Munda family. They live in Chota Nagpur and Bengal, Orissa, and Bihar and presently number over 4 million individuals. They are historically known for a series of rebellions against the colonial presence, the most important of which was the 1855 Santhali Rebellion, which targeted merchants and missionaries. Santhals lived, for the most part, on the fringes of caste society and the colonial economy.

30. The American Baptist Mission had a normal school in Bhimpur, and the British Baptist Mission had one in the Santhal Pargannahs. Wesleyan Mission had a boarding institution for Santhals in Bankura.

31. *General Report on Public Instruction, 1871-72* (Calcutta: Bengal Military Orphan Press, 1872), app. A, 37-38.

32. *General Report on Public Instruction, 1874-75* (Calcutta: Bengal Secretariat Press, 1875), 109.

33. *General Report on Public Instruction, 1874-75,* 109.

34. *Report of the Baptist Missionary Society,* no. 82 (London: Haddon Bros., and Co., 1884), 218.

35. *Report of the Baptist Missionary Society,* no. 82, 218.

36. *General Report on Public Instruction, 1876-77* (Calcutta: Bengal Secretariat Press, 1877).

37. The CMS decided that it would move the school to Krishnagur, under the able leadership of Reverend Gmelin, who not only began offering English but also turned the institution into a "first grade" normal school funded by the Department of Public Instruction in 1882. As Gmelin insisted, "only those boys who have had a careful preparation before hand, and who have shown by good behavior and diligence that they may turn out good teachers, should be received into the Institution." Reverend Gmelin, Plan for CMS Normal Training School at Krishnagar, 1862, Calcutta Corresponding Committee, CI 1/0117/12. Church Missionary Society Archives, Birmingham, UK.

38. By the early twentieth century, the colonial government abandoned any pretense of funding the expansion or improvement of teaching for primary schools. Instead, by 1897, the only normal schools still funded by the Department of Public Instruction were higher-grade institutions that offered English and attracted upper-level *pandits* (precisely what Croft and Mukhopadhyay had tried to resist). Of the 20 lower-grade schools that had been established in the 1870s, only three remained. *General Report on Public Instruction, 1897-98* (Calcutta: Bengal Secretariat Press, 1877), 80.

39. Bhudev Mukhopadhyay, *Bhūdeba-racanāsambhāra* (Calcutta: Mitra & Ghosh, 1962), 483.

40. Mukhopadhyay, *Bhūdeba-racanāsambhāra,* 484.

41. Pradip Kumar Bose, "Sons of the Nation," in *Texts of Power,* ed. Partha Chatterjee (Minneapolis: University of Minnesota Press, 1995), 118.

42. Bose comments that "Satischandra completely rejects the school or any other educative institution as the proper site of character formation. The only

reference in the whole text to the school appears where he says that 'irresponsible cane-and-wage-dependent teachers' cannot fulfill this task nor should parents be content sending their children to schools." Bose, "Sons of the Nation," 140.

43. Pratapchandra Majumdar, *Stricaritra,* quoted in Bose, "Sons of the Nation," 25.

5. TEACHING GENDER IN THE COLONY

1. Mary Carpenter, *Suggestions on Prison Discipline and Female Education in India* (London: Longman's and Co., 1866), 12–13.

2. In England, there was a feminization of the teaching profession at the primary level. In 1870, there were 99 female teachers for every 100 male teachers. But by 1890, there were 207 female teachers for every 100 male teachers. Michael Apple, *Teachers and Texts: A Political Economy of Class and Gender Relations* (New York: Routledge & Kegan Paul, 1986), 60.

3. Mary Carpenter, *Six Months in India* (London: Longmans, Green & Co., 1868), 185–186.

4. Zenana instruction consisted of private tutorials by missionaries, European governesses, and native Christians in the inner quarters of upper-caste Hindu and upper-class Muslim homes for women observing *pardah.*

5. Carpenter submitted a proposal to the colonial government in 1867 to open a normal school in Calcutta. It was taken up by the Brahmo Samaj and eventually established by the Department of Public Instruction but closed in 1872.

6. While there exists considerable debate about the precise relationship between women's education (and the "woman question" more generally) and nationalism in late-nineteenth-century Bengal, there is a consensus that efforts to reform the *bhadramahila* were connected to the transformation of the "nation." See Sonia Amin, *The World of Muslim Women in Bengal* (New York: EJ Brill, 1996); Himani Bannerji, *Inventing Subjects* (New Delhi: Tulika, 2001); Dipesh Chakrabarty, *Provincializing Europe: Postcolonial Thought and Historical Difference* (Princeton, N.J.: Princeton University Press, 2000); Partha Chatterjee, *The Nation and Its Fragments: Colonial and Postcolonial Histories* (Princeton, N.J.: Princeton University Press, 1993); Geraldine Forbes, *Women in Modern India* (Cambridge: Cambridge University Press, 1996); Mahua Sarkar, *Visible Histories, Disappearing Women: Producing Muslim Womanhood in Late Colonial Bengal* (Durham: Duke University Press, 2008); and Tanika Sarkar, *Hindu Wife, Hindu Nation* (London: Hurst, 2001).

7. Partha Chatterjee, "The Nationalist Resolution of the Women's Question," in *Recasting Women,* ed. Kumkum Sangari and Sudesh Vaid (New Brunswick, N.J.: Rutgers University Press, 1990), 247.

8. Even the most progressive upper-caste Bengalis, the Brahmos, were largely unwilling to have their educated daughters or wives work as teachers. There were a few attempts in the 1870s, including the normal school attached to Bethune College, the Chandra Nath Female Normal School in Rajshashi, and Keshub Chunder Sen's Mirzapore Normal School. By 1897, the only non-Christian normal school was the Hindu Boarding and Training School for widows, which

had ten students. See *General Report on Public Instruction in Bengal, 1897–98* (Calcutta: Bengal Secretariat Press, 1898), 76.

9. I have chosen to use the term *"Bairagi,"* usually used to refer to mendicant Vaishnava men, rather than *"Boshtomi,"* the term used for women, to retain consistency. In most of the government sources, the trainees are referred to as *"Bairagi* women," not *Boshtomi*.

10. It is difficult to say how many native women trained as teachers and even more difficult to trace their histories after leaving school. Many missionary schools that trained teachers were never counted in the Department of Public Instruction records, and mission organizations rarely kept detailed or systematic records of the numbers of students and schools they supported. This is even more true when trying to trace where, when, and how students were placed. This has meant that in this chapter, I have had to rely on correspondence about students and anecdotal stories from mission and governmental sources to piece together the histories of native Christian women. For a longer discussion of the archival challenges of doing women's history, see Antoinette Burton, *Dwelling in the Archive: Women Writing House, Home and History in Late Colonial India* (New York: Oxford University Press, 2003).

11. When *Bairagi* and native Christian women figure in historical accounts, they are often relegated to merely being the "other" against which the modernizing *bhadramahila* is defined (and defines herself). Even historians like Sumanta Banerjee, who is interested in the lives of non-elite women, see Vaishnavite women primarily as examples of "folk" or "popular" culture that were incrementally purged from *bhadra* society. See Sumanta Banerjee, "Marginalization of Women's Popular Culture in Nineteenth Century Bengal," in Sangari and Vaid, *Recasting Women*, 127–79.

12. Maina Singh Chawal and Michelle Maskiell have detailed the complexity (for a later period and in other parts of North India) of colonial institutions for higher education. But the institutions they focused on, particularly Kinnaird College, belonged to a much later period and were primarily aimed toward wealthier Christian, Hindu, and Muslim families. Padma Anagol's essay on Indian Christians focused primarily on such high-caste Christian converts as Pandita Ramabia, Krupabai Satthianadhan, and Soonderbai Powar. See Maina Singh Chawal, *Gender, Religion and "Heathen" Land* (New York: Garland, 2000); Michelle Maskiell, *Women between Cultures: The Lives of Kinnarid College Alumnae in British India* (Syracuse, N.Y.: Maxwell School of Citizenship and Public Affairs, 1984); and Padmna Anagol, "Indian Christian Women and Indigenous Feminism, 1850–1920," in *Gender and Imperialism*, ed. Clare Midgley (Manchester, UK: Manchester University Press, 1998). Apart from missionary work, an important exception to the dominance of upper-caste education is the efforts of Jotirao Phule, the nineteenth-century Maharashtran social reformer, and his wife, Savitribai. In fact, when Phule opened his school for low-caste girls and women in Pune in 1848, he had difficulty locating women teachers, and Savitrabai became the first woman instructor at the school. See Rosalind O'Hanlon, *Caste, Conflict and Ideology: Mahatma Jotirao Phule and Low Caste Protest in Nineteenth-Century Western India* (Cambridge: Cambridge University Press, 1985), 118.

13. *General Report on Public Instruction in Bengal, 1859–1860* (Calcutta: Bengal Military Orphan Press, 1861), 20.

14. As the school inspector for Jessore noticed, "[I]n many circles there are girls who attend the schools along with their brothers and cousins. Indeed I have found by experience that female education in this shape seems never to be objected to, while education in schools professed for girls has invariably to contend with some prejudice more or less strong." See *General Report on Public Instruction in Bengal, 1871* (Calcutta: Bengal Military Orphan Press, 1872), 20.

15. *Bala Bodh* (Dacca: Srimathlabkra Printers, 1868), 5.

16. See Syed Nurullah and J.P. Naik, *A History of Education in India* (Bombay: Macmillan & Co., 1951), 170.

17. *General Report on Public Instruction in Bengal, 1883–1884* (Calcutta: Bengal Military Orphan Press, 1885), 123.

18. Forbes, *Women in Modern India*, 44.

19. In 1867, Bhudev Mukhopadhyay, the eminent reformer and school inspector, suggested that *pathshala gurus* be paid for every four girls they taught. See *General Report on Public Instruction in Bengal, 1867–88* (Calcutta: Bengal Military Orphan Press, 1888), 48.

20. Forty-one thousand girls attended single-sex schools, while 37,000 girls attended boys' schools. Another significant distinction is between "aided" and "unaided" schools, the aid referring to government funding. Mixed primary schools were almost never aided, while single-sex girls' schools were given nominal support by the Bengal Department of Public Instruction. See *General Report on Public Instruction in Bengal, 1884–1885* (Calcutta: Bengal Military Orphan Press, 1885), 93.

21. By the early twentieth century, there was a convergence of evangelical and more orthodox Hindu views on girls' education. Gopal Mukhopadhyay argues that the revival of orthodox Hinduism (particularly after the controversies over the 1892 Age of Consent bill) led to the removal of girls from mixed and single-sex schools in various parts of Bengal. See Gopal Mukhopadhyay, *Mass Education in Bengal, 1882–1914* (Calcutta: National Publishers, 1984), 117.

22. *General Report on Public Instruction in Bengal, 1905–1906* (Calcutta: Bengal Military Orphan Press, 1906), 33–34.

23. Harishchandra Sharma Kavivarta, *Barnabodhini* (Calcutta: Girish-Bidhratna, 1868), 3.

24. Tanika Sarkar, *Words to Win: The Making of Amar Jiban, a Modern Autobiography* (New Delhi: Kali for Women, 1999), 62–63.

25. "The assertion of Brahmanical dominance in a religious movement which was rooted in mysticism, and which was anti-caste and anti-intellectual, inevitably led to the growth of deviant orders." In Ramakanta Chakravarti, *Vaishnavism in Bengal, 1486–1900* (Calcutta: Sanscrit Pustak Bhandar, 1985), 324.

26. *General Report on Public Instruction in Bengal, 1863–64* (Calcutta: Bengal Military Orphan Press, 1864), 86.

27. Martin reported that there was a *Bairagi* woman teaching in a village school for girls (for Rs. 8 and food) near Dhaka and also mentioned that a local *zemindar* had written him about the employment of a *Bairagi* woman as a teacher in his household. See *General Report on Public Instruction in Bengal,*

1863–64, 364. Sumanta Banerjee also discusses *Bairagi* women instructors in "Women's Popular Culture," in Sangari and Vaid, *Recasting Women*, 135.

28. *General Report on Public Instruction in Bengal, 1863–64*, 86.

29. There are various suggestions that Vaishnava nuns and mendicants were recruited from "unchaste widows of the lower classes"; see Chakravarti, *Vaishnavism in Bengal*, 332. Reverend Lal Behari De, a Presbyterian minister and scholar, describes in his novel *Govinda Samanta* the ways in which Aduri, a young widow, was "seduced" by the Vaishnavas; see Lal Behari De, *Govinda Samanta* (Calcutta: Editions Indian, 1969), 159.

30. The curriculum at the school was "Literature, Chaurapat Part I; Kobeitaboly Part II (poetry); Composition: short essays on objects. Each mistress is likewise required to bring to school every Monday a short diary of the past week. Dictation from the books they study; grammar, Sundhee as in Beeakorna Probesh; Arithmetic: 4 simple and 3 compound rules, mental arithmetic, the tables; History:History of Bengal II; Geography: Asia with a particular account of India, map-drawing; Needlework." See R. L. Martin to Department of Public Instruction, in *General Proceedings: Education*, August 1864 (Calcutta: Bengal Secretariat Press, 1865), 8.

31. Usha Chakrabarty has consistently cited Vaishnavite women as the main source of social and sexual "delinquency" in colonial Bengali society (she has argued that they made up the majority of prostitutes, beggars, and thieves). Usha Chakrabarty, *Condition of Bengali Women around the Second Half of the Nineteenth Century* (Calcutta: Sr Harlal, 1963).

32. Somaprakash, c. 1866 (Paush 3, B.S. 1273), quoted in Banerjee, "Women's Popular Culture," in Sangari and Vaid, *Recasting Women*, 154.

33. There is an interesting parallel to this debate in Tamil Nadu over the inclusion of *teyvadiyals* (temple dancers) in girls' schools. Sita Anantha Raman, *Getting Girls to School: Social Reform in the Tamil Districts 1870–1930* (Calcutta: Stree, 1996), 35.

34. "Around 1867–68, the Faridpur school had employed another well-known woman teacher, Bhagabati Debi, trained by the teachers' training (Normal) school at Dacca, at the considerable salary of Rs. 20 a month." Sarkar, *Words to Win*, 68.

35. *General Proceedings: Education*, March 1873 (Calcutta: Bengal Secretariat Press, 1874), file 34-1.

36. H. H. Risley, *Tribes and Castes of Bengal* (Calcutta: Bengal Secretariat Press, 1892), 344.

37. Manna Manorama. "The Kharaday's Girls' Missionary School of Another Era," *Nagaropantha* (January 2, 1991): 42.

38. Reverend (Dr.) Murray Mitchell to H. Luttman-Johnson, private secretary to Lieutenant Governor Bengal, in *General Proceedings: Education*, March 1872 (Calcutta: Bengal Secretariat Press, 1873), file 154.

39. In fact, a part of the "Indianization" of Christianity involved the adaption of *bhakti* forms of devotion and worship. Pandita Ramabai, for instance, used the *kirtan* to convey the message of Christianity. Padma Anagol, "Indian Christian women and indigenous feminism, c. 1850 -c. 1920," in *Gender and Imperialism*, ed. Clare Midgley (Manchester: Manchester University Press, 1998), 97.

40. There is an extensive historiography on European women teachers and nurses in colonial India. These include Nupur Chaudhuri and Margaret Strobel, eds., *Western Women and Imperialism* (Bloomington: Indian University Press, 1992); Mary Taylor Huber and Nancy Lutkehaus, eds., *Gendered Missions: Women and Men in Missionary Discourse and Practice* (Ann Arbor: University of Michigan Press, 1999); Geraldine Forbes, "In Search of the 'Pure Heathen': Missionary Women in Nineteenth Century India," *Economic and Political Weekly* 21, no. 17 (1986): ws2–ws8; and Antoinette Burton, *Burdens of History: British Feminists, Indian Women, and Imperial Culture, 1865–1915* (Chapel Hill: University of North Carolina Press, 1994).

41. Indrani Chatterjee, "Colouring Subalternity: Slaves, Concubines and Social Orphans in Early Colonial India," in *Subaltern Studies X*, ed. Gautam Bhadra, Gyan Prakash, and Susie Tharu (Delhi: Oxford University Press, 1999), 49–97.

42. Michael A. Laird, *Missionaries and Education in Bengal, 1793–1897* (Oxford: Clarendon Press, 1972), 140.

43. Mary Weitbrecht, *Letters from a Missionary's Wife Abroad to a Friend in England* (London: James Nisbet & Co., 1843), 134.

44. *News of Female Missions in Connexion with the Church of Scotland*, no. 9 (April 1861): 396–97.

45. Mr. Johnson, Calcutta Committee, 1 June 1882, Box 13: Incoming Correspondence (Bengal) 1877–80, Collection of the Wesleyan Methodist Missionary Society, School of Oriental and African Studies Archives and Manuscripts, London.

46. *Baptist Missionary Herald*, May 1866, 338.

47. *Baptist Missionary Herald*, May 1866, 308.

48. Ladies' Association, *Report of the Ladies' Association, for the Support of the Zenana Work and Bible Women in India* (London: Yates and Alexander, 1890), 25.

49. *News of Female Missions in Connexion with the Church of Scotland*, no. 3 (October 1859): 134.

50. Baptist Missionary Society, *Report of the Baptist Missionary Society* (London: Haddon Bros., & Co., 1881), 68, emphasis mine.

51. Indian Female Normal School, *Indian Female Normal School, 12th Annual Report* (London: Suter and Alexander, 1864), 5.

52. *News of Female Missions*, no. 10 (July 1861), 421.

53. Ladies' Association, *Report of the Ladies Association for the Support of the Zenana Work and Bible Women in India* (London: Yates and Alexander, 1882), 15. The Calcutta Normal School functioned as a normal school before being turned into a teachers' home and normal school in 1881.

54. *News of Female Missions in Connexion with the Church of Scotland*, no. 4 (October 1863): 168.

55. Baptist Missionary Society, *Report of the Baptist Missionary Society* (London: Haddon Bros. & Co., 1919), 33.

56. *Report on the Progress of Female Education in the Presidency and Burdwan Divisions* (Calcutta: Bengal Secretariat Book Depot, 1919), 13.

57. *India's Women: The Magazine of the Church of England Zenana Missionary Society* (London: James Nisbet & Co., 1881), 23.

58. *General Report on Public Instruction in Bengal, 1897–98* (Calcutta: Bengal Military Orphan Press, 1898), 76.

59. In spite of her caste status, rules of pollution and purity kept the widow teacher on the fringes of respectable Hindu society, even as she was called upon to reproduce it. Nita Kumar has a wonderful essay on the ambiguous position of widow teachers within nationalism. Nita Kumar, "Oranges Are for the Girls," in *Women as Subjects,* ed. Nita Kumar (Charlottesville: University Press of Virginia, 1994).

6. MISSION SCHOOLS AND QUR'AN SCHOOLS

1. Abdul Karim, *Muhammadan Education in Bengal* (Calcutta: Metcalfe Press, 1900), 23.

2. Bernard Cohn points out how this theory was buttressed by the new demographic information provided by the census to colonial administrators. "Questions were being raised about the balance between Hindus and Muslims in the public services, about whether certain castes or 'races' were monopolizing access to new educational opportunities, and a political theory was beginning to emerge about the conspiracy which certain castes were organizing to supplant British rule." In Bernard Cohn, "The Census and Objectification in South Asia," in Bernard Cohn, *An Anthropologist among Historians* (Delhi: Oxford University Press, 1987), 243.

3. Sanjay Seth argues that the notion of the "backward" Muslim was produced by state census practices through the "cross-tabulation" of statistics on religious identity and levels of education. See Sanjay Seth, *Subject Lessons: Western Education of Colonial India* (Durham, N.C.: Duke University Press, 2007).

4. Faisal Devji suggests that we might understand nineteenth-century Indian *ashraf* attitudes as constituting something he calls "an apologetic modernity." See Faisal Devji, "Apologetic Modernity," *Modern Intellectual History* 4, no. 1 (2007): 61–76.

5. My focus is on primary schooling, but for a discussion of the colonial reform of *madrassah* education, see Muhammad Qasim Zaman, *The Ulama in Contemporary Islam: Custodians of Change* (Princeton, N.J.: Princeton University Press, 2002).

6. For a longer discussion of Hunter's text, see Peter Hardy, *The Muslims of British India* (Cambridge: Cambridge University Press, 1972); and Francis Robinson, *Separatism among Indian Muslims* (Cambridge: Cambridge University Press, 1974). For a discussion of the Wahhabi trials, see Muin-ud-Din Ahmad Khan, ed., *Selections from Bengal Government Records on Wahhabi Trials (1863–1870)* (Dacca: Asiatic Society of Pakistan, 1961). In part, the notion of a "conspiracy" was related to the assumption that the various kinds of anticolonial movements in the subcontinent were all connected. Thus, calling the movement in Bengal "Wahhabi" assumed its connection to the Wahhabi movements in other parts of the Muslim world.

7. William Hunter, *The Indian Musalmans: Are They Bound in Conscience to Rebel against the Queen?* (London: Trubner and Company, 1871), 3.

8. Hunter, *The Indian Musalmans*, 190–91.

9. Ibid., 164.

10. In fact, Hunter declared in a speech delivered a speech to the Royal Society of Arts his "conviction that English missionary enterprise is the highest modern expression of the world-wide national life of our race. I regard it as the spiritual complement of England's instinct for colonial and imperial rule." In "Sir William W. Hunter on the Religions of India," *The Mission Field* (April 1888): 130–40. Quoted in Andrew Porter, *Religion versus Empire: British Protestant Missionary and Overseas Expansion, 1700–1914* (Manchester, UK: Manchester University Press, 2004), 284.

11. This tendency was largely the result, as Ashok Sen notes, of British imperial policy that encouraged *bhadralok* educators to fund their own schools to ensure "the only means of living and respectability available to them." See Asok Sen, *Vidyasagar and His Elusive Milestones* (Calcutta: Riddhi—India, 1977), 41.

12. Hunter, *The Indian Musalmans*, 483

13. Ibid., 165.

14. *General Report on Public Instruction, 1871–72* (Calcutta: Bengal Secretariat Press, 1872).

15. *Correspondence on the Subject of the Education of the Muhammadan Community in British India and Their Employment in Public Service Generally* (Calcutta: Superintendent of Government Printers, 1886).

16. "Proposals of the Education Commission Regarding Muhammadan Education, 1883," in *Correspondence*, 359.

17. "Home Dept. Resolution on Muhammadan Resolution, July 15, 1884," in *Correspondence*, 384.

18. For the broader context of this debate, see Ayesha Jalal, *Self and Sovereignty: Individual and Community in South Asian Islam since 1850* (London: Routledge, 2000).

19. "Home Dept. Resolution," in *Correspondence*, 384.

20. "Proposals," in *Correspondence*, 360.

21. Ibid., emphasis added.

22. Sanjay Seth, *Subject Lessons*, 144.

23. "Home Dept. Resolution, July 15, 1884," in *Correspondence*, 381.

24. Karim, *Muhammadan Education*, 29.

25. Ibid., 39.

26. Ibid., 30.

27. Zaman, *The Ulama in Contemporary Islam*, 7.

28. Anonymous, "Vernacular Education for Bengal," 334.

29. It is worth noting that apart from educational change, there were also efforts from below to reform Bengali Islam. Raifuddin Ahmed argues that the main cultural brokers in reformulating the identity of rural Bengali Muslims were the low-level *mullahs*, many of whom graduated from the *madrassahs* and taught at the *maktabs* or the junior *madrassahs*. Rafiuddin Ahmed, *The Bengal Muslims, 1871–1906: A Quest for Identity* (Delhi: Oxford University Press, 1996), 84.

30. Government of Bengal, to the Department of Public Instruction, January 18, 1892, Home Department: Education, Nos. 40–41, National Archives, New Delhi.

31. Bombay Presidency, to the Department of Public Instruction,, July 1892, Home Department: Education, Nos. 25–34, National Archives, New Delhi.

32. Government of Bengal, to the Department of Public Instruction, August 1892, Home, Nos. 56–59, National Archives, New Delhi.

33. Bombay Presidency, to the Department of Public Instruction, July 1892, Nos. 25–34, National Archives, New Delhi.

34. Francis Robinson, *Islam and Muslim History in South Asia* (New Delhi: Oxford University Press, 2001), 70.

35. For a discussion of the particular constraints on Muslim education in producing a Muslim intelligentsia, see Tazeen Murshid, *The Sacred and the Secular* (Calcutta: Oxford University Press, 1995).

36. Jalal, *Self and Sovereignty*, 157.

37. The other part of Muslim society—one that became more important in terms of their leadership in the twentieth century—was the emergence of Muslim landlords who were socially and culturally closely connected to their rural Muslim peasants. This group, sometimes referred to as "*mofussil* Muslims," would become increasingly important in Bengali Muslim politics in the twentieth century. See Joya Chatterji, *Bengal Divided: Hindu Communalism and Partition, 1932–47* (Cambridge: Cambridge University Press, 1994).

38. Foucault sees the conception of pastoral care as central in the rise of the new kind of "governmentality" arising in Europe—concern about the welfare of one's flock (however defined) was a central concept in modern statecraft. See, Michel Foucault, "Governmentality," in *The Foucault Effect: Studies in Governmentality*, ed. Graham Burchell, Colin Gordon, and Peter Miller (Chicago: University of Chicago Press, 1991).

39. *Report of the Baptist Missionary Society, 1859* (London: Haddon Bros., and Co.), 29.

40. Mustafa Nurul Islam, *Bengali Muslim Public Opinion as Reflected in the Bengali Press, 1901–1903* (Dhaka: Bangla Academy, 1973).

41. Hardy, *The Muslims of British India*, 126.

42. See David Lellyveld, *Aligarh's First Generation: Muslim Solidarity in British India* (Princeton, N.J.: Princeton University Press, 1978); and Barbara Metcalf, *Islamic Revival in British India: Deoband, 1860–1900* (Princeton, N.J.: Princeton University Press, 1982).

43. David Gilmartin, "Partition, Pakistan and South Asian History: In Search of a Narrative," *The Journal of Asian Studies* 57, no. 4 (November 1998): 1075.

44. Woodrow, the head inspector in Bengal, had proposed that special funds should be set aside specifically to target Muslim boys and that inspectors shouldn't be promoted unless they increased the number of Muslims and achieved other similar goals. But the lieutenant governor asserted that "he (lieutenant governor) must maintain the principle that the general funds set apart for the education of the people generally must be administered w/out favor to one religion or another." In *Selections from Important Orders in the Educational Department during the Year 1872–73* (Calcutta: Bengal Secretariat Press, 1873), 81.

45. Syed Nawab Ali Choudury, *Vernacular Education in Bengal* (Calcutta: Caxton Press, 1900), 4.

46. In Bengal, the efforts to support Muslim educational and employment opportunities, however limited, were also meant to stem the growing power of the Hindu *bhadralok* and ensure that a balance was maintained between different "races" within the colonial administration and economy. In 1889, two Muslim assistant inspectors were appointed for East Bengal and Bihar. Sufia Ahmed, *Muslim Community in Bengal, 1884–1912* (Bangladesh: Oxford University Press, 1974), 27.

47. Karim, *Muhammadan Education*, 25.

48. Choudury, *Vernacular*, 17.

49. M. Azizul Huque, *History and Problems of Moslem Education in Bengal* (Calcutta: Thacker, Spink & Co., 1917), 3.

50. Karim, *Muhammadan Education*, 31.

51. Ibid., 30.

CONCLUSION

1. David Stow, *The Training System of Education* (London: Longman Green, Co., 1859), 7.

2. Sana Aiyar, "Fazlul Huq, Region and Religion in Bengal: The Forgotten Alternative of 1940-43," *Modern Asian Studies* vol. 42, no.6 (July 2007): 4.

3. Promesh Acharya, "Education and Communal Politics in Bengal: A Case Study," *Economic and Political Weekly* (July 29, 1989): PE-81. Acharya's article examines the communal debates over the Bengal Secondary Education Bill in 1940, arguing for the importance of communal differentiation rooted in the autonomous realm of cultural identity as expressed through education.

4. The act, like those being enacted in other provinces, proposed having a school board in each district that would survey the educational needs of the area and develop a plan for educational expansion. The act gave the board the authority to implement a cess (tax) to fund compulsory primary education.

5. To give a comparative sense, the United Provinces had only 15 percent single-teacher schools versus Bengal's 76 percent, the United Provinces had 66 percent trained teachers whereas Bengal had 25 percent, and Bengali primary school teachers were paid an average of Rs. 8-6-0 to Bombay's 47-0-0 (although this was clearly an exaggeration). See J.P. Naik and Syed Nurullah, *A History of Education in India* (Bombay: Macmillan & Co., 1951), 673.

6. It is in "the 'separate' schools that the Muhammadan pupils suffer most from the relative inefficiency of the segregate institutions—madrasahs, maktabs and Koran schools—which they attend." According to the report, Bengal had almost 20,000 lower-level *maktabs* ("special institutions"), greater than all of the other provinces combined. Quoted in Naik and Nurullah, *History of Education*, 721.

7. All-India Educational Committee, *Report of the Kamal Yar Jung Education Committee* (Calcutta: AM Kureishy, 1942), 31.

8. All-India Educational Committee, *Report of the Kamal Yar Jung*, 43.

9. Moslem Education Advisory Committee, *Report of the Moslem Education Advisory Committee* (Alipore: Bengal Government Press, 1935), 31.

10. Moslem Education Advisory Committee, *Report of the Moslem Education Advisory Committee*, 31.

11. Talal Asad, *Genealogies of Religion* (Baltimore: Johns Hopkins Press, 1993), 207.

12. In the appendix of the 1935 *Report of the Moslem Education Advisory Committee*, committee members outline the appropriate "Curriculum for Religious Instruction." According to the suggested curriculum, religious instruction should be introduced in class 1 for 1 1/2 hours per week, and by class 4 it should take up three hours per week. The actual curriculum, which was divided into practical work, reading, and writing, lays out the specific rituals and texts that should be followed. Moslem Education Advisory Committee, *Report of the Moslem Education Advisory Committee*, 49.

13. All-India Educational Committee, *Report of the Kamal Yar Jung*, 204.

14. Moslem Education Advisory Committee, *Report of the Moslem Education Advisory Committee*, 31.

15. For a further elaboration on the Muslim minority as a political identity, see Faisal Devji, "The Minority as Political Form," in *From the Colonial to the Postcolonial: India and Pakistan in Transition*, ed. Dipesh Chakrabarty, Rochona Majumdar, and Andrew Sartori (Delhi: Oxford University Press, 2007).

16. Moslem Education Advisory Committee, *Report of the Moslem Education Advisory Committee*, 43.

17. Ibid.

18. All-India Educational Committee, *Report of the Kamal Yar Jung*, 288.

19. William Connolly, "Populism and Faith," in *Political Theologies*, ed. Hent de Vries and Lawrence Sullivan (New York: Fordham University Press, 2006), 286.

20. All-India Educational Committee, *Report of the Kamal Yar Jung*, 301.

Bibliography

LIBRARIES AND ARCHIVES CONSULTED

Angus Library and Archives of the Baptist Missionary Society, Oxford
Archives of Christian Missions and Overseas Aid Organisations, London
Archives of the Church Missionary Society and Society for Promoting Female Education, Birmingham
Archives of the Government of West Bengal, Calcutta
Bangladesh National Archives, Dhaka
Carey Library of Serampore College, Serampore
Dhaka University Library, Dhaka
India Office Library, London
Jaykrishna Mukherjee Library, Uttarpara, West Bengal
National Archives of India, New Delhi
National Library, Calcutta
National Library of Scotland, Edinburgh
Ramakrishna Mission Library, Calcutta
Regent's Park College, Oxford
School of Oriental and African Studies, London
University of Birmingham Library, Birmingham

GOVERNMENT PROCEEDINGS AND REPORTS

Correspondence Relative to the Expedience of Raising an Educational Cess in Bengal. 1870. Simla: Government Central Press.
Four Articles on Mr. A.M. Monteath's Report on the State of Education in India in 1867. 1867. Calcutta: Englishman Press.
General Reports on Public Instruction in the Lower Provinces of the Bengal Presidency, 1857–1905 (Calcutta: Baptist Mission Press).

Note on the State of Education in India, 1865–66. 1866. Calcutta: Home Secretariat Press, 1867.
Report of the Indian Education Commission. 1883. Calcutta: Superintendent of Government Printing.
Report on the Committee Appointed by the Bengal Government to Consider Questions Connected with Muhammadan Education. 1915. Calcutta: Bengal Secretariat Depot.
Report on the Progress of Female Education in the Presidency and Burdwan Divisions. 1919. Calcutta: Bengal Secretariat Book Depot.
Report on the Survey of Primary Education, Bengal. 1918. Calcutta: Bengal Secretariat Book Depot.
Rules and Order of the Education Department, Bengal. 1908. Calcutta: Bengal Secretariat Book Depot.
Selections from Educational Records of the Government of India, vol. 1. 1960. New Delhi: National Archives of India.
Selections from Important Order in the Educational Department during the Year 1872–73. 1873. Calcutta: Bengal Secretariat Press.
Suggestions to Masters of Colleges and Schools. 1842. Calcutta: Bengal Military Orphan Press.

UNPUBLISHED MANUSCRIPT SOURCES

Calcutta Corresponding Committee Reports and Papers of the Church Missionary Society, University of Birmingham Library, Birmingham

Female Education Society, Administration Minutes, Church Missionary Society, University of Birmingham Library, Birmingham

Letter Book of the Chairwoman of the Women's Association for Foreign Missions Scottish Foreign Mission Society, Scottish National Archives, Edinburgh

Letter Books of the Church Missionary Society, University of Birmingham Library, Birmingham

London Missionary Society, North India—Bengal Incoming Correspondence, School of Oriental and African Studies Library, London

Minutes of Foreign Missions Committee, Free Church of Scotland, Scottish National Archives, Edinburgh

Wesleyan Methodist Missionary Society Synod Minutes, School of Oriental and African Studies Library, London

MAGAZINES, NEWSPAPERS, AND ANNUAL REPORTS

Annual Reports of the Baptist Missionary Society
Annual Reports of the Christian Vernacular Education Society for India
Annual Reports of the Indian Female Normal School and Instruction Society
Annual Reports of the Ladies' Association for the Support of the Zenana Work and Bible Women in India in Connection with the Baptist Missionary Society
Bamabodhini Patrika

The Church of Scotland Home and Foreign Missionary Record
The Free Church Monthly
India's Women
The Indian Female Evangelist
Journal of the National Indian Association in Aid of Social Progress in India
Missionary Herald of the Baptist Mission Society
News of Female Missions in Connexion with the Church of Scotland
Reports of the Local Committee of the Calcutta Female Normal School, Church of England Zenana Mission Society
The Missionary Record of the United Free Church of Scotland

OTHER PRINTED MATTER

Acharya, Poromesh. 1988. "Is Macaulay Still Our Guru?" *Economic and Political Weekly* (May 28): 1124–30.

———. 1989. *Banglar Deshaj Shikhaguru*. Calcutta: Anushoopapookashani.

———. 1989. "Education and Communal Politics in Bengal: A Case Study." *Economic and Political Weekly* (June 29): PE81–PE90.

———. 1981. "Politics of Primary Education in West Bengal: The Case of *Sahaj Path*." *Economic and Political Weekly* (June 13): 1069–75.

Adam, William. 1824. *Queries and Replies Respecting the Present State of the Protestant Missions in the Bengal Presidency*. Calcutta: Thacker & Co.

A Handbook of Foreign Missions: Containing on Account of the Principal Protestant Missionary Societies in Britain. 1888. London: Protestant Missionary Society in Great Britain.

Ahmed, Rafiuddin. 1996. *The Bengal Muslims, 1871–1906: A Quest for Identity*. Delhi: Oxford University Press.

Ahmed, Sharif Uddin. 1986. *Dacca: A Study in Urban History and Development*. London: Curzon.

Ahmed, Sufia. 1974. *Muslim Community in Bengal, 1884–1912*. Bangladesh: Oxford University Press.

Alam, Shahanara, and Husniara Huz. 1996. *Azizul Huque: A Biographical Account of His Life and Work*. Dhaka: S. Alam & H. Huq.

All-India Educational Committee. 1942. *Report of the Kamal Yar Jung Education Committee*. Calcutta: AM Kureishy.

Almutt, S. S. 1894. *The Present Needs of an Educational Enterprise*. Cambridge: Cambridge University Press.

Amin, Sonia. 1996. *The World of Muslim Women in Colonial Bengal, 1876–1939*. Leiden; New York: E.J. Brill.

Anderson, R. D. 1995. *Education and the Scottish People, 1759–1918*. Oxford: Clarendon Press.

Andrews, C. F. 1912. *The Renaissance in India*. London: Church Missionary Society Press.

Annett, Edward A. 1923. *The Natural Method of Bible Teaching for India*. Madras: Christian Literature Society.

Anti-Caste (Anonymous). 1859. *Christian Government and Education in India*. London: John F. Shaw.

Apple, Michael. 1986. *Teachers and Texts: A Political Economy of Class and Gender Relations.* New York: Routledge & Kegan Paul.

Asad, Talal. 1983. *Genealogies of Religion.* Baltimore: Johns Hopkins University Press.

The Avon Object Lesson Handbook, no. III. 1897. London: Sir Isaac Pitman & Sons.

Bagal, Jogesh Chandra. 1956. *Women's Education in Eastern India: The First Phase.* Calcutta: The World Press Private, Ltd.

Balachin, Richard. 1905. *Common Objects of Daily Life,* book 1 of *Clive's Object Lesson Readers.* London: W.B. Clive.

Balagangadhara, S. N. 1994. *The Heathen in His Blindness: Asia, the West and the Dynamic of Religion.* Leiden: E.J. Brill.

Ballhatchet, Kenneth. 1998. *Caste, Class and Catholicism in India, 1789–1914.* Surrey: Curzon Press.

Bakhle, Janaki. 2005. *Two Men and Music: Nationalism in the Making of an Indian Classical Tradition.* New York: Oxford University Press.

Bala Bodh. 1874. Dhaka: Sri Mathlabkra Printers.

Bandhyopadhyay, Gopal Chunder. 1872. *Shiksha Pranali,* 3rd ed. Calcutta.

Bandhyopadhyay, Sekhar. 1997. *Caste, Protest and Identity in Colonial India: The Namasudras of Bengal 1872–1947.* Surrey: Curzon Press.

Bandhopadhyay, Sibaji. 2001. *Gopal-Rakhal Dwandasamas: Uponibeshbad O Bangla Sishu-Sahitya.* Calcutta: Papyrus.

Banerjea, K. M. 1841. *A Prize Essay on Native Female Education.* Calcutta: Bishop's College Press.

Banerjee, Prathama. 2006. *Politics of Time: "Primitives" and History-Writing in a Colonial Society.* Delhi: Oxford University Press.

Banerji, Bibhuti Bhushan. 1987. *Panther Panchali.* London: Lokamaya Press.

Bannerjee, Sumanta. 1989. *The Parlour and the Streets: Elite and Popular Culture in Nineteenth-Century Calcutta.* Calcutta: Seagull Books.

Bannerji, Himani. 1991. "Fashioning a Self: Education Proposals for and by Women in Popular Magazines in Colonial Bengal." *Economic and Political Weekly,* October 26, (WS50–WS62).

Bannerji, Himani. 2001. *Inventing Subjects.* New Delhi: Tulika.

Barnard, H. C. 1947. *A Short History of English Education.* London: University of London Press.

Basu, Priyanantha. 1897. *The Education of Mahomedans and Christians in India: A Thought,* vol. 1. Benares: Chandraprabha Press.

Basu, Subho, and Sikata Banerjee. 2006. "The Quest for Manhood: Masculine Hinduism and Nation in Bengal." *Comparative Studies of South Asia, Africa and the Middle East* 26, no. 3: 476–90.

Bayly, Susan. 1989. *Saints, Goddesses and Kings: Muslims and Christians in South Indian Society, 1700–1900.* Cambridge: Cambridge University Press.

Bhabha, Homi. 1994. *The Location of Culture.* New York: Routledge).

Bell, Andrew. 1827. *Manual of Public and Private Education Founded on a Discovery "by Which a School or Family May Teach Itself under the Superintendence of the Master or Parents," Made, Recorded and Promulgated at Madras in 1789–98.* London: C & J Rivington.

Bellenoit, Hayden. 2007. *Missionary Education and Empire in Late Colonial India, 1860–1920*. London: Pickering and Chatto.
Bengali Primer (Parts I and II): Barnamala. 1872. Calcutta: Baptist Mission Press.
Besant, Annie. 1943. *Essentials of an Indian Education*. Madras: Theosophical Publishing House.
Bhabha, Homi. 1994. *The Location of Culture*. New York: Routledge.
Bhattacharya, Debipada. 1968. *Rebharenda Lalbihari De O Candramukhitra UPakhyana*. Calcutta.
Bhattacharya, Tithi. 2005. *The Sentinels of Culture*. New Delhi: Oxford University Press.
Biklen, Sari. 1995. *Schoolwork: Gender and the Cultural Construction of Teaching*. New York: Teachers College Press.
Bird, Elizabeth. "To Cook or to Conjugate: Gender and Class in the Adult Curriculum 1865–1900 in Bristol, United Kingdom." *Gender and Education* 3, no. 2 (1991):183–198 .
Birla, Ritu. 2009. *Stages of Capital: Law, Market and Governance in Late Colonial India*. Durham, NC: Duke University Press.
Borthwick, Margaret. 1984. *The Changing Role of Women in Bengal, 1849–1905*. Princeton, NJ: Princeton University Press.
Bose, Pradip Kumar. 1995. "Sons of the Nation." In *Texts of Power*, edited by Partha Chatterjee,118–144 . Minneapolis: University of Minnesota Press.
Boyd, William. 1914. *From Locke to Montessori*. London: George G. Harrap & Co.
Brander, Isabel. 1899. *Kindergarten Teaching in India: Stories, Object Lessons, Occupations, Songs and Games*. London: Macmillan and Co.
Breckenridge, Carol, and Peter Van der Weer, eds. 1993. *Orientalism and the Postcolonial Predicament: Perspectives on South Asia*. Philadelphia: University of Pennsylvania, Press.
Broomfield, J. H. 1968. *Elite Conflict in a Plural Society: Twentieth-Century Bengal*. Berkeley: University of California Press.
Brown, J. H. 1911. *Frances E. Brockway: Memoirs*. London: Unwin Bros. Ltd.
Brown, J. Jenkyn. 1867. *Woman's Work in the Church*. London: Pewtres Brothers and Gould.
Brumberg, Johan Jacobs. 1982. "Zenanas and Girlless Villages: The Ethnology of American Evangelical Women, 1870–1910." *Journal of American History* 69, no. 2 (September):347–371 .
Burton, Antoinette. 1994. *Burdens of History: British Feminists, Indian Women and Imperial Culture, 1865–1915*. Chapel Hill: University of North Carolina Press.
———. 2003. *Dwelling in the Archive: Women Writing House, Home and History in Late Colonial India*. New York: Oxford University Press.
Carey, William. 1895. *Our Village Schools in Bengal*. London: Mission House.
Carpenter, Mary. 1868 . *Six Months in India*. London: Longmans, Green & Co.
———. 1866. *Suggestions on Prison Discipline and Female Education in India*. London: Longmans and Co.

Chakrabarty, Dipesh. 2000. *Provincializing Europe: Postcolonial Thought and Historical Difference*. Princeton, NJ: Princeton University Press.

Chakraborty, Thakurdas. 1873. *Popular Education in Bengal*. Calcutta: Banders, Cones and Co.

Chakravarti, Ramakanta. 1985. *Vaishnavism in Bengal, 1486–1900*. Calcutta: Sanscrit Pustak Bhandar.

Chakravarti, Uma. 1998. *Rewriting History: The Life and Times of Pandita Ramabai*. New Delhi: Kali for Women.

Chalmers, Thomas. 1846. *Churches and Schools for the Working Classes*. Edinburgh: Miller and Fairly.

Chambers, Robert, and William Chambers. 1860. *Rudiments of Knowledge*, new ed. Edinburgh: William and Robert Chambers.

Chapman, Priscilla. 1839. *Hindoo Female Education*. London: R.B. Seeley.

Chatterjee, Indrani. 1999. "Colouring Subalterneity: Slaves, Concubines and Social Orphans in Early Colonial India." In *Subaltern Studies X*, edited by Gautam Bhadra, Gyan Prakash, and Susie Tharu, 49–97. Delhi: Oxford University Press.

Chatterjee, Partha. 1984. *Bengal 1920–1947: The Land Question*. Calcutta: K.P. Bagchi & Co.

———. 1996. *The Nation and Its Fragments*. Delhi: Oxford University Press.

Chaudhuri, Nupur. 1988. "Memsahibs and Motherhood in Nineteenth-Century Colonial India." *Victorian Studies* (Summer): 517–526.

Chaudhuri, Nupur, and Margaret Strobel, eds. 1992. *Western Women and Imperialism*. Bloomington: Indiana University Press.

Choudury, Syeed Nawab Ali. 1900. *Vernacular Education in Bengal*. Calcutta: Caxton Press.

Christian Education for India in the Mother Tongue: A Statement on the Formation of the Christian Vernacular Education Society. 1857. London: William Nichols.

The Church of Scotland in Calcutta: Its History and Work. N.d. Calcutta: Thacker, Spink & Co.

Cohn, Bernard. 1987. *An Anthropologist among Historians and Other Essays*. Delhi: Oxford University Press.

Comaroff, John, and Jean Comaroff. 1991. *Of Revelation and Revolution*. Chicago: University of Chicago Press.

Connolly, William. 2006. "Populism and Faith." In *Political Theologies*, edited by Hent de Vries and Lawrence Sullivan, 278–297. New York: Fordham University Press.

Cooper, Fred, and Ann Stoler, eds. 1997. *Tensions of Empire: Colonial Cultures in a Bourgeois World*. Berkeley: University of California Press.

Copley, Anthony. 1997. *Religions in Conflict: Ideology, Cultural Contact and Conversion in Late Colonial India*. Delhi: Oxford University Press.

Cowan, Minna G. 1912. *The Education of the Women of India*. Edinburgh: Oliphant, Anderson & Ferrier.

Cox, Jeffrey. 2002. *Imperial Fault Lines: Christianity and Colonial Power in India, 1818–1940*. Stanford, CA: Stanford University Press.

Dalmia, Vasudha, and Heinrich von Stietencron, eds. 1995. *Representing Hinduism: The Construction of Religious Traditions and National Identity.* New Delhi: Sage.

Davidoff, Leonore and Catherine Hall. 1987. *Family Fortunes: Men and Women of the English Middle Class, 1780–1850.* Chicago: University of Chicago Press.

Davis, Richard. *Lives of Indian Images.* 1999. Princeton, NJ: Princeton University Press.

De, Lal Behari. 1869. *Primary Education in Bengal: A Lecture Delivered at the Bethune Society.* Calcutta: Barham, Hill & Co.

———. 1969. *Bengali Peasant Life, Folktales of Bengal, Recollections of My Schooldays.* Edited by Mahadevprasad Saha. Calcutta: Editions India.

Dena, Lal. 1988. *Christian Missions and Colonialism.* Sillong.

Denney, J. H. K. 1902. *Toward the Surprising: A History of Work for the Women of India Done by Women from England.* London: Marshall Bros.

Deshpande, Prachi. 2007. *Creative Pasts: Historical Memory and Identity in Western India, 1700–1960.* New York: Columbia University Press.

Devji, Faisal. 2007. "Apologetic Modernity." *Modern Intellectual History* 4, no. 1: 61–76.

———. 2007. "The Minority as Political Form." In *From the Colonial to the Postcolonial: India and Pakistan in Transition,* edited by Dipesh Chakrabarty, Rochona Majumdar, and Andrew Sartori, 85–95. Delhi: Oxford University Press.

DiBona, Joseph, ed. 1983. *One Teacher, One School: The Adam Reports on Indigenous Education in Nineteenth Century India.* New Delhi: Sita Ram Goel.

Dick, Malcom. 1980. "The Myth of the Working-Class Sunday School." *History of Education* 9, no. 1.

Dieter, Jedan. 1981. *Johann Heinrich Pestalozzi and the Pestalozzian Method of Language Teaching.* Bern: Peter Lang.

Dirks, Nicholas. 2001. *Castes of Mind: Colonialism and the Making of Modern India.* Princeton, NJ: Princeton University Press.

Donald, James. 1992. *Sentimental Education: Schooling Popular Culture and the Regulation of Liberty.* London: Verso.

Dube, Saurabh. 1998. *Untouchable Pasts: Religion Identity and Power among a Central Indian Community, 1780–1950.* Albany: State University of New York Press.

———. 2004. *Stitches on Time: Colonial Textures and Postcolonial Thought.* Durham, NC: Duke University Press.

Duff, Alexander. 1872. *Foreign Missions: An Address Delivered before the General Assembly.* Edinburgh: Ballantyne and Co.

———. 1988. *India and Indian Missions.* New Delhi: Swati Publications.

Dutt, Hurchunder. 1856. *An Address on Native Female Education.* Calcutta: Calutta Gazette Office.

Dutta, Akshay Kumar. 1878. *Charupath: Entertaining Lessons in Science and Literature,* part 1. Calcutta: New Sanskrit Press.

Ealand, A. F. 1915. "Religious Education in India." *The East and the West* (April).
Eaton, Richard. 1997. *The Rise of Islam and the Bengal Frontier, 1204–1760.* Delhi: Oxford University Press.
The Educational Destitution in Bengal and Behalf and the London Christian Vernacular Society for India. 1858. Calcutta: Baptist Mission Press.
Etherington, Norman, ed. 2005. *Missions and Empire.* Oxford: Oxford University Press.
Ferguson, Niall. 2003. *Empire: The Rise and Demise of the British World Order and the Lessons for Global Power.* New York: Basic Books.
Forbes, Geraldine. 1986. "In Search of the 'Pure Heathen': Missionary Women in Nineteenth Century India." *Economic and Political Weekly* 21, no. 17 (April 26): WS2–WS8.
———. 1998. *Women in Modern India.* Cambridge: Cambridge University Press.
Forrester, Duncan. 1980. *Caste and Christianity.* Calcutta: Firma KLM.
Foucault, Michel. 1991. "Governmentality." In *The Foucault Effect: Studies in Governmentality,* edited by Graham Burchell, Colin Gordon, and Peter Miller, 87–104. Chicago: University of Chicago Press.
Frykenberg, Robert, and Judith Brown, eds. 2002. *Christians, Cultural Interaction and India's Religious Traditions.* London: Routledge Curzon.
Ghosal, Sarala Devi. 1901. *A Scheme for an India Girls' School, Mahabodhi Society.* .
Ghosh, Anindita. 2006. *Power in Print: Popular Publishing and the Politics of Language and Culture in a Colonial Society.* New Delhi: Oxford University Press.
Ghosh, Kamakhacharan. 1870. *Ratnasar: First Part.* Calcutta.
Ghosh, Kaushik. 1999. "A Market for Aboriginality: Primitivism and Race Classification in the Indentured Labour Market of Colonial India." In *Subaltern Studies X,* edited by Gautam Bhadra, 8–48. Delhi: Oxford University Press.
Gmelin, Frederic. 1872. *Adhapanna Paddati.* Bhowanipore.
Gordon, Leonard. 1974. *Bengal: The Nationalist Movement, 1876–1940.* New York: Columbia University Press.
Gould, F. J. 1911. "Moral Education in India." *East and the West* (April).
Guha, Ranajit. 1998. *A Rule of Property for Bengal.* Durham, NC: Duke University Press.
Gupta, Aruna. 1988. *Nirab Kahini.* Calcutta: Sushil Printers.
Hall, Catherine. 2002. *Metropole and Colony in the English Imagination, 1830–1867.* Cambridge: Polity Press.
———. 2002. *White Male and Middle-Class: Explorations in Feminism and History.* Cambridge: Polity Press.
Hardy, Peter. 1972. *The Muslims of British India.* Cambridge: Cambridge University Press.
Hartog, Phillip. 1939. *Some Aspects of Indian Education: Past and Present.* Oxford: Oxford University Press.
Hassell, Joseph. 1866. *From Pole to Pole: A Handbook of Christian Missions for the Use of Ministers, Teachers and Others.* London: James Nisbet & Co.

Hatcher, Brian. 1996. *Idioms of Improvement: Vidyasagar and Cultural Encounter in Bengal*. Calcutta: Oxford University Press.
Hilton, Boyd. 1988. *The Age of Atonement*. Oxford: Clarendon Press.
Hobsbawm, Eric J. 1962. *The Age of Revolution, 1789–1848*. New York: New American Library.
Huber, Mary Taylor, and Nancy Lutkehaus, eds. 1999. *Gendered Missions: Women and Men in Missionary Discourse and Practice*. Ann Arbor: University of Michigan Press.
Hunter, Ian. 1994. *Rethinking the School: Subjectivity, Bureaucracy, Criticism*. Sydney: Allen & Unwin Private Ltd.
Hunter, W. W. [1871] 1975. *The Indian Musalmans*. Bangladesh: W. Rahman.
———. 1895. *The Old Missionary*. Oxford: Horace Hart.
———. 1897. *The Annals of Rural Bengal*. London: Smith, Elder and Co.
Huque, M. Azizul. 1917. *History and Problems of Moslem Education in Bengal*. Calcutta: Thacker, Spink & Co.
Islam, Mustafa Nurul. 1973. *Bengali Muslim Public Opinion as Reflected in the Bengali Press, 1901–1903*. Dhaka: Bangla Academy.
Jalal, Ayesha. 2000. *Self and Sovereignty: Individual and Community in South Asian Islam since 1850*. London: Routledge.
Jayawardena, Kumari. 1995. *The White Woman's Other Burden: Western Women and South Asia during British Colonial Rule*. New York: Routledge.
Jenkins, David. 1994. "Object Lessons and Ethnographic Displays: Museum Exhibitions and the Making of American Anthropology." *Comparative Studies in Society and History* 36, no. 2: 242–70.
Karim, Abdul. 1900. *Muhammadan Education in Bengal*. Calcutta: Metcalfe Press.
Karlekar, Malavika. 1986. "Kadambini and the Bhadralok: Early Debates over Women's Education in Bengal." *Economic and Political Weekly* 21, no. 17 (April 26): WS25–WS31.
Kaviraj, Sudipta. 1995. *The Unhappy Consciousness*. New York: Oxford University Press.
Kavivarta, Harishchandra Sharma. 1868. *Barnabodhini*. Calcutta: Girish-Bidhratna.
Kawashima, Koji. 1998. *Missionaries and a Hindu State: Travancore, 1858–1936*. Delhi: Oxford University Press.
Keane, Webb. 2007. *Christian Moderns: Freedom and Fetish in the Mission Encounter*. Berkeley: University of California Press.
Kent, Eliza. 2004. *Converting Women: Gender and Protestant Christianity in Colonial South India*. New York: Oxford University Press.
Khan, Muin-ud-Din Ahmad, ed. 1961. *Selections from Bengal Government Records on Wahhabi Trials (1863–1870)*. Dacca: Asiatic Society of Pakistan.
Kiernan, Victor. 1952."Evangelicalism and the French Revolution." *Past and Present*, no. 1 (February): 44–56.
Kopf, David. 1969. *British Orientalism and the Bengal Renaissance: The Dynamics of Indian Modernization, 1773–1835*. Berkeley: University of California Press.

Kumar, Krishna. 1991. *Political Agenda of Education: A Study of Colonialist and Nationalist Ideas.* New Delhi: Sage.
Kumar, Nita. 1994. "Oranges Are for Girls, or the Half-Known Story of the Education of Girls in Twentieth-Century Banaras." In *Women as Subjects: South Asian Histories,* edited by Nita Kumar, 211–232. Charlottesville: University Press of Virginia.
Laird, M. A. 1972. *Missionaries and Education in Bengal, 1793–1837.* Oxford: Clarendon Press.
Laqueur, Thomas. 1976. *Religion and Respectability.* New Haven, CT: Yale University Press.
Lellyveld, David. 1978. *Aligarh's First Generation: Muslim Solidarity in British India.* Princeton, NJ: Princeton University Press.
———. 2002. "Talking the National Language: Hindi/Urdu/Hindustani in Indian Broadcasting and Cinema." In *Thinking Social Science in India: Essays in Honor of Alice Thorner,* edited by Sujata Patel, 355–366. New Delhi: Sage.
Long, James. 1848. *Handbook of Bengal Missions in Connexion with the Church of England.* London: John Farquhar Shaw.
———. 1871. *Scripture Truth in Oriental Dress.* Calcutta: Thacker, Spink & Co.
———. 1918. *A Descriptive and Classified Catalogue of Bengali Christian Literature Published up to 1917.* Calcutta: Council of Missions.
Loomba, Ania. 1993. "Dead Women Tell No Tales: Issues of Female Subjectivity, Subaltern Agency and Tradition in Colonial and Post-Colonial Writings on Widow Immolation in India." *History Workshop Journal,* no. 36: 209–227.
Ludden, David. 2006 "Territorial Politics, Spatial Inequality, and Economic Development: The Case of the Province of Eastern Bengal and Assam." Paper presented at Carleton College.
Lukose, Ritty. 2009. *Liberalization's Children: Gender, Youth and Consumer Citizenship in Globalizing India.* Durham, NC: Duke University Press.
Macpherson, G. 1900. *Life of Lal Behari Day, Convert, Pastor, Professor, and Author.* Edinburgh: T & T Clark.
Majumdar, Rochona. 2009. *Marriage and Modernity: Family Values in Colonial Bengal.* Durham, NC: Duke University Press.
Mani, Lata. 1990. "Contentious Traditions: The Debate on *Sati* in Colonial India." In *Recasting Women,* edited by Kumkum Sangari and Sudesh Vaid, 88–126. New Brunswick, NJ: Rutgers University Press.
Maskiell, Michelle. 1984. *Women between Cultures: The Lives of Kinnaird College Alumnae in British India.* Syracuse, NY: Maxwell School of Citizenship and Public Affairs.
Masuzawa, Tomoko. 2005. *The Invention of World Religions.* Chicago: University of Chicago Press.
Mathur, Saloni. 1997. "Re-visualizing the Missionary Subject: History, Modernity and Indian Women." *Third Text,* 10. Issue 37: 53–61. (Winter): 53–61.
McCann, Phillip. 1977. *Popular Education and Socialization in the Nineteenth Century.* London: Methuen and Co. Ltd.
McClymont, Andrew W. 1947. *The Traveling Bookman: John Murdoch of Madras.* London: Lutterworth Press.

McCully, B. T. 1963. *English Education and the Rise of Indian Nationalism.* New York: Columbia University Press.
McGuire, John. 1983. *The Making of a Colonial Mind: A Quantitative Study of the Bhadralok in Calcutta, 1857–1885.* Canberra: Australian National University Press.
McLean, David. 1991. *Education and Empire: Naval Tradition and England's Elite Schooling.* London: British Academic Press.
Metcalf, Barbara. 1982. *Islamic Revival in British India: Deoband, 1860–1900.* Princeton, NJ: Princeton University Press.
———. 1990. *Perfecting Women: Maulana Ashraf 'Ali Thanawi's Bihishti Zewar: A Partial Translation with Commentary.* Berkeley: University of California Press.
Metcalf, Thomas. 1964. *The Aftermath of Revolt: India, 1857–1870.* Princeton, NJ: Princeton University Press.
Midgley, Clare, ed. 1998. *Gender and Imperialism.* Manchester, UK: Manchester University Press.
Minault, Gail. 1998. *Secluded Scholars: Women's Education and Muslim Social Reform in Colonial India.* Delhi: Oxford University Press.
Mir, Farina. 2010. *The Social Space of Language: Vernacular Culture in British Colonial Punjab.* Berkeley: University of California Press.
Moore, R.J. 1965. *The Composition of Wood's Despatch.* London: Longman Press.
Morris, Henry. 1906. *The Life of John Murdoch: The Literary Evangelist of India.* London: Christian Literature Society for India.
Morrison, Thomas. 1860. "Oral Lessons on Common Things." In *Object Teaching and Oral Lessons on Society Science and Common Things,* edited by Henry Barnard. New York: FC Brownell.
Mufti, Aamir. 2007. *Enlightenment in the Colony: The Jewish Question and the Crisis of Postcolonial Culture.* Princeton, NJ: Princeton University Press.
Mukherjee, S. N. 1966. *History of Education in India: The Modern Period.* Baroda: Acharya Book Depot.
———. 1976. "Bhadralok in Language and Literature: An Essay on the Understanding of Caste and Status." *Bengal Past and Present* 181, pt. 1.
Mukhopadhyay, Bhudev. 1856. *Sikhavidhyaka Pastava: An Introduction to the Art of Teaching.* Calcutta.
———. 1962. *Bhūdeba-racanāsambhāra.* Calcutta: Mitra & Ghosh.
Mukhopadhyay, Gopal. 1984. *Mass Education in Bengal.* Calcutta: National Publishers.
Mukhopadhyay, Somnath. 1870. *Shiksha Paddhati,* 3rd ed. Dhaka.
Mullens, Hannah. 1852. *Phulmani O Karunnar Bibaran.* Calcutta: Chrsitian Tract and Book Society.
Murdoch, John. 1865. *Letter to Babu Ishwar Chandra Bidyasagar on Bengali Typolography.* . National Library, Calcutta.
———.1872. *Education as a Missionary Agency in India.* Madras: Foster Press.
———. 1885. *The Indian Teacher's Manual: With Hints on the Management of Vernacular Schools.* Madras: Christian Vernacular Education Society.

———. 1898. *Indian Educational Reform as Suggested by the Sedition Act and the Bloomsbury Meeting.* Madras: Christian Literature Society for India.

———. 1908. *My Duties: A Junior Moral Text-Book.* Madras: Christian Literature Society.

Murshid, Tazeen. 1995. *The Sacred and the Secular: Bengal Muslim Discourses, 1871–1977.* Calcutta: Oxford University Press.

Nandy, Ashish. 1983. *The Intimate Enemy: Loss and Recovery of Self under Colonialism.* Delhi: Oxford University Press.

Naregal, Veena. 2001. *Language Politics, Elites and the Public Sphere: Western India under Colonialism.* New Delhi: Permanent Black.

Nayar, Usha. 1988. *Women Teachers in South Asia.* Delhi: Chanakya Publications.

Neill, Stephen. 1985. *A History of Christianity in India.* Cambridge: Cambridge University Press.

Nurullah, Syed, and J. P. Naik. 1951. *A History of Education in India.* Bombay: Macmillan & Co.

Nutan Barnamala. 1877. Calcutta: Bengal Press.

Oberoi, Harjot. 1997. *The Construction of Religious Boundaries: Culture, Identity and Diversity in the Sikh Tradition.* Delhi: Oxford University Press.

Object Teaching and Oral Lessons on Social Science and Common Things. 1860. New York: F.C. Brownell.

Oddie, G. A. 1979. *Social Protest in India.* New Delhi: Viking Press.

O'Hanlon, Rosalind. 1985. *Caste, Conflict and Ideology: Mahatma Jotirao Phule and Low Caste Protest in Nineteenth-Century Western India.* Cambridge: Cambridge University Press.

The Opinions of the Press and the Resolution to the Bengal Government on the Pamphlet of Syed Ameer Hossein Khan Bahadur on Mohammedan Education. 1882. Calcutta: PSD Razario and Co.

Oswill, G. D. 1901. *Paper on Religious Education in State Schools and Colleges.* Calcutta: Thackeray, Spink & Co.

Owen, David. 1964. *English Philanthropy: 1600–1960.* Cambridge, MA: Belknap Press.

Pandey, Gyanendra. 1992. *The Construction of Communalism in Colonial North India.* Delhi: Oxford University Press.

Pestalozzi, Johann. 1898. *How Gertrude Teaches Her Children.* New York: C.W. Bardeen.

Pietz, William. 1985. "The Problem of the Fetish I." *Res* 9 (Spring): 5–17.

Porter, Andrew. 2004. *Religion versus Empire? British Protestant Missionaries and Overseas Expansion, 1700–1914.* Manchester, UK: Manchester University Press.

Potts, Daniel. 1967. *British Baptist Missionaries in India.* Cambridge: Cambridge University of India.

Prakash, Gyan, ed. 1995. *After Colonialism: Imperial Histories and Postcolonial Displacements.* Princeton, NJ: Princeton University Press.

Purvis, Jane. 1989. *Hard Lessons.* Cambridge: Polity Press.

Qasim Zaman, Muhammad. 2002. *The Ulama in Contemporary Islam: Custodians of Change.* Princeton, NJ: Princeton University Press.

———. 2007. *Schooling Islam: The Culture and Politics of Modern Muslim Education.* Princeton, NJ: Princeton University Press.

Rafael, Vicente Rafael. 1988. *Contracting Colonialism: Translation and Christian Conversion in Tagalog Society under Early Spanish Rule.* Ithaca, NY: Cornell University Press.

Ram, Kalpana, and Margaret Jolly. 1998. *Maternities and Modernities: Colonial and Postcolonial Experience in Asia and the Pacific.* Cambridge: Cambridge University Press.

Raman, Sita Anantha. 1996. *Getting Girls to School: Social Reform in the Tamil Districts 1870–1930.* Calcutta: Stree.

Ramaswamy, Sumathi. 1997. *Passions of the Tongue: Language Devotion in Tamil India, 1871–1900.* Berkeley: University of California Press.

Ray, Bharati, ed. 1997. *From the Seams of History: Essays on Indian Women.* New Delhi: Oxford University Press.

Ray Chaudhuri, Tapan. 1988. *Europe Reconsidered: Perceptions of the West in Nineteenth-Century Bengal.* Delhi: Oxford University Press.

Report of the Moslem Education Advisory Committee. 1935. Alipore: Bengal Government Press.

Richardson, Allen. 1994. *Literature, Education and Romanticism: Reading as Social Practice, 1780–1832.* Cambridge: Cambridge University Press.

Risley, H. H. 1891. *Tribes and Castes of Bengal.* Calcutta: Bengal Secretariat Press.

Robinson, Frances. 1974. *Separatism among Indian Muslims.* Cambridge: Cambridge University Press.

Robinson, Rowena, and Sathianathan Clarke, eds. 2003. *Religious Conversion in India: Modes, Motivations and Meanings.* New Delhi: Oxford University Press.

Roy, Gautam. 1995. "The Pathshala and the School: Experiences of Growing up in Nineteenth and Twentieth Century Bengal." In *Mind, Body and Society,* edited by Rajat Kanta Ray. Calcutta: Oxford University Press.

Roy, Krishna Chandra. 1992. *Education in India.* Calcutta: KL Addy.

Sanyal, Hriteshranjan. 1992. "British Purba Athihagoth Shikkababastha." *Yogasutra* (January–March).

———. 1981. *Social Mobility in Bengal.* Calcutta: Papyrus.

Sarkar, Mahua. *Visible Histories, Disappearing Women: Producing Muslim Womanhood in Late Colonial Bengal.* 2009. Durham: Duke University Press.

Sarkar, Sumit. 1998. "Vidyasagar and Brahminical Society." In Sumit Sarkar, *Writing Social History.* Delhi: Oxford University Press.

Sarkar, Tanika. 1999. *Words to Win: The Making of Amar Jiban, a Modern Autobiography.* New Delhi: Kali for Women.

———. 2001. *Hindu Wife, Hindu Nation.* London: Hurst.

Sartori, Andrew. 2008. *Bengal in Global Concept History.* Chicago: University of Chicago Press.

Schwartz, Joel. 1999. "Robert Chambers and Thomas Henry Huxley, Science Correspondents: The Popularization and Dissemination of Nineteenth Century Natural Science." *Journal of the History of Biology* 32:343–383.

Scott, J. J. 1896. *A Brief History of the Indian Sunday School.* Calcutta: India Sunday School Union.

Scott, Joan Wallach. 1988. *Gender and the Politics of History.* New York: Columbia University Press.

Sen, Ashok. 1977. *Iswarchandra Vidyasagar and His Elusive Milestones.* Calcutta: Riddhi.

Sen, Satadru. 2007. "The Orphaned Colony: Orphanage, Child and Authority in British India." *The Indian Economic and Social History Review* 44, no. 4:463–488.

Sengupta, Parna. 2003. "An Object Lesson in Colonial Pedagogy." *Comparative Studies in Society and History* 45, no. 1 (January): 96–121.

———. 2005. "Teaching Gender in the Colony: The Education of 'Outsider' Teachers in Late Nineteenth Century Bengal." *The Journal of Women's History* 17, no. 4 (December): 32–55.

Seth, Sanjay. 2007. *Subject Lessons: The Western Education of Colonial India.* Durham, NC: Duke University Press.

Shahidulla, Kazi. 1987. *Patshalas into Schools.* Calcutta: Firma KLM.

Singh Chawal, Maina. 2000. *Gender, Religion and "Heathen Lands."* New York: Garland.

Singha, Abha. 1998. *Idarpane Barisal.* Calcutta.

Sinha, Mrinalini. 1995. *Colonial Masculinities.* Manchester, UK: Manchester University Press.

———. 2006. *Specters of Mother India: The Global Restructuring of Empire.* Durham, NC: Duke University Press.

Sinha, Soumitra. 1995. *The Quest for Modernity and the Bengali Muslims, 1921–1947.* Calcutta: Minerva Associates.

Sister Nivedita. 1907. *Cradle Tales of Hinduism.* London: Longmans, Green and Co.

———. 1923. *Hints on National Education in India,* 3rd ed. Calcutta: Ubodhan Office.

Sketch of the official career of the Hon'ble Ashley Eden : with an appendix containing the hon'ble Ashley Eden's evidence before the indigo commississon, the Treaty with Sikhim, and Sir Charles Wood's Despatch to the Government of India. 1877. Calcutta: Kally Prosono Dey.

Smith, George. 1864. *Christianity in India: With Reference to the Scotch System of Missionary Operation and to Female Education.* Edinburgh: John Maclaren.

———. 1879. *Fifty Years of Foreign Missions or the Foreign Missions of the Free Church of Scotland in their Year of Jubilee, 1879–80.* Edinburgh: John Maclaren and Son.

Southey, Robert. 1844. *Life of Andrew Bell.* London: J. Murray.

Special Appeal on Behalf of the Calcutta Normal School. 1858. London: Suter and Alexander.

Speech of the Duke of Marlborough upon the Exclusion of the Bible from Government Schools. 1860. London: W.H. Dalton.

Spivak, Gayatri Chakravorty. 1999. *A Critique of Postcolonial Reason: Toward a History of the Vanishing Present.* Cambridge, MA: Harvard University Press.

Steedman, Carolyn. 1990. *Childhood and Culture in Britain: Margaret McMillan, 1860–1931.* New Brunswick, NJ: Rutgers University Press.

———. 1995. *Strange Dislocations: Childhood and the Idea of Human Interiority, 1780–1930*. Cambridge, MA: Harvard University Press.
Steedman, Carolyn, Cathy Urwin, and Valerie Wakerdine, eds. 1985. *Language Gender and Childhood*. Boston: Routledge and Kegan Paul.
Stocking, George. 1985. *Objects and Others: Essays on Museums and Material Culture*. Madison: University of Wisconsin Press.
Stokes, Eric. 1990. *The English Utilitarians in India*. Oxford: Oxford University Press.
Stoler, Ann. 1995. *Race and the Education of Desire*. Durham, NC: Duke University Press.
Storrow, Edward. 1856. *The Eastern Lily Gathered: A Memoir of Bala Shondoree Tagore*. London: John Snow.
———. 1916. *Our Indian Sisters*. London: Religious Tract Society.
Stow, David. 1834. *Moral Training, Infant and Juvenile, as Applicable to the Conditions of Large Towns*. Glasgow: William Collins.
———. 1839. *Supplement to Moral Training and the Training System, with Plans for Erected and Fitting up Training School*. Glasgow: W.R. M'Phun.
———. 1860. "Stow's Gallery Training Lessons." In *Object Teaching and Oral Lessons on Social Science and Common Things*, ed. Henry Barnard. New York: FC Brownell.
Taylor, Charles. 1989. *Sources of the Self: The Making of the Modern Identity*. Cambridge, MA: Harvard University Press.
Tharu, Susie, and K. Lalita. 1993. *Women Writing in India*, vol. 1. Delhi: Oxford University Press.
Thorne, Susan. 1999. *Congregational Missions and the Making of an Imperial Culture in Nineteenth-Century England*. Stanford, CA: Stanford University Press.
Trautmann, Thomas. 1997. *The Aryans and British India*. Berkeley: University of California Press.
Tropp, Asher. 1957. *The School Teachers: The Growth of the Teaching Profession in England and Wales from 1800 to the Present*. London: William Heinemann Ltd.
Tyndale-Biscoe, C. E. 1914. "Social Service in Education Institutions: The CMS Boys; Schools, Srinagar." *International Review of Missions* (January).
Uddin, Sufia. 2006. *Constructing Bangladesh: Religion, Ethnicity, and Language in an Islamic Nation*. Chapel Hill: University of North Carolina Press.
Underhill, E. B. 1896. *The Principles and Methods of Missionary Labour*. London: Alexander and Shephard.
Van der Veer, Peter, ed. 1996. *Conversion to Modernities: The Globalization of Christianity*. New York: Routledge.
———. 2001. *Imperial Encounters: Religion and Modernity in India and Britain*. Princeton, NJ: Princeton University Press.
Vedatirtha, Sakuntala. 1937. *Development of Female Education in England and Utilization of Western Methods of Education in Bengal*. Calcutta: University of Calcutta Press.
"Vernacular Education for Bengal." 1854. *Calcutta Review*, no. 44.

Vicinus, Martha. 1985. *Independent Women: Work and Community for Single Women, 1850–1920*. Chicago: Chicago University Press.

Vidyasagar, Iswar Chandra. 1868. *Bodhodoy*, 33rd ed. Calcutta: Sanskrit Press.

Village Education in India: The Report of a Commission of Inquiry (Fraser Report). 1920. London: Oxford University Press.

Viswanathan, Gauri. 1998. *Masks of Conquest: Literary Study and British Rule in India*. Delhi: Oxford University Press.

———. 1998. *Outside the Fold: Conversion, Modernity and Belief*. Princeton, NJ: Princeton University Press.

Walker, J. 1876. *The Handy Book of Object Lessons from a Teacher's Note Book*. London: Jarrold & Sons.

Weitbrecht, Mary. 1843.*Letters from a Missionary's Wife Abroad to a Friend in England*. London: James Nisbet & Co.

Western, F .J. 1911. "Religious Training in Indian Missionary Schools." *The East and the West* (April).

Western, M. P. 1911. "Problems Regarding Female Education in N. India." *The East and the West* (January).

Whitehead, Henry. 1924. *Indian Problems in Religion, Rducation and Politics*. London: Constable and Co., Ltd.

Widdowson, Frances. 1980. *Going up into the Next Class: Women and Elementary Teacher Training, 1840–1914*. London: Women's Research and Resources Centre Publications.

Wood, Ella N. 1897. *Object Lessons for Junior Work*. New York: Fleming H. Revell Company.

Wyburn, W. M. 1934. *The Theory and Practice of Christian Education*. London: Oxford University Press.

Zupanoav, Ines. 1999. *Disputed Missions: Jesuit Experiments and Brahmanical Knowledge in Seventeenth-Century India*. New Delhi: Oxford University Press.

Index

Adam, William, 23–24, 27, 127
adivasis, 64, 77–79, 95–99
Ahmed, Raifuddin, 142, 184n29
Ahmed, Sufia, 136
Aligarh Anglo-Oriental College, 140–141
Ali, Karamat, 148
All-India Mohammedan Educational Conference, 18–19
All-India Muslim League, 149
ambivalence, about rural Muslim Bengalis, 132–133
American Baptist Mission, 177n30
Anglicism, 14, 23–24
Anglo-vernacular schools, 34–35
anjuman, 144
anschauung, 65, 66, 172n18
antislavery movement, 37–38, 167n36
Asad, Talal, 156
ashraf: *atrap* and, 141–142; "conspiracy" and, 123–124, 126; modernization of Muslims and, 142–148; as proponents of educational reform, 5; religious education and, 125; schoolbooks and, 43; writings of, 3
ashramas, 76
atrap: *ashraf* and, 141–142; "backwardness" of, 125, 128; education of, 136, 143, 145

"backwardness," 124–126, 135, 140–142, 148, 183n3

Bairagi women, 103–105, 107–113, 121–122, 179n9, 179n11
Bala Bodh (Knowledge for Girls), 48, 105, 169n15
Bandhopadhyay, Gopal Chunder, 74, 94, 95–96, 99
Banerjee, Prathama, 64
Banerjee, Sumanta, 179n11
Baptist Home Society, 33
Baptist Missionary Society (BMS), 33, 116
Baptist Normal School, 119, 120
Baptists, 117
Barisal boarding school, 118, 120
Barnabodhini (Knowledge of Letters), 106–107, 112
Barnamala, 53, 56–57
Barnaparichay (Vidyasagar), 49–53, 59, 169n15
Batris Sinhasan, 46
Battala publications, 47
beels, 120
Bell, Andrew, 84
Bellenoit, Hayden, 161n6
Bengal: education in, 14–16; education and social mobility in, 17–19; elementary schooling in, 27–30; gallery lessons in, 90–95; missionary activity and, 13; social history of Islam in, 141–142
Bengali schoolbooks, 46–54, 59–60
Bengal (Rural) Primary Education Act (1930), 153, 186n4

205

Index

"Bengal system," 133–134
Bentinck, Lord, 23
bhadralok: adivasis and, 77–78; *Bairagi* women and, 110; cultural change and, 95; education under, 3, 4–5; female education and, 102–104; grants-in-aid and, 129; as headmasters, 88–89; object lessons and, 62–64, 79; pedagogic models of, 19–20; religious prejudices of, 123–124; schoolbooks and, 7–8, 41; social mobility and, 17; teacher training and, 82, 90–95, 98; vernacular education and, 16, 25, 34
Bible, 44, 137
bidha-shikha, 77–79
boarding institutions, 92, 114, 115–118
Bodhodoy (Vidyasagar), 54, 57, 74–76
Bomwetch, Reverend, 57, 89
Bose, Pradip Kumar, 101, 177n42
Britain: education in, 11–12; feminization of teaching profession in, 178n2
British and Foreign School Book Society, 45
British Baptist Mission, 177n30
Brockway, Frances, 69–70
Burdwan, Mr., 89

Caitainya, Sri, 108
Calcutta School Book Society, 40, 54
Carey, William, 12–13, 26, 28–30, 45–46, 52, 164n22
Carpenter, Mary, 102, 178n5
caste. *See* hierarchy
census (1872), 123, 183n2
cess, 35–38
Chakrabarty, Dipesh, 16
Chakrabarty, Thakurdas, 37
Chakrabarty, Usha, 181n31
chakri, 176n18
Chambers brothers, 74–76
Charupath: Entertaining Lessons in Science and Literature (Dutta), 77–78
Choudury, Syed Nawab Ali, 144–147, 149
Christianity, revitalization of, 11. *See also* conversion; missionary activity
Christian patriarch, 85–90
Christian publishers, 168n11
Christian Vernacular Education Society (CVES), 42, 50, 53, 55–57
Christian women teachers, 113–118, 179n11
Church Missionary Intelligencer, 58
Church Missionary Society (CMS), 33
Church of England Zenana Missionary Society, 121

"civilization": of lower caste Christians, 143; of native teachers, 118–121; of Santhali teachers, 96–99
coconut object lesson, 67–68
colonial India: pedagogic institutions' impact on, 4–5, 10–11; 1857 Rebellion in, 55
Comaroff, Jean, 10
Comaroff, John, 10
community identity, hierarchy and, 17–19
concrete language, 67
Congregationalist London Missionary Society (LMS), 33
Connolly, William, 159
conversion: imperialism and, 9, 12–13; of lower castes, 143; missionary normal schools and, 85–90; obstacles to, 26–27; through literacy, 40, 44, 54–57
Cook, James, 26
Croft, Mr., 97–98
cultural identity: education reports and, 153–160; religious education and, 150–153
cultural pluralism, 151, 159–160

death, 76
Debi, Bhagabati, 181n34
De, Lal Behari, 38, 175n13, 181n29
"demussalmanising," 156–157
Deobandi *madrassah,* 140, 141
Department of Public Instruction (DPI): *bhadralok* reformers and, 4–5; Dhaka Normal School and, 107–113; establishment of, 31; expectations of, 157; funding increase by, 14–15; Karim and, 123; missionary normal schools under, 121; Muslim subjectivity and, 136–140; object lessons and, 79; primary school funding and, 177n38; records of, 32; Santhali schools and, 97–98; sex-segregated schooling and, 105–107; teacher training and, 91, 103–104; vernacular schoolbooks and, 46, 47; Wood's "Despatch" and, 34
Dhaka Normal School, 103–104, 107–113, 114
Dissenting Protestantism, 12, 25, 28–29
dobhashi Bangla, 43, 59–60, 146
domestic service, 115–117
Duff, Alexander, 29–30, 55–56, 166n16
"Dusky Darlings," 69–70
Dutta, Akshay Kumar, 75, 77–78, 79

Dutt, O. C., 57
dvijya, 76

East India Company, 13, 14, 23–24, 28–29, 164n22
education: in Britain, 11–12; cultural identity and, 150–153; funding for, 35–38; impact of, on colonial India, 4–5; imperialism and, 6–12; modernization of religious ideas through, 140; Muslim theories on, 3–4; religious identity and, 21–22; reports on Muslim, 153–160; social mobility and, 17–19; twentieth-century debates over, 6
Education in India with Special Reference to Vernacular Schools (Murdoch), 87
elementary schooling: in Bengal, 27–30; evangelicalism and, 25–27
English-language schools, 90–91
An Enquiry into the Obligations of Christians to Use Means for the Conversion of the Heathen (Carey), 12–13
Entally Boarding and Normal School, 117, 118–119, 120
evangelicalism: female teacher training and, 102, 104; literacy and, 114; masculinity and, 82; missionary activity and, 8–10; modern elementary schooling and, 25–27; schoolbooks and, 44–47

family: affection in, 81; child-rearing and, 100–101; Christian patriarch and, 87–88; Mukhopadhyay on, 93
fathers: Christian patriarch, 85–90; Mukhopadhyay on, 93–94; role of, in families, 81, 82
female teacher training: argument for, 105–107; conclusions on, 121–122; Dhaka Normal School and, 107–113; in England, 178n2; hierarchy and, 178n8; introduction to, 102–105; native teachers and, 118–121, 179n10; personal stories of, 113–118; widows and, 122, 183n59
fetishism, 70–72, 172n15, 172n17, 172n18
Foucault, Michel, 174n5, 185n38
Free Church institutions, 117
funding: debate over, 35–38; for mass education, 149, 167n32, 185n44; for primary schools, 177n38; for Qur'an schools, 137–138, 139, 145. *See also* grants-in-aid

"gallery lessons," 81, 83–85, 90–95
Garbett, Reverend, 84–85
gendered education. *See* sex-segregated schooling
Ghosh, Anindita, 47
Ghosh, Kamakhacharan, 78–79
Ghosh, Kaushik, 64
Gilmartin, David, 144
Glasgow Seminary and Normal School, 49, 81, 83
Gmelin, Reverend, 87–88, 175n12, 177n37
Grant, Charles, 12
grants-in-aid, 31–34, 129, 131–134. *See also* funding
gurumahashoy, 83, 91, 94, 103–106, 109

Hall, Catherine, 9, 10
The Handy Book of Object Lessons from a Teacher's Note Book (Walker), 67–68
Haq, A. K. Fazlul, 152, 155
Haq, Azizul, 152, 158, 160
Hardy, Peter, 124, 144
Hastings, Warren, 14
Hatcher, Brian, 46
headmasters, 88–90, 91
Hebron, Frances, 116, 118, 119, 120
Herdman, Mr., 116
hierarchy: *Bairagi* women and, 107–112; Christian civilization and, 119–120; community identity and, 17–19; education funding and, 24–25, 35–38, 129; female teacher training and, 102–105, 115, 178n8; headmasters and, 88–90; missionary normal schools and, 86; object lessons and, 78–79; as obstacle to Christian conversion, 26–27; *pathshalas* and, 145; teacher training and, 81–83, 94–95; tribal teachers and, 96–99; in vernacular schoolbooks, 48; Wood's "Despatch" and, 34–35
Hinduism: conversion to Christianity from, 26–27; idolatry and, 70–72
Hints on Education in India (Murdoch), 77
Hitopadesha, 46
Hooghly Normal School, 81, 82, 92
humanitarianism, 24, 25–26, 38
Hunter Commission (1882), 106, 129–131, 133–134, 146
Hunter, Ian, 174n5

Index

Hunter, William Wilson, 2–3, 21, 124–131, 141, 184n10
Huque, Azizul, 147

idolatry, 70–72, 173n23
imperialism: education and, 6–12; missionary activity and, 9–13; object lessons and, 67–68
The Indian Musalmans: Are They Bound in Conscience to Rebel against the Queen? (Hunter), 2–3, 124–131, 141
Indian National Congress, 155
India's Women, 121
Ireland, 45

jat, 112. *See also* hierarchy
Jinnah, M. A., 19

Karim, Abdul, 123, 124, 134–135, 145, 147–148
Khan, Syed Ahmed, 140–141
Kharaday Mission Girls' School, 113
Kiernan, Victor, 25
kindergarten, 101
knowledge, object lesson on, 77–79
Knox, John, 29–30, 166n19

Laird, Michael, 45, 115
Lancaster, Joseph, 84
landlords, Muslim, 185n37
language: in Bengali education, 14–16; concrete and stylistic, in object lessons, 67; in Muslim education, 146; religious identity and, 42
language primers, 7–8, 41–43, 48–54, 59–60, 154–58. *See also* schoolbooks
literacy: conversion through, 44; evangelicalism and, 114; as heart of religious epistemology, 2; Murdoch and Vidyasagar and, 52–53; Muslim subjectivity and textual, 136–140. *See also* language primers; schoolbooks
London Missionary Society, 117
Long, James: on imperialism and education, 37; language primers and, 53–56; as missionary source, 8; *Nil Darpan* and, 167n34; teacher training and, 85–86, 92
Ludden, David, 19

Macaulay, Thomas Babington, 14, 31, 90–91
madrassahs, 28, 128–129
maktabs, 128–129, 133–135, 137, 154–157
Mana, Manorama, 113

mantras, 136–138
A Manual of Education for the Use of Vernacular Teachers (Gmelin), 87, 175n12
Marshman, Joshua, 28, 45
Martin, Mr., 108–109, 113, 180n27
masculinity: Hindu identity and, 175n18; teacher training and, 82–83, 90–95; tribal teachers and, 96–99
mass education: conclusions on, 38–39; education reports' plan for, 159; elementary schooling and, 27–30; evangelicalism and, 25–27; funding for, 35–38, 149, 167n32; introduction to, 24–25; Primary Education Act and, 153
Masuzawa, Tomoko, 172n15, 172n17
maulavis, 142
Mayo, Charles, 174n37
Mayo, Elizabeth, 67–68
Mayo, Lord, 2, 127, 161n3
memorization, 136–138
Metcalf, Barbara, 140
Metcalf, Thomas, 166n20
mianji, 135
Miftah-ul-Janna (The Key to Paradise) (Ali), 148
"Minute on Indian Education" (Macaulay), 14, 90–91
missionary activity: in *adivasi* communities, 96–97; in Britain and colonies, 11–12; caste and, 27, 142–143; Christian women teachers and, 113–118; cultural change and, 95–96; education and, 4, 8–9; gender norms and, 20; government aid and, 32–33; imperialism and, 9–13; influence of, on modern politics, 20–21; object lessons and, 68–72; pedagogic models and, 19–20; pluralist curriculum and, 57–59; schoolbooks and, 44, 54–57; vernacular education and, 15–16, 23–25; as "Victorian NGO," 1
missionary normal schools: Christian women teachers and, 113–118; female teacher training and, 102–104; native teachers and, 118–121; in Santhal Pargannahs, 96–99; teacher training and, 85–90
Missions and Empire, 11
mission schools: Bengali Muslim education and, 131–136; conclusions on, 148–149; "conspiracy" and "backwardness" and, 126–131; introduction to, 123–126; modernization of religious ideas through, 140–142; modern religious education

and, 142–148; textual literacy and Muslim subjectivity in, 136–140
Mitra, Baboo Rajendra Lall, 36–37
modernization: of Muslims, 142–148; of religious ideas, 140–142; religious identity and, 151
"*mofussil* Muslims," 185n37
Mohammedan Educational Conference, 18–19
monitorial system, 84, 174n3
Mookerjee, Baboo Joykishen, 167n32
morality: in language primers, 48; in object lessons, 69–70
More, Hannah, 29
mothers, child education and, 101
Mrityunjay Vidyalankar, 45–46, 52
Mukhopadhyay, Bhudev: as education reformer, 16, 34, 51; on gurus and students, 81; on guru wages, 180n19; object lessons and, 72–74, 79; scholarly views on, 176n21; teacher training and, 87, 91–95, 100–101
Mukhopadhyay, Gopal, 180n21
Mukhopadhyay, Somnath, 74
Murdoch, John: Christian education and, 54–57; methods of, 170n41; object lessons and, 77; schoolbooks and, 42–44; on secular teaching, 58; teacher training and, 87; vernacular schoolbooks and, 49–50, 51–53
Muslim Community in Bengal (Ahmed), 136
Muslim Education Committee, 157
Muslim landlords, 185n37
Muslim League, 19, 155
Muslims: "conspiracy" and "backwardness" and, 124–131, 135, 140–142, 148, 183n3; educational theories of, 3–4; education for Bengali, 131–136, 153–160; education and social mobility and, 17–19; loyalty of, 2–3; modernization of, 142–148; prejudice against, 123–124; subjectivity of, 136–140
Mussalmani Bangla, 59–60

Nagaropantha, 113
National Society, 45
native Christians, 116–119, 122
newspapers, *ashraf* class and, 144
Nil Darpan, 167n34
Nonconformist Protestants, 12, 25–26, 28–29, 32–33
Nutan Barnamala (Bomwetch), 57, 170n38

object lessons: conclusions on, 79–80; idolatry and fetishism and, 70–72; introduction to, 61–64; in missionary schools, 68–70; origins of, 64–68; "other" and, 76–79; societal norms and, 72–76
Object Lessons for Junior Work, 70
Object Teaching and Oral Lessons (Stow), 61
object theory, 61–62, 64–65
Orientalism, 14, 23–24
orphanages, 114–120
orthography, 51, 169n22, 169n23

pardah, 101, 103–107, 116
pastoral care, 143, 185n38
pathshalas: accessibility of, 144–145, 165n12; Adam and, 23–24; curriculum in, 154–155; dismantling of, 30; education in, 40; Muslim education and, 132, 135, 146–147; organization of, 27–28; religiosity of, 157; schoolbooks in, 46; sex-segregation in, 105–107
patriarch, 85–90
Perkins, Mr. and Mrs., 69, 172n13
Permanent Settlement, 36–38
Pestalozzi, Johann, 61–62, 64–66, 72, 171n6
philanthropy, 25–26
Pietz, William, 70, 172n15, 172n18
Pious Clause (1813), 164n22
play, teacher training and, 93
pluralism, cultural, 159–160
pluralist curriculum, 57–59
Porter, Andrew, 9
Pratt, Archdeacon, 55–56
Primary Education Act (1930), 153, 155, 158, 186n4
privatization of education, 24
punthis, 142

Qur'an schools: Bengali Muslim education and, 131–136; conclusions on, 148–149; "conspiracy" and "backwardness" and, 126–131; introduction to, 123–126; modernization of religious ideas through, 140–142; modern religious education and, 142–148; textual literacy and Muslim subjectivity in, 136–140
Qur'an, study of, 139

Ramabai, Pandita, 181n39
Ratnashar (Ghosh), 78–79
Rebellion and Mutiny (1857), 55, 127

Religion versus Empire? (Porter), 9
religious education: cultural identity and, 150–153; modern, 142–148; for Muslims, 125, 128–129, 148, 155–157; object lessons and, 62–63; standardization of, 5–6; through repetition, 136–137. *See also* Qur'an schools
religious holidays, 18
religious identity: language primers and, 40–44, 48–54; mass schooling and, 21–22; modernization and, 151; religious education and, 142–148; Western education and, 1–4, 6–12
religious revitalization, 11, 25–27
repetition, 136–138
Report of the Kamal Yar Jung Education Committee (1942), 153–160
Report of the Moslem Education Advisory Committee (1935), 153–160, 187n12
respectability, 112–113, 121
rice, 61, 62, 73–74
"rice" Christians, 143
Risley, H. H., 111–112
Robinson, Francis, 139
Rose, Jacqueline, 66–67
Roy, Ram Mohan, 23, 79
Rudiments of Knowledge (Chambers), 74–76
ryot, 37–38

sadhu-bhasa, 50, 54, 170n30
Santhali teachers, 96–99
Santhal Pargannahs, 97
Santhals, 177n29
Santipore Normal and Training School, 85–86, 89
Sarkar, Tanika, 107–108
schoolbooks: Bengali, 47–48, 59–60; Christian publishers of, 168n11; conversion through, 54–57; evolution of evangelical, 44–47; introduction to, 40–43; in *maktabs* and *pathshalas*, 154–155; Muslim Education Committee on, 157–158; object lessons and, 63, 67, 79, 80; pluralist curriculum and, 57–59; religious identity and, 48–54; Vidyasagar and, 169n15. *See also* language primers
Schur, Reverend, 89–90
Schwarz, Joel, 74
science, object lessons and, 79
Scottish Free Church, 33, 116
Scottish Free Church orphanage, 118, 119, 120

Sen, Ashok, 25, 184n11
Serampore Baptist Training School, 98–99
Serampore Normal School, 99
Seth, Sanjay, 6, 124, 134, 183n3
sex-segregated schooling: argument for, 105–107; conclusions on, 121–122; Dhaka Normal School and, 107–113; introduction to, 102–105; native teachers and, 118–121; overview of, 20; personal stories of, 113–118
shambhramayar, 93, 94
Shastras, 94
shikha pranali, 100
Shikha Vidyak Prasatava (Mukhopadhyay), 81–82
shradhashpada, 93, 94
Sibler, Kate, 171n6
"simultaneous method," 83–85, 174n5, 174n6
Skresfrud, Mr., 98
slavery, 35–38, 167n36
social mobility. *See* hierarchy
spelling, 51, 169n22, 169n23
Spurgeon, Rev. R., 120
Storrow, Edward, 33
Stow, David: education and cultural identity and, 150–151; on monitorial system, 174n3; Normal Seminary started by, 49; object lessons and, 61, 67, 73–74; teacher training and, 81–85
stylistic language, 67
subjectivity, of Muslims, 136–140, 142–148
Sunday schools, 26, 29, 44
"sympathy of numbers," 81, 83–85

taxation, 35–38
teacher training: in Bengal, 90–95; certification for, 175n9; Christian patriarch and, 85–90; conclusions on, 100–101; cultural change and, 95–96; introduction to, 81–83; Stow and, 83–85; tribal teachers and, 96–99. *See also* female teacher training
textual literacy, 136–140
Thomason, Thomas, 28–29
tols, 27, 28
trade, 12–13
The Training System of Education (Stow), 150
tribal teachers, 96–99
The Tribes and Castes of Bengal (Risley), 111–112

Uddin, Suffia, 18

Vaishnavism, 107–110, 181n29, 181n31
vanaprastha, 76
vernacular education: in Bengal, 14–16; conclusions on, 39; elementary schooling and, 28–30; hierarchy and funding for, 17–19, 35–38, 129; missionary activity and, 23–25; Murdoch and Vidyasagar and, 49–54; for Muslims, 132–133; pluralist curriculum and, 57–59; religious equity in, 135–136; religious identity and, 1–3, 7–8; schoolbooks and, 42–43, 46–48; Wood's "Despatch" and, 31–35
Vidyasagar, Iswar Chandra: as education reformer, 16, 34; object lessons and, 75–76, 79; orthography and, 169n22; pluralist curriculum and, 58; rejection of Christian schoolbooks and, 55, 57; schoolbooks and, 41–44, 49–54, 169n15
village teaching, 91–92
Viswanathan, Gauri, 12

Vivekananda, Swami, 173n23
voluntarism, 24–25, 32

Walker, J., 67–68
Ward, William, 28
Weitbrecht, Mary, 115–116
Wesleyan Mission, 177n30
Western education: impact of, 6–12; religious identity and, 1–4, 21–22
widow teachers, 122, 183n59
Wilson, Bishop, 55–56
women teacher training. *See* female teacher training
Wood, Charles, 4, 31–35, 105–106, 129
Woodrow (head inspector), 185n44
"Wood's Education Despatch," 4, 31–35, 105–106, 129
writing, 167n1
Wylie, Macleod, 55–56

Zaman, Muhammad Qasim, 136
zemindars, 36–38
zenana, 102, 178n4
zillah schools, 34–35, 118

TEXT
10/13 Sabon
DISPLAY
Sabon
COMPOSITOR
Westchester Book Services
INDEXER
Rachel Lyon

www.ingramcontent.com/pod-product-compliance
Lightning Source LLC
Chambersburg PA
CBHW030651230426
43665CB00011B/1041